The Seminole Baptist
Churches of Oklahoma

The Civilization of the American Indian Series

For my parents

The Seminole Baptist
Churches of Oklahoma

MAINTAINING A TRADITIONAL COMMUNITY

By Jack M. Schultz

University of Oklahoma Press : Norman

Library of Congress Cataloging-in-Publication Data

Schultz, Jack M. (Jack Maurice), 1957–
    The Seminole Baptist churches of Oklahoma : maintaining a
traditional community / by Jack M. Schultz.
        p.   cm. — (The civilization of the American Indian series ;
    v. 233)
    Includes bibliographical references and index.
    ISBN 0-8061-3117-9 (cloth : alk. paper)
    1. Seminole Indians—Oklahoma—Ethnic identity.   2. Seminole
Indians—Oklahoma—Religion.   3. Baptists—Oklahoma.   I. Title.
II. Series.
E99.S28S37   1999
306.6'861'089973—dc21   98-48406
                                                          CIP

*The Seminole Baptist Churches of Oklahoma: Maintaining a Traditional
Community* is Volume 233 in The Civilization of the American Indian Series.

The paper in this book meets the guidelines for permanence and durability
of the Committee on Production Guidelines for Book Longevity of the
Council on Library Resources, Inc.∞

Contents

Illustrations

Preface

This study is the result of over four years of fieldwork under-taken during the years 1990–94. During that time I was present in the community of the Seminole Baptists at least one day each week (from early afternoon to early the next morning) and often on multiple days. I attended many gatherings, both formal (weekly Prayer Meetings and Fourth Sunday Meetings, for example, as described in chapter 6) and informal (e.g., church grounds maintenance, auto repair). I interviewed members in English and Mvskoke in their homes, around dinner tables, at church grounds, and in vehicles traveling to and from gatherings.[1] I was regularly welcomed as an over-night guest. I ran errands with members and assisted in the demolition and maintenance of camp houses (see chapter 5 for a description of camp houses). I witnessed and participated in many aspects of the members' social lives (eating, shopping, repairing automobiles, watching television, playing with chil-dren, chatting on porches and over car hoods). I was assigned a clan (see chapter 2), a specific seat in the sanctuary, and a Mvskoke nickname.[2] I participated fully in the church services. I was regularly asked to lead Mvskoke songs and prayers in public gatherings, "fulfilling my work" for the congregation. Most of my visits were to one particular congregation (here called Eufaula); however, I attended and participated in eight of the twenty-eight churches in the rotation (see chapter 6) on multiple occasions.[3] More than twenty members (pastors, ministers, deacons, women's leaders, and floor members) from eight different churches were interviewed. The interviews, many of them taped and transcribed, and my observations serve as the primary database for this study.

It is probably impossible to state adequately my feelings of appreciation and indebtedness to the many Seminoles who embraced me during my field experience. I was regularly overwhelmed by the graciousness extended to me and by the fact that they incorporated me into their lives and community. Perhaps in the account that follows some of that graciousness will be conveyed.

Some readers will no doubt find it curious that a study focusing on a church virtually ignores beliefs and the issues of faith and meaning (chapter 4 does address beliefs, however briefly). This curiosity may be diminished when one recognizes the distinction between theology and anthropology. Whereas theology focuses on what one can learn about the deities in religion, the anthropology of religion focuses on what one can learn about humans by investigating their religions.

Anthropologists have used various approaches to the study of religion, all explicating the *human* elements. There are two basic anthropological approaches to the study of the human activities generally grouped under the rubric of religion. The first may be labeled as idealism. This approach views religion as expressions of human ideas and emphasizes religion as a meaning system. Dimensions of this approach include semiotics, symbolic anthropology, hermeneutics, structuralism, and interpretive anthropology. Using this approach, the anthropologist seeks to reveal the logic systems—the internal structures of the religious system—or to discover the meaning that the religion holds for its members. Elements of religion are viewed as "symbols" strung together in a structure, or system, used and interpreted by its practitioners. Contemporary anthropologists using this approach often couch their analysis in metaphors involving language; their analysis is, then, an "interpretation of meaning."

The second approach, materialism, usually views religion as epiphenomena, the primary phenomena being some social and material constraints. Included in this approach is Marxist materialism and various functionalisms (including variations of Durkheim's social functionalism). Using one of these approaches, the anthropologist connects religion (something nonmaterial) to some empirical element necessary for the group's material survival. This necessary element is often some aspect of the economic, political, or social structure.

Each of the two approaches brings insight to our understanding of religion. Whereas the first approach emphasizes *cultural* aspects of religion and provides a humanistic accounting aimed at understanding, the second emphasizes the *social* aspects and reveals the role of religion in the organization and maintenance of groups of people. The present study weds the two approaches. I will demonstrate how the Seminole Baptist church system (cultural aspects) functions in maintaining community and identity (social aspects) for its participants.

My approach is considerably different from that taken in the past. Previous anthropological studies have usually viewed the adoption of Christianity as an element of assimilation, that is, as a step toward the inevitable total immersion into the dominant Anglo world. Such a perspective does not adequately explain the Seminole Baptist situation. The Seminole Baptists are not assimilated; they are culturally unique and maintain a distinct identity. Moreover, rather than being a huge step toward assimilation into the dominant Anglo system, their adoption of Christianity—their church system—actually functions to maintain their unique identity as Seminoles within the dominant Anglo system.

Acknowledgments

I would like to acknowledge those who assisted in the completion of this book. Foremost are my dissertation committee members: Morris W. Foster, John H. Moore, Susan Vehik, Joseph Whitecotton, and Tom Boyd. I am particularly indebted to Morris Foster, for his guidance throughout this process and for his careful reading of various drafts of this book. I would also like to acknowledge Raymond D. Fogelson and William C. Sturtevant, readers secured by the University of Oklahoma Press, for their careful critiques of my study and for their suggestions, which moved a manuscript from a narrow dissertation to a broader, more useful book. Patricia Bell, Sociology Department Head at Oklahoma State University, has been very supportive and has provided continued opportunities for me to complete this work.

I graciously acknowledge the Seminole people who freely gave of their time and knowledge over the course of some five years to this *cepanhvtke* ("white boy"). I am particularly indebted to Bunny, Louella, and Billy Porter, Webster Fixico, Joe Spain (recently deceased), Dorsey and Agness Nero, Walter and Josephine Wise, Aggie West, Amos Factor, Houston Tiger, Houston Palmer, Jerry Deer, Dave Bowlegs, George and Belinda Harjoce, and Joammie Harrison. I consider myself fortunate to be counted as their friend and brother.

Early in my field experience, Bunny Porter served as my guide, interpreter, guardian, and consultant. Later, his health became such that I did not want to burden him with my questions and needs. I sorely miss our hours together under the arbor. Toward the end of my field experience, Webster Fixico looked out for me. Webster regularly opened his home to me, and our countless fishing trips became a real source of pleasure. Joe Spain spent many long hours conversing with me, drinking strong coffee in front of a tape recorder. He viewed his time with me as an act of service for future Seminoles, patiently moving me toward understanding Seminole beliefs and practices so that I might faithfully record them ("You don't know how God might use you to minister to Indian people," he once said to me). Joe playfully suggested that I entitle this book "My Life as an Indian." I gratefully acknowledge these three men for their assistance and contributions to the completion of this project.

Linda Alexander, Margaret Mauldin, and George Bunny assisted greatly in Mvskoke-language issues and translation questions. I was privileged to work with Linda and Margaret in teaching Mvskoke-language classes at the University of Oklahoma. Linda Alexander was particularly patient, helpful, and gracious. She answered any question I put before her, drawing from her vast knowledge, experience, and understanding of her people and mine.

I would like to thank Jimmy Dunlop for his diagram of the church interior. My wife, Christine Schultz, provided all other drawings and careful transcriptions of my interviews.

I want to thank and acknowledge the members of my family who assisted in this project: my children, Joshua, Anna, and Abigail, who heartened me throughout this process and patiently did without; my in-laws, W. D. "Bill" and Marie Crow, for their support and encouragement; and my wife, Christine, without whose love and faith, my own work would be unfulfilled. This book is dedicated to my parents, Arthur R. Schultz and Leona Rosenthal Schultz, who together encouraged me to look further.

The Seminole Baptist
Churches of Oklahoma

CHAPTER 1

Introduction

This is a study of a community of people who call themselves Seminole Baptists. That self-characterization is significant. They are Baptist: gathering several times each week in steepled churches, they meet for prayers, hymns, and sermons expounding biblical texts. They are Seminole: conducting worship services primarily in the Mvskoke language, the participants are descendants of the Muskogean people of the Florida peninsula who were forcibly removed to Indian Territory in the mid–nineteenth century.

One might suppose that Indians identifying themselves as Baptist would have assimilated into the larger Anglo world, but such is not the case here. The Seminole Baptists do not seek to identify themselves with the Anglo Baptist church (the Seminole Baptist congregations are fiercely independent and are opposed to any affiliation with a larger Baptist assembly), and non-Seminole Baptists would find the community's ideologies, practices, and gatherings quite foreign. The Seminole Baptist community, whether from necessity or from choice, remains a distinct, vital, and *traditional* Seminole entity within the dominant Anglo world.

This may appear to be a contradiction—Seminole *and* Christian. One might assume that "Christian" is synonymous with assimilated, that is, that by adopting this foreign faith, the natives have lost their native soul. One might also assume that in embracing a foreign faith, they have lost an aspect of their identity, if not their whole identity. I will show, however, the converse: the practices and beliefs that the Seminole Baptists share are themselves instruments in the maintenance of their identity as a distinct ethnic unit within the dominant Anglo world.

To understand how this group can be both Christian and traditional Seminole, one must begin by understanding the term *traditional*. If one views a community of indigenous people as a "culture," one would conclude that a traditional culture is one in which the patterns of traits, behaviors, and structures are relatively static and self-reproducing. Trait lists can be compiled and compared,[1] and perhaps people can be ranked according to degrees of conservation and assimilation, yet little else is learned from such a characterization of a traditional community.

A better approach emphasizes community as the *interactions of people*. A traditional community, therefore, denotes a shared history of interaction, communication, negotiation, and face-to-face encounters between people of a social group— not a fixed set of traits, behaviors, structures, or modes of production. *Traditional* does not, then, mean that the community is unchanging but rather that changes are structured in culturally meaningful ways, allowing a social group to sustain its identity while being engaged in changing circumstances. *Traditional* does not necessarily imply immutability, or dusty vestigial characteristics of a culture in the process of assimilation; rather, *traditional* describes a dynamic social group sharing a history, adapting to changed circumstances, and demonstrating vitality. When such a view is espoused, one can go beyond trait list comparisons and can probe the questions of *how* communities maintain identity while adapting to a changing situation. I suggest that the best way to understand the maintenance of the Seminole Baptist church of Oklahoma as a traditional community is by recognizing the interdependence of cultural factors (i.e., conceptual frameworks such as belief systems, worldviews, morals, and church rituals) and social factors (i.e., action and interaction between and among individuals and groups). To illustrate such continuity in the midst of change, this book will investigate the social interactions within a traditional congregation and between congregations of the Seminole Baptist church community.

A Critique of Assimilation, Acculturation, and Ethnicity Models

Ethnographers have tended to disregard Christianized native peoples, apparently assuming that they have assimilated into the larger Anglo world. Ethnographers (e.g., Linton 1940; Powers 1977; Hudson 1976) who have studied them have done so only to contrast Christian natives with more "conservative" and "traditional" native religionists. This is no less true with ethnographies of the Seminoles and Creeks. John Swanton (1922; 1928a; 1928b), in his voluminous descriptions of the Creeks and Seminoles of Oklahoma, ignored the Indian churches even though they were thriving all around him. In his work *Oklahoma Seminoles,* James Howard (1984:18, 104, 161) contrasted "conservative" and "traditional" Stomp grounds participants[2] with "the native Christian element." He asserted that the former were traditional, unchanged, and therefore the genuine Seminoles, whereas the latter were more assimilated and somehow less Seminole. It is as if Christianized Indians were somehow less authentic and possibly even less Indian.

This lack of anthropological attention to Christianized native peoples is the result, at least in part, of the bias of the assimilation and acculturation models that continue to dominate the way in which contemporary native peoples are interpreted by anthropologists and historians. To many, *Christian* is assumed to be synonymous with *assimilated.* This is unfortunate because the Seminole Baptists, at least, maintain a unique sociocultural system of language, organization, ideology, worldview, and values. Assimilation and acculturation models fail to recognize the integrity of this difference.

A basic thesis of the assimilation and acculturation models (Linton 1940; Spicer 1961; Trigger 1986) is that change is the result of contact with a foreign, dominant force, namely, Euro-American economic and political formations. These models presume that precontact native communities were relatively static and were in their "purest" forms before contact. The events since contact are, then, a chronicle of native culture loss and assimilation into the dominant, Euro-American system. Christian natives are characterized as being more assimilated than those "conservatives" who adhered to "traditional" beliefs and practices. But to gloss Seminole Baptists as assimilated fails to recognize the viability of the Seminole community and the dynamic nature of its social life. Because assimilation and acculturation models obscure distinctly Seminole features, they are inadequate as explanations of the Seminole Baptist community.

Proponents of the assimilation and acculturation models also fail to account for the many individuals who shift back and forth between those traits or behaviors deemed "assimilated" and those called "traditional." One can see this movement among the Seminoles. Howard (1984:104) defined traditional Seminoles as those who were active in the Stomp Dance religion, implying that the churched Seminoles were nontraditional (assimilated). However, many Seminoles participate in both arenas (Stomp grounds and Indian churches) concurrently. There also is sequential movement between arenas among both leaders and laypeople. Most church members whom I have encountered, particularly leaders, participated in the Stomp grounds ceremonies at some point in their lives.[3] Many former Stomp grounds leaders assume leadership roles within the church system. Howard was either unaware of or ignored the highly salient fact that his "ultra-conservative" informant, Willie Lena, was, since childhood, a participating member of a Seminole Baptist church.

An especially problematic aspect of the acculturation and assimilation models is the supposed passivity of the native community. As Fowler (1987:6) observed: "The acculturation framework often presents Native peoples as essentially passive, or at best unsuccessful; change is viewed not as resulting from resourceful and creative acts of choice but as capitulation to pressures from the wider society. The underlying assumption is that eventually 'Natives' will assimilate or, if they do not, become hopelessly disorganized, marginal people. Ethnographers who take this approach tend also to overemphasize the shaping of Indian culture and history by social contacts with and adoption of ideas of non-Indians."

Native communities *actively* respond to changing external environments and adapt to them. Assimilation models have failed to recognize this historical as well as ongoing reinterpretation and reorganization. Within the Seminole Baptist churches, traditional Seminole symbols are extended, renamed, or redefined to suit the prevailing situation. Religious symbols, with their established credibility and inherent ambiguity, are vehicles for interpretations that reinforce traditional categories of meaning while adapting to changes in the surrounding social conditions.[4] One can see that by extending symbols—both Seminole and Baptist—Seminoles have adapted their cultural or congregational structures while maintaining a social system that functions to integrate their community. The Seminole community's innovations expressed in the Baptist churches are not passive responses to a dominant society, nor are they an abandonment of cultural integrity; rather, they are creative, deliberate adaptations that ensure community survival within a locally meaningful framework.

The more general criticism of the assimilation and acculturation models is their emphasis on cultural factors (conceptual frameworks such as belief systems, worldviews, and morals) to the exclusion of social factors (action and interaction between and among individuals and groups). "Social factors" and "cultural factors" are reifications that are constructed by academics and that are often treated as separate realities, but the phenomena conceptualized as "social" or "cultural" are interdependent. As noted, assimilation and acculturation models have often neglected this interdependence and have focused on cultural aspects at the expense of social aspects. This has often led to the conclusion that any use of cultural features external to the native community was tantamount to assimilation, particularly when the feature adopted is termed "religion." Hence, in adopting Christianity, natives lose their "otherness" and, therefore, their academic appeal. However, by focusing on conceptual frameworks as ends in themselves, ethnographers have often neglected to inquire into how these ideas were used.

When one defines Christianity as a conceptual framework, it is treated as a set of ideas or beliefs. Those who hold such views conclude that Christianity has been adopted at the expense of an indigenous set of ideas or beliefs that have been held since before contact. These latter cultural features are labeled "traditional" and are assumed to be the antithesis of Christianity. However, when one looks beyond the ideas or beliefs to the actions that they inform, one sees that Christianity can fulfill ongoing social needs in much the same way as did prior beliefs.

Similarly, theories of ethnicity (Barth 1969; Blu 1980; Gumperz 1982; Spicer 1961) explain changing Indian identity as reaction to outside forces. These theories define Indian action in terms of dominance and dependency. Individuals mobilize interest groups (around symbols and markers that identify or characterize their "ethnic" group) in opposition to the dominant, external, sociopolitical forces while accommodating choices and actions to these dominant forces. Although relationships of domination and dependency may account for some actions, and although the dominant forces do limit (yet not prescribe) actions, the Seminole Baptist community is not *defined by* these forces. Community definition and maintenance results primarily from intragroup interaction, not from the community's relationship to dominant outsiders.

Assimilation, acculturation, and ethnicity models fail to identify continuous community-specific social dynamics that make use of changing cultural symbols. The Seminole Baptists are best understood by focusing on the social uses of their Christian beliefs and symbols. Church gatherings, as social occasions, function to regulate and organize social relations, within both the local congregation and the larger Seminole community, in a manner that parallels the function of the ceremonial Stomp grounds.

A Sociology of Interaction

Sapir (1949:515) recognized the interdependence of culture and social interaction: "The true locus of culture is in the interaction of specific individuals and, on the subjective side, in the world of meaning which each one of these individuals may unconsciously abstract for himself from his participation in these interactions." It is in the social dimensions—the history of interaction, communication, negotiation, and face-to-face encounters between members of a social group or community—that cultural dynamics are better understood. In viewing the social, one can go beyond compiling trait-list comparisons and assimilation continuums to probing the question of how communities maintain a distinct identity while adapting to a changing context. Seminole Baptists have developed a system that is responsive to their needs for faith, tradition, values, and worldview as well as to their needs for community organization and maintenance.

A sociology of interaction provides an effective means to analyze social action. One such vocabulary of interaction is found in the works of Erving Goffman (1959; 1961; 1963; 1967; 1969). The prolific Goffman is utilized by academics identifying themselves as dramaturgists, symbolic interactionists, symbolicists, and the like. I do not intend to use Goffman as a theoretical body here; rather, I will use some of his concepts and terminology, specifically those that are useful for identifying the processes of interaction and delineating the social units in which interaction occurs. I will also extend some of Goffman's concepts to accommodate the Seminole Baptist social situation.

Central to Goffman's processes of interaction is the notion of "impression management." He argues that participants in a social occasion will present themselves and their activities to others at the social occasion in ways that strategically guide or control the impression that others have of them and the present situation. Impressions are managed to effect desired social outcomes, most of which involve maintenance or enhancement of a person's "face." Face is "the positive social value a person effectively claims for himself by the line others assume he has taken during a particular contact. Face is an image of self delineated in terms of approved social attributes" (Goffman 1967:5). A person in a social encounter brings into that encounter a face that he or she must maintain or enhance. The person must manage the flow of events to ensure that a particular impression, or expressive order, is maintained: "By automatically appealing to face, he knows how to conduct himself in regard to talk. By repeatedly and automatically asking himself the question, 'If I do or do not act in this way, will I or others lose face?' he decides at each moment, consciously or unconsciously, how to behave" (Goffman 1967:36). Paradoxically, a person's social face is his "most personal possession and the center of his security and pleasure," yet it is only "on loan to him from society." It may be withdrawn from him by his social peers "unless he conducts himself in a way that is worthy of it" (Goffman 1967:10). Attention to face (face maintenance and face enhancement), therefore, becomes a primary consideration in virtually all social encounters; and strategic consideration of one's face can easily be viewed as the primary explanation for choices in social action. Socialized members of a community have deep feelings attached to their faces, making them vulnerable to the scrutiny of peers and exposing them to social sanctions. Appeal to face is the instrument of social maintenance in communities that do not have formal, centralized social structures (Foster 1991:29).

The primary arenas for face work often are "social occasions." Social occasions are one of three analytical units that Goffman identifies in which the processes of interaction are enacted. The other two units are "gatherings," and "situations." The term *gathering* refers "to any set of two or more individuals whose members include all and only those who are at the moment in one another's immediate presence" (Goffman 1963:18). Gatherings result from the simple fact of copresence. Interaction within gatherings may be "focused" or "unfocused." Focused interaction occurs "when people effectively agree to sustain for a time a single focus of cognitive and visual attention" (Goffman 1961:7). Unfocused interaction occurs consciously and unconsciously whenever two or more people are simply present in a gathering. It is necessary to distinguish *gathering* from *group*. Groups are the enduring units made up of community members who have some corporate rights and/or duties in common. Gatherings, conversely, end when people are no longer physically present with one another.

Gatherings occur within "situations." Goffman defines *situation* as "the full spatial environment anywhere within which an entering person becomes a member of the gathering that is (or does then become) present. Situations begin when mutual monitoring occurs, and lapse when the second-last person has left" (Goffman 1963:18). This concept is the basis for "social occasions" (sometimes referred to as "situations"): "*Social occasion . . .* is a wider social affair, undertaking, or event, bounded in regard to place and time and typically facilitated by fixed equipment; a social occasion provides the structuring social context in which many situations and their gatherings are likely to form, dissolve, and re-form, while a pattern of conduct tends to be recognized as the appropriate and (often) official or intended one" (Goffman 1963:18). Social situations are more institutionalized expressions of situations. Social occasions among Seminole Baptists include the Prayer Meetings, Fourth Sunday Meetings, and Big Meeting weekends.

Individual and group behavior occurring within social occasions is governed by *situational proprieties* (Goffman 1963:24). Situational proprieties are culturally specific social norms, or conventions, that organize social interactions, including social occasions. They are the shared expectations held by interacting participants according to the kind of occasion the participants understand to be ongoing. Situational proprieties are conceptual frameworks that participants use to interpret behavior. One may speak of "situational presence," or "involvement," as a way of describing one's adherence to situational proprieties. When the situational proprieties are followed, participants are likely to feel comfortable in the interaction. They will know how to respond, how to feel, and how to act: the norms regulate the communication traffic. While in a social encounter, a participant must give attention to face as well as to situational proprieties—both of which may be strategically manipulated by individuals to achieve desired social ends.

In addition to functioning as a vehicle for accomplishing social tasks, situational proprieties are also moral norms that serve as a matrix for social cohesion—they serve to identify and maintain a social group. Situational proprieties define a moral community, providing a valid statement of a community's collective self-definition. Social processes, therefore, may often have a moral component; thus, social categories may be considered sacred. Within the Seminole worldview, the distinction between sacred and secular is not a traditional means for demarcating social interactions, and social processes often take on a sacred, or moral, dimension (social identities, behaviors, and relationships are often defined in terms of divine imperatives). The Seminole Baptist church participants constitute a moral community governed by situational proprieties.

By adhering to situational proprieties within social occasions, individuals express their identities as members of the same moral community. Social situations provide a means for individuals to express their identities not only as members of the community but also as members of its constituent social units (such as a particular congregation). A person's social identity is intrinsically linked to participation in social occasions. Within the Seminole community there are two competing and ostensibly exclusive social divisions—church people and Stomp grounds people. Participation in the social occasions of these divisions marks alliances that obligate and empower social action in accord with situational proprieties and strategic considerations of face. Interdivisional tension is ameliorated by the fact that many people participate within both divisions simultaneously. There are, therefore, more shared standards of conduct across divisional boundaries than may first appear evident. Thus, participation in occasions of either division exposes relationships, identities, and faces to regulation by the larger unit of the Seminole community. This is particularly evident when one considers the high degree of obligatory interaction required by the Fourth Sunday network of the churches and by the dance rotations of the Stomp grounds.

Goffman's approach emphasizes the role and motivations of individual actors within a community. This emphasis is appropriate, particularly for mainstream American culture. Social relationships in the mainstream American system are relatively fluid. We are given considerable freedom to unattach ourselves from one social network (such as a job, a church, or a club) and reattach to another. The individual is a relatively autonomous social actor, and individual motivations for social interaction, namely strategic consideration of one's face, can easily be viewed as the primary explanation for choices in social action. Within the Seminole community, however, there is not the same degree of freedom to unattach from and reattach to social networks. As participants within the community, Seminoles are enmeshed in networks of family, clan, churches, Stomp grounds, and political and economic ties that make movement costly, if not impossible. There are few anonymous interactions between community members. As a result, individuals are constrained by obligations to their immediate social units. Within the churches this translates to a primary level of orientation situated between individual self-interest and membership in the larger community. I will call this level "congregational face." By this I mean that as a member of a congregation, a participant in a social occasion additionally presents a face reflecting the social worth and intention of his or her own congregation. Each time members of different congregations interact, they risk their own as well as their congregation's face.

Congregational face may be viewed as an extension of two of Goffman's concepts: "honor" and "social relationships" (Goffman 1967:9–10, 41–42). According to Goffman, honor is displayed when a person manages impressions and events in a situation out of "duty to wider social units, and receives support from these units in doing so." For Seminole Baptists, the immediate "wider social units" are congregations. Members are obligated to perform certain behaviors (most notably, attend church gatherings and participate fully in them) and to avoid other behaviors (such as drinking, playing bingo, dancing, and playing in ball games) because of their membership in a church. In addition to such obviously identifying behaviors, a whole host of other, more subtle actions are subject to interpretation by other community members. Members are ever-mindful of how opinions, values, and beliefs are expressed and of how others may interpret their expressions and actions. Unlike membership in Anglo congregations, membership within a particular Seminole congregation is relatively permanent. A participant does not freely move among congregations. A person does not leave a congregation to join another without a considerable loss of face. Members of Seminole congregations are bound within social relationships in which they are compelled to support each other's face on a regular basis. Here Goffman's (1967:42) explanation of "social relationships," the second of his concepts extended for congregational face, is helpful:

> It seems to be a characteristic obligation of many social relationships that each of the members guarantees to support a given face for the other members in given situations. To prevent disruption of these relationships, it is therefore necessary for each member to avoid destroying the others' face. At the same time, it is often the person's social relationship with others that leads him to participate in certain encounters with them, where incidentally he will be dependent upon them for supporting his face. Furthermore, in many relationships, the members come to share a face, so that in the presence of third parties an improper act on the part of one member becomes a source of acute embarrassment to the other members. A social relationship, then, can be seen as a way in which the person is more than ordinarily forced to trust his self-image and face to the tact and good conduct of others.

Members of the same congregation share an enduring social relationship in which they are dependent on each other to support an individual face as well as a shared, or congregational, face. A congregation, therefore, closely monitors the behavior of its members, for all members' face is at risk. It is not surprising, therefore, that great care is extended in selecting congregational leaders. Members identified for leadership positions within a congregation are most likely those whose individual faces most closely reflect the face of the congregation. In general, though, impressions are managed by all church participants in social occasions, to maintain and enhance their own as well as their congregation's face.

The approach that I am using is a micro-sociology. I am investigating the actual processes by which real people, individuals within a web of social interactions and groups, maintain community and its concomitant sense of ethnicity, tradition, and self. Those favoring a macro-sociology will no doubt criticize this study for its failure to investigate the larger political and economic dimensions of the Seminole context. This failure is not one of oversight but rather is one of paradigmatic choice and analytical focus. Granted, the political and economic situation is significant, but these considerations run tangentially to the primary considerations of this study: the interdependence of cultural and social factors in the maintenance of a traditional community.

"Fulfilling the Work": The Social Functions of Seminole Baptist Church Gatherings

When native Christianity is defined as a conceptual framework introduced by nonnative sources and is therefore interpreted as a product of acculturation, leading to assimilation, ethnographers have failed to recognize the function of Christianity in maintaining traditional forms of social organization in Native American communities. The Seminole Baptist churches, as a social formation parallel with the Stomp grounds, serve to regulate and maintain social life within the Seminole community. Consequently, Seminole Christianity is better explained by the dynamic demands of community organization than by assimilation, acculturation, or culture loss. From a cursory glance, Seminole Baptists may appear to have accommodated to the dominant Anglo world; however, this is not so. Seminole Baptists maintain a distinct (i.e., traditional) cultural and social system that integrates their larger community. For Seminole church members, participation in church gatherings and occasions is the primary vehicle of social integration into the wider Seminole community. Occasions, which are governed by culturally specific situational proprieties, draw participants into encounters in which their faces are exposed to the scrutiny of peers. A participant's face is enhanced when his or her behavior is judged by other participants to be appropriate. Conversely, a participant who behaves inappropriately experiences a loss of face. Consideration of face—individual and congregational face within social occasions—provides the mechanism for community regulation, integration, and maintenance.

Face, of course, is an intrinsically social process. Face is contingent on people interacting. Social occasions provide the medium of interaction. Within Seminole Baptist churches, the power of social occasions to function as a primary vehicle of social integration lies in their compulsory nature—members are obligated into participation. Members speak of this obligation as *vtotkv esfaceces* ("fulfilling the work"). To understand the motivations that inform gatherings, one must consider the Seminole notion of *vtotketv* ("to work"). Members say they are *vtotketv esfacecares* ("going to fulfill the work"), meaning they are going to have a worship service. Participants in the service are said to be *vtotkv esfaceces* ("fulfilling the work") when they offer prayers, lead songs, or direct any aspect of the worship. Members are often referred to as *vtotkv* ("worker") or the plural *vtotkike* ("workers"). Early in my field experience, I asked a deacon for his understanding of a "good Christian." He responded, "I would say that a good Christian is one who is always in church." He reasoned: "God created our spirits; they come from God, and he wants them back. The only way that he'll get them back is if we make him number one in our lives." On further inquiry, the deacon stated that making God "number one" means that a person "goes to church and doesn't get slack in his work." A pastor spoke of work this way: "When a person is a Christian, he is supposed to fulfill the work of God. He does the work, and then he'll get the reward. We're supposed to 'work while it is day.' That means while we're alive, then we'll get the reward." I asked him, "What is the work that Christians are supposed to do?" He looked at me somewhat dumbfounded, as if the answer was self-evident. He said that the work was "doing church, you know, fulfilling the work. Doing church is the work that God requires of Christians." Moral behavior is, of course, necessary—"living what you believe"—but fulfilling the work of church is the divine imperative.

As will be shown, fulfilling the work requires a substantial commitment from the members. The obligations are not simply an hour each week on Sunday mornings. There are multiple gatherings each week, some beginning on Wednesday evening and continuing throughout the weekend. The simple Sunday-morning attendance expected in Anglo churches is criticized by Seminoles as being "slack," that is, a failure to fulfill the obligatory work of Christians. For the Seminoles, this work is paramount. Individuals are directed to the church gatherings not for whatever psychological benefits they might receive from the experience (i.e., inspiration, existential comfort, or support); rather, it is the *work* that is being done that merits people's attendance.

Seminole Baptists are neither "persistent relics" of aboriginal life nor Indians who have been assimilated into a white-oriented way of life. Nor is it appropriate to describe them as something in between. Rather, Seminole Baptist congregations constitute a segment of the culturally and socially distinct Seminole community in Oklahoma. Appeal to face, both individual face and congregational face, during obligatory social occasions is the instrument of social organization and regulation of the Oklahoma Seminole Baptist community. As the primary locus of Seminole social interaction, the Seminole Baptist church system also serves to integrate and maintain the larger Seminole community. By investigating the cultural symbols or conceptual frameworks (or, in Goffman's terminology, the "situational proprieties") of the Seminole Baptist church, this book will analyze how participants use those symbols (their actions and interactions) to achieve social ends—particularly the maintenance of the *traditional* community.

CHAPTER 2

A Brief History of the Seminoles

The body of literature concerning the Seminoles is necessarily interconnected with the literature regarding the Creeks. The Seminoles are a rather recent offshoot of the southeastern native people historically identified as Creek. The split resulted from a gradual relocation to the south of a portion of people who had associated with the loosely organized Creek Confederacy. The first documented reference to "Seminoles" was in 1765, but the distinction between the two groups was not formally recognized until after the Creek War of 1813–14. Yet even after that time some people still moved between Creek and Seminole communities, and the histories of the two groups remain interconnected today.[1]

The distinction between Creek and Seminole is problematic. Culturally and linguistically, the Oklahoma Seminoles are virtually indistinguishable from the Oklahoma Creeks. Those Seminoles in Florida whose ancestors were not removed to Indian Territory are more different, culturally and linguistically, from their Oklahoma relatives than the Oklahoma Creeks are from the Oklahoma Seminoles. Politically, however, the distinction between the Seminoles and the Creeks in Oklahoma is clear: they represent two tribes with separate tribal complexes that house governments administering distinct policies. The Oklahoma Seminoles are quick to point out that they are Semelone (Seminole) and not Mvskoke (Creek), yet there is a considerable amount of intermarriage between the two tribes.

The distinction between the two tribes is often voiced when both groups are represented at large gatherings, such as church and Stomp grounds gatherings. There are few, if any, exclusively Seminole or Creek activities. Yet even though there is considerable interaction between Creek and Seminole churches, only a few of the sixty or so Indian Baptist churches are recognized as Seminole. This study is limited to those churches—churches that are identified by Seminole Baptists as Seminole Baptist churches. The identification of churches as Seminole is largely determined by location—within or immediately adjacent to Seminole County. Thus, in this book I will use "Seminole" to define an analytical unit.

In the literature, the Seminoles have usually been treated as an aspect of the Creek community. The perceived singularity of the Seminoles in the literature has been their involvement with runaway slaves and their unique relationship with black freedmen. The Seminole literature is primarily historical, emphasizing the interactions between the Seminoles and the Euro-American forces and the relationships that those interactions fostered. There are very few ethnographic works devoted exclusively to the Oklahoma Seminoles; most treat the Seminoles as adjunct to the Creeks. Those ethnographies that do describe the Seminoles focus on the Florida community, whose development was much different from that of the Oklahoma community.

Nevertheless, there are some useful works that address the Oklahoma Seminoles. Swanton (1922, 1928a, 1928b) treats the Seminoles as an aspect of the Creek Confederacy, yet his descriptions of the Seminoles are indispensable. Swanton's *Early History of the Creek Indians and Their Neighbors* (1922:9) is, in his own words, an "account of the distribution, interrelationship, and history of these people gathered rather from documentary sources than from field investigations. . . . [The aim has been] to furnish something in the nature of an encyclopedia of information regarding the history of the southeastern Indians for the period covered, and hence has usually included direct quotations instead of attempting to recast the materials." Swanton makes liberal use of such primary sources as William Bartram, James Adair, and Benjamin Hawkins. In "Social Organization and Social Usages of the Indians of the Creek Confederacy" (1928a), Swanton uses an ethnographic approach. He describes social institutions such as kinship terminology, clanship, government, crime and punishment, and general customs. This broad work serves as a useful introduction for the peoples incorporated into the Creek Confederacy. The companion study to "Social Organization" is "Religious Beliefs and Medical Practices of the Creek Indians" (1928b). In this work Swanton, relying heavily on field observations, seeks to determine aboriginal beliefs and ceremonies. The volume is highly descriptive and informative yet fails to consider the social processes involving these cultural conceptualizations.

Grant Foreman's *Indian Removal* (1932) and Angie Debo's *And Still the Waters Run* (1940) and *The Road to Disappearance* (1941) are valuable historical accounts. Foreman's study addresses each of the Five Civilized Tribes and recounts in detail the Seminole "Trail of Tears." Debo's *And Still the Waters Run* meticulously documents unscrupulous governmental policy bent on the liquidation of the Five Tribes. Her *Road to Disappearance* focuses, with equal care, specifically on the Creek situation. In this work, the Seminoles are only occasionally considered.

Alexander Spoehr turned his attention to the Seminoles in two important ethnographic works. The first, "Oklahoma Seminole Towns" (1941), is a brief introduction to the organization of Seminole social and political life through the *etvlwv*, or town or band system (discussed below). His *Kinship System of the Seminole* (1942) traces changing kinship patterns of the Oklahoma Seminoles. In this work he demonstrates that the changing terminological system allowed the Seminoles to adapt a portion of their social organization to the surrounding Anglo world while maintaining their distinctness. He attributes this change to acculturation.

Edwin McReynolds's *The Seminole* (1957) was the first detailed history devoted exclusively to the Oklahoma Seminoles. It is a straightforward account of Seminole and Euro-American interactions. His account follows the Seminoles to Indian Territory after the Third Seminole War, and it ends at statehood.

Charles Hudson, in *The Southeastern Indians* (1976), includes the Seminoles in his ethnological survey of southeastern cultures. *The Southeastern Indians*, a synthesis of archaeology, history, and ethnology, serves as an introduction to the native peoples of the Southeast. In this work, Hudson locates the Seminoles within the larger "Mississippian tradition." His emphasis is on similarities among the native peoples and a "description of the major social institutions before they were fundamentally changed by European invaders" (Hudson 1976:viii). His representation may be criticized in that he presents precontact groups as pristine and static; through history, the peoples experience what he calls "deculturation." Hudson fails to consider the internal social dynamics of Indian communities.

Oklahoma Seminoles: Medicines, Magic, and Religion (1984), by James Howard, is the only ethnography concerned exclusively with the Oklahoma Seminoles. Howard cites the lack of anthropological attention to the Oklahoma Seminoles as his motivation to present Seminole culture "as it is seen and interpreted by its more traditional members" (Howard 1984:xvi). This work is highly descriptive, yet after reading it, one is still left with little sense of the Seminole people. Howard's interpretation goes only as far as explaining that "traditional" cultural practices result from the "stubborn persistence" of conservatives such as his informant, Willie Lena.

The Newberry Series of critical bibliographies has consistently produced excellent reference works, and this is no less true with Harry Kersey's *The Seminole and Miccosukee Tribes: A Critical Bibliography* (1987). His introductory historical essay concisely reports the important interactions between the Seminoles and the Euro-Americans. Unfortunately, from the removal period forward, he cites only works dealing with the

Seminoles who remained in Florida. Regarding the Oklahoma Seminoles he warns, "One must look elsewhere for the body of literature on these people" (Kersey 1987:ix). One must look long and hard, for there is a dearth of ethnographic materials on the Oklahoma Seminoles. Adequate histories have been produced, but these accounts end at statehood—the Oklahoma Seminoles, however, did not.

The Seminoles, as a distinct polity, are a relatively recent development. The people who became known as Seminoles came out of the loose affiliation of tribes called Creek. The history of the Seminoles is thus interconnected with the history of the Creeks.

The earliest historical accounts of the people who became known as Creeks, and the part of the Creeks who later became known as the Seminoles, placed them in central Georgia and Alabama (Adair 1930; Bartram 1928; Hawkins 1980). In the early seventeenth century, settlements of Muskogean-speaking peoples were scattered along the fertile river bottoms. The term "Creek" (initially "Ochese Creek," after the name of the river that supported a major concentration of these people) was originally used by the British in reference to all of the native peoples of the region, regardless of language or of ethnic or political affiliations. For European traders, settlers, and politicians, it was convenient to group all these native peoples together. The native peoples' self-designation was, however, considerably different. For the native peoples, primary self-identification was through their "band" affiliation. Thus, before proceeding with the history, we need to understand the nature of "band."

The fundamental political and ethnic unit of those groups called Creek and, later, Seminole was the *etvlwv* (translated by contemporary Seminoles as "band" and by Creeks as "town").[2] The *etvlwv* should not be thought of as a physical group of residences but rather as a group of people associated with a ceremonial center, or square ground, and its sacred central fire.

There were from twelve to twenty-four named Creek bands in the early seventeenth century (Sturtevant 1971:93). The number of bands fluctuates through time, with perhaps as many as eighty at one time. Bands have been relatively unstable, their makeup and size adjusting to changing circumstances. Fission and fusion was the pattern. For example, when a band became too large and unwieldy, a faction could split off. The departing faction, if it still "shared the fire"—that is, if it still participated in the ceremonial life of the original band— was considered an *ecuswv* ("daughter"), with the original band being the *etske* ("mother"). Conversely, if a band became too small through population loss resulting from war or disease, the band survivors could be adopted into a more stable band. Bands also experienced fission or fusion for political reasons.

Each band was politically autonomous, providing its own leadership, both civic and religious. Each band retained a degree of social and cultural autonomy—various Muskogean languages were spoken—and all bands had some idiosyncratic ceremonial practices. It is therefore more useful to understand the *etvlwv* as tribes rather than as simple enclaves of residences.

The ceremonial cycle of the *etvlwvlke* (the plural form of *etvlwv*) centered around the annual *posketv* ("to fast, or busk"), or Green Corn Festival. This festival of ritual renewal, purification, and thanksgiving marked the new year. Homes were swept and cleaned; old pottery was discarded and replaced with new. Past grievances, injuries, and crimes were forgiven. Old fires were extinguished, and a new fire was ritually kindled. This new fire, representing birth and renewal, was lit in the ceremonial center, or square ground. Embers were taken from the new sacred fire to light the fires of each of the hearths in the band. Swanton (1928b:548–49) described the symbolic significance of the busk fire:

> The busk with its fire, its medicines, and its ceremonial was a great unifying element between the several members of the Creek confederacy, all the tribes which united with it either adopting such a ceremonial or altering their own to agree with it. And further than that it was a special unifying institution

within each town [band], bringing together for a definite purpose in which the good of each and the good of all were bound up. . . . It is to be added that at the time of this ceremonial everyone must speak in a low, gentle tone of voice, if children begin to cry, they must be quieted at once without disturbance, and a general air of harmony must be preserved.

This theme of unity displayed ritually in the busk would later be displayed in the Seminole Baptist churches in their Communion Meetings (described in chapter 6).

During the Green Corn Festival, participants, after a period of fasting, consumed an emetic "black drink," or "medicine," as part of the ritual purification. The ceremony included all-night dances around the fire. Gourd and turtle-shell rattles accompanied the singing dancers. An additional aspect of the festival was playing stickball.[3] The game was played band against band, clan against clan, or men against women. The outcome had political and religious significance, determining future ritual leadership and interband alliances.

The *posketv* or Green Corn Festival continues in the present Seminole community with the activities at the Gar Creek Stomp grounds in northern Seminole County. Gar Creek sponsors at least four gatherings each summer. The gatherings include the Green Corn Festival, dances, medicine, and stickball games. Ball games occur every weekend in good, warm weather. During winter, benefit bingos are frequently held to raise money for the grounds. Many Seminoles also participate in the neighboring Creek Green Corn ceremonies.

The historical *etvlwv* owned and maintained agricultural lands. Portions of the arable land were assigned to matrilineal clans within the band. Corn agriculture provided the bulk of their subsistence economy and was the center of their ceremonial cycle. Squash, beans, sunflower seeds, and later sweet potatoes, pumpkin, rice, and peas were also cultivated. Agriculture was supplemented by gathering wild nuts and fruits and also by hunting. Deer, bear, and bison were the most important game animals. Waterfowl and fish were harvested by the more coastal bands.

Residential units were usually one or more structures surrounding a central square plaza. More-affluent homes included separate winter residences, cookhouses, and storage houses. Residences were often rectangular and constructed of logs, with thatch or bark shingles. Other types of dwellings were circular wattle-and-daub structures or skin- or bark-covered frames. Bartram, in his 1789 *Observations* (quoted in Swanton 1928a:172–73), described Seminole residences:

> Their private habitations consist generally of two buildings: one a large oblong house, which serves for a cook room, eating house, and lodging rooms, in three apartments under one roof; the other not quite so large, which is situated eight or ten yards distant, one end opposite the principal house. This is two stories high . . . and divided into two apartments, transversely, the lower story of one end being a potato house, for keeping such other roots and fruits as require to be kept close, or defended from cold in winter. The chamber over it is the *council*. At the other end of this building, both upper and lower stories are open on their sides; the lower story serves for a shed for their saddles, pack-saddles, and gears, and other lumber; the loft over it is a very spacious, airy, pleasant pavilion, where the chief of the family reposes in the hot seasons, and receives his guests, etc.

These dwellings are described as generous and comfortable.

By the late eighteenth century, the bands were entrenched in the European trade economy. Early in that century, Indians traded slaves, pelts, and deerskins for cloth, hardware, cooking vessels, knives, beads, and firearms. By the end of the century, many natives "depended more on selling deerskins than growing maize" (Wright 1986:42).

Within the bands, people were organized into clans. Clans served to regulate many aspects of Seminole life, including conduct, education of children, marriage, punishment of incest[4] and adultery, legal protection, ownership and inheritance of property, and social welfare. Until about the nineteenth century, the clans were responsible for punishing murderers.

In Swanton's (1928a:114) description of clans he commented, "The whole subject of clanship is not, however, entirely clear even yet, and some features of it probably never can be understood, owing to the death of those persons who were familiar with them and the breakdown of the entire institution." "Breakdown" should probably be understood here to mean that the clanship institution was undergoing modification in response to the changing social situation at the time of Swanton's research, for even contemporary Seminoles are well aware of their clan identities, and clan membership defines some social roles in both churches and Stomp grounds.

There have been as many as twenty-eight Seminole clans (Spoehr 1942:52); presently at least fourteen clans are represented in the Seminole community. I have heard people who, meeting for the first time, exchange names and then their clans, defining, at least in part, their relationship to each other. I have also seen a church flyer announcing a "Clan Day," in which clan identity would be determined for those people unsure of their clan.[5]

Swanton (1928a:168) observed the function of clanship for the Creeks and the Seminoles:

Clanship had an important influence on the relations between men, extending into the smallest matters of everyday life, and much of Creek etiquette was based upon it. Thus a Creek could tell by the attitude of any two members of his tribe toward each other—whether they joked with one another and so on—in what manner they were related. Persons having parents of the same clan used to joke with each other. This "joking relationship" thus included the entire clan of the mother; it also included all of those whose fathers belonged to one's own father's clan. . . . It was etiquette to talk disparagingly of one's own clan, even in the presence of other members of it, what was said being understood in a contrary sense. On the other hand one must always back up his father's clan and those belonging to it and must speak well of it and of them.

This description is apropos for the contemporary role of clan-ship among Seminole church people. I was a little alarmed when two men I had known to be very cordial, soft-spoken, and polite sat next to each other and began insulting each other and calling each other names, laughing in between insults. This was my introduction to a "joking relationship." The "backing up" that Swanton mentions includes providing assistance to a relative when the need is recognized or defending the clan reputation. One woman told me how her aunt took a man's brand-new Stetson off his head and threw it in the trash after he made fun of her father's clan.

Each band had an executive political leader called the *mekko* ("king"). In some bands the *mekko* served as the ceremonial leader as well. In other bands the ceremonial direction was the responsibility of the *heles hayv* ("medicine maker"). Assisting the mekko in the political leadership of the band was the *heneha*, who advised the *mekko* in practical administrative matters. Additional officers included the following: the *mekko*'s attending *emponvkv* ("one who speaks"), who spoke on behalf of the *mekko*; a head military officer called *tvstvnvke* ("warrior"); a group of councilors; and women's leaders. Together, all these leaders oversaw the civic government and made decisions regarding commerce, war, and other affairs that affected the band. The contemporary Seminole Stomp grounds employs leaders in positions parallel to these historical positions. The same terms are used, although their duties have, of course, been modified. Similarly the Seminole Baptist church leadership roles resemble the historical arrangement of band leadership posi-tions. Chapter 5 gives a comparison between these historical positions and the contemporary church leadership positions.

Bands enjoyed autonomy, but there was also cooperation between and among bands. Although there were differences, bands shared a similar "Southeastern culture" (Hudson 1976; Kersey 1987). Various languages were spoken in the bands, yet Mvskoke served as the lingua franca between bands. The extent of this cooperation is debatable, however, at least in the seventeenth and eighteenth centuries (Sturtevant 1971; Champagne 1992:64–67). There is some evidence of a union or confederacy of bands, but the confederacy was loose at best. In the mid–eighteenth century, Adair (1930:460) noted: "Every town [band] is independent of another, their own friendly compact continues the union. An obstinate war leader will sometimes commit acts of hostility, or make peace for his own town [band], contrary to the good liking of the rest of the nation." Bands were, to a large degree, independent of each other. At times bands even competed with each other, or at least had competing agendas. This was most clearly seen in military affairs. Opler (1972:35) noted, "Towns [Bands] could and did act alone in military affairs, and no town [band] accepted as valid treaties or agreements affecting it unless ratified by its own officers." The failure, whether intentional or not, of the Europeans and later the Americans to recognize band autonomy resulted in many misunderstandings. Euro-American diplomatic negotiators would hold the whole, loose confederacy responsible for the actions and treaty ratifications of single bands.

It is important to understand that the band structure was not static. New bands (or tribes) were incorporated regularly into the loose confederacy. Conversely, bands or parts of bands sometimes chose to cease affiliating with other bands. During this period, the invasion of Europeans and Americans brought war, disease, and land encroachment, disrupting many aspects of Indian life. Some bands experienced population decimation. During these turbulent years, bands underwent periods of fission and fusion, as noted earlier. Surviving band members were incorporated into other, stronger bands or joined with other survivors to form a new band. Just as the political structuring of bands was adjusted to changing external conditions, so too were cultural practices. New people brought new ideas. It was this fluid structuring of bands that led to the formulation of the Seminoles.

The genesis of the Seminole people is interwoven with the geopolitics of the European expansion into the New World. After destroying a French colony, the Spanish took over the site and founded St. Augustine on the present-day northeastern Florida peninsula in 1565. The Franciscans soon after began operating a mission system out of St. Augustine. The missionaries were relatively successful among the native Timucua and Guale and later among the Apalachee peoples. Spanish interests in Florida were pursued in peace until the English establishment of Charles Town to the north in 1670.

The fledgling English colony required large numbers of laborers. The English employed local Yamasee and Creek Indians to supply Indian slaves. By 1680, slaving sent the Yamasees and Creeks farther south to capture more Indians for slaves. As the need for Indian slaves at Charles Town diminished, the English pursued the skin and fur trade. Thousands of slaves were still needed elsewhere, however. The Spanish governor's 1708 report to the king (in Boyd, Smith, and Griffin 1950:90) estimated that ten thousand to twelve thousand natives of the Apalachee region of northern Florida were enslaved. Most had been exported to West Indies plantations and to New England. The Florida mission population was virtually destroyed, leaving perhaps only three hundred native refugees at St. Augustine. As a result, St. Augustine withdrew its outposts. Spain's influence in the region was waning. The fertile northern Florida region, often referred to as the Alachua region, was left nearly vacant.

As the pool of native slaves dried up at the beginning of the eighteenth century, the Creeks and Yamasees became more involved in the English fur trade. Indian hunters traded fur and tanned hides for manufactured goods. English traders often extended credit to the Indian hunters, providing supplies for fall and winter hunts with the expectation of payment in the spring. As credit levels increased and the availability of fur-bearing animals decreased, Creek and Yamasee hunters found themselves in chronic debt to the traders. Some traders would enslave a debtor's family as payment. Such actions created very hostile feelings between traders and indebted Indian hunters, resulting in conflict that often led to the murder of traders by Indians. Not surprisingly, the hostilities escalated into war.

The Yamasee War of 1715 was an attempt by the allied forces of Yamasee, Creek, Choctaw, Catawba, and other tribes to drive the English, French, and Spanish out of the Southeast. The Indian forces attacked the Carolina colonies, killing many. But the well-armed colonists struck back, and the allied Indian forces were mercilessly routed. This defeat began a massive movement of native peoples.

Fearing reprisals, the Yamasees moved en masse from the Carolina region and settled in northern Florida. The Apalachee, Apalachicola, Oconee, Yuchi, and other Lower Creek bands all moved west and south (the terms "Lower" and "Upper" were applied by Europeans beginning at this time to distinguish the eastern or Lower from the western or Upper Creeks). The southern movement of native peoples was encouraged by the Spanish, who needed a buffer between Spanish Florida and the English settlements to the north.

During the fifty years following the Yamasee War of 1715, military and economic pressures continued to push native people south. Hunters had to travel farther in search of deer and fur-bearing animals. Groups of hunting families began to spend large parts of the year in the Florida frontier. Gradually, large portions of some bands established more permanent settlements in the Florida region, and the bands grew. By 1765, the bands of Eufaula, Oconee, Tamathli, Apalachicola, Hitchiti, and Yuchi had settled into the Alachua region of northern and central Florida. It was to these bands, composed primarily of Hitchiti-speakers, that the term "Seminole" was first applied.

Sturtevant (1971:105) notes that "Seminole" was used on two levels: first, as a general term for all Florida Indians; and second, more specifically, as a term for the Alachua-region settlements. Sturtevant records the etymology of the term: "The ethnonym is of Muskogee origin: *simanoli* (earlier *simaloni*, surviving in some dialects) means 'wild, runaway,' as applied to animals and plants. It was originally borrowed by Muskogee from the Spanish word *cimarron*, which has the same meaning. A more appropriate translation of the Muskogee word in its extended, perhaps metaphorical, use as an ethnonym is probably 'emigrants,' 'pioneers,' or 'frontiersmen.'" Through time, the Florida bands became more independent of the Creeks to the north. The term "Seminole" came to be used to distinguish the Florida bands from their northern Creek relatives.

The third quarter of the eighteenth century marked a period of British hegemony in the Southeast. At the end of the French and Indian War, France was eliminated as a contender for territory in the Southeast, and Spain ceded Florida to British control. Southeastern natives continued to participate in the fur trade industry with the British. British political policy, seeking to preserve cheap Indian labor for the fur industry, sought to restrict colonists to coastal settlements. The constraints failed as more and more agriculturally minded colonists encroached on Indian lands. The resulting tensions between the colonists and the English led in part to the Revolutionary War.

Competitive geopolitics among English, Spanish, and the emergent Americans accompanied the Revolutionary War. Florida was returned to Spanish control. In most instances, which of these competing forces controlled a particular piece a land did not affect Indian life. Native people attempted to play the Euro-American forces to their own best interest. Toward the end of the eighteenth century, the United States became the dominant force in the Southeast. Spanish and British support of the natives ceased, and natives were left to oppose U.S. expansion without external aid. During this period, the deerhide trade also collapsed, destabilizing economic life in the region.

During the first quarter of the nineteenth century, Indian people were forced to cede lands, originally to pay increasing trade debts. After the War of 1812, the Southeast, except Spanish Florida, was under U.S. hegemony. The Americans continued to use the strategy of allowing increased trade debts as a means to acquire Indian land. Indians were encouraged to accrue debts so large that the only means they had to settle the debts was to cede land. A policy of acculturation and assimilation was also instituted to reduce the Indians' need for land. The U.S. government reasoned that moving the Indians away from hunting and toward subsistence agriculture would free large tracts of land for American expansion.

A significant event in defining the Seminole people as a community distinct from that of the Creeks was the Creek or Red Stick War of 1813–14. The eastern Lower Creeks had been serving as a buffer for the western Upper Creeks against encroaching Europeans and Americans. The Lower Creeks, with their longer and more intimate interactions with the Euro-Americans, were more economically assimilated. When the American agent Benjamin Hawkins began his work among the Creeks, he sponsored a new Creek National Council as a means of organizing and controlling the Creek bands. Hawkins planned to maneuver the more compliant Lower Creek *mekkos* into positions of authority in the Creek National Council. The Upper Creeks opposed the proposed innovations. The visit of Tecumseh, a Shawnee political leader (whose mother was Mvskoke), to the Upper Creeks exacerbated the already volatile relationship with the Lower Creeks. Tecumseh's nativistic, anti-U.S. message urged insurrection against the Americans. Several Creeks responded immediately and attacked and killed a number of American families. The Lower Creeks, desiring to maintain good relations with the Americans, tracked down the guilty Upper Creeks and executed them. The conflict accelerated into a civil war. The makeup of the two opposing factions was quite complex: in some cases whole towns supported a side, but other towns were divided in their support; some young people sided against their more conservative elders. The turning point of the war came when one faction received U.S. aid. Andrew Jackson and the state militia joined the more progressive-minded faction and handily defeated the conservative-minded side. In the war's aftermath, many of the defeated refugees emigrated to Florida to join the Seminoles there. The Creeks who remained in the north were forced to cede about two-thirds of their land to the U.S. government.

Some of the emigrant refugees established new bands among the Seminoles. Others were incorporated into existing Seminole bands. Before the Red Stick War there were estimated to be perhaps 3,500 Seminoles in Florida; after the war, there were about 6,000 (Sturtevant 1971:106). The prewar Seminole population had a majority of Hitchiti-speakers. After the war, the majority of the Seminoles spoke Mvskoke.

The situation in Spanish Florida was vexing for the U.S. government, which feared that Florida was becoming an attractive locale for troublemakers. In addition to the Red Stick refugees were many escaped slaves and their offspring. Some of these blacks, called freedmen, had organized into *etvlwvlke* that affiliated with the Seminoles. The Seminoles had been armed by the British during the War of 1812 and were encouraged to cross the border into Georgia to conduct raids. Many southern Americans feared an Indian-black uprising.

In 1818, Andrew Jackson and his Georgia militia entered Spanish Florida in retaliation, starting the First Seminole War. Jackson destroyed Seminole bands and black settlements. Many freedmen were captured during this war and forced north to become slaves. The Americans then negotiated with the battered Seminoles, resulting in the 1823 Treaty of Moultrie Creek. With the defeat of the Indians, Spain could no longer hold Florida and relinquished it to the United States in 1821.

In the Treaty of Moultrie Creek the Seminoles gave up claim to all of their Florida territory except for four million acres, in the center of the state, which would serve as a reservation. The Seminoles were to receive $5,000 each year for the next twenty years and $1,000 to establish and maintain a reservation school. Charles Fairbanks (cited in Sturtevant 1971:107) later reported that at the time of the treaty signing, the Seminoles in Florida maintained at least thirty-two *etvlwvlke*, or bands. These included eight Red Stick refugee bands, two Yuchi bands, and three black bands.

In 1829, Andrew Jackson was elected president. With his presidency came aggressive policies to deal with the Indians, most notably the Indian Removal Act of 1830. The act gave states the authority to deal with Indians within their boundaries. States, of course, favored removal. As a result, the Seminoles were engaged in removal negotiations resulting in the Treaty of Payne's Landing of 1832.

In this treaty the Seminoles relinquished all their land claims in Florida and were to remove to Indian Territory in the west and settle among the Creeks there. The treaty contained a clause stating that a delegation of Seminoles was to examine land in Indian Territory to find a satisfactory location among the Creeks. That delegation, while exploring Indian Territory, was maneuvered into signing an additional treaty. The Treaty of Fort Gibson stated that the Seminoles were to be considered a constituent unit of the Creek nation and placed in an undetermined location within the Creek nation. The exploratory delegation, of course, had no authority to negotiate a treaty. Nevertheless, both the Treaty of Payne's Landing and the Treaty of Fort Gibson were ratified by Congress in 1834.

The Seminoles were greatly upset by the report of the returning exploratory delegation. They were adamantly opposed to merging with the larger Creek nation, particularly considering that many of those Creeks had been enemies during the Red Stick War earlier in the century. When it came time for removal according to the treaties, the Seminoles violently refused. Charley Emathla, a Seminole who had supported the removal effort, was murdered by fellow Seminoles. Other Seminoles, led by Osceola, killed the Indian agent and several agency employees. That same day another party of

Seminoles and freedmen attacked and destroyed a company of U.S. troops en route to assist the removal efforts. Thus began the Second Seminole War.

The Second Seminole War lasted for seven years. Considered to be one of the most expensive of the Indian wars, it cost the U.S. government 1,500 soldiers' lives and $20 million. It resulted in the destruction of Seminole bands, livestock, and provisions and the removal of 4,420 Seminoles to Indian Territory (Sturtevant 1971:108). Remaining in the Florida everglades after the war were approximately 500 Seminoles, who would form the nucleus of the surviving Florida Seminole community.

Once in Indian Territory, the Seminoles continued to have problems with the Creeks. Since some Creeks had assisted the United States during the Second Seminole War against the Seminoles, hard feelings were still harbored. According to the Treaty of Fort Gibson, the Seminoles were expected to incorporate into the Creek nation and be subject to Creek laws. The Seminoles objected, fearing that they would be absorbed into the larger Creek nation and that Seminole identity would be lost. Some Seminoles refused to settle with the Creeks and instead remained at Fort Gibson in Cherokee territory.

The Seminole freedmen reestablished their two bands as settlements in Indian Territory. The Creeks objected to the large settlements of blacks on their land and were continually making fraudulent claims for ownership of the slaves and freedmen that accompanied the Seminoles into Indian Territory. In 1845, General Thomas Jesup, who had negotiated peace and the removal from Florida, reminded all of the Seminole blacks who had surrendered in Florida that they were considered free under the removal agreement. Almost all of the blacks, taking General Jesup at his word, fled from Indian Territory to Fort Gibson. Jesup's declaration was later voided, and in 1848 the Seminole blacks were forced to return. The once-amicable relationship that had existed between the blacks and the Seminoles began to deteriorate.

For the Seminoles in Indian Territory, life was difficult. Provisions promised in the treaty were of poor quality and low quantity. Many Seminoles starved. Additionally, the Seminoles faced raiding parties of Plains Indians, to whom they lost horses and property.

Back in Florida, another conflict arose between the remaining Seminoles and the Americans, and the Third Seminole War erupted. This war was of a much smaller scale then the previous one. Only a handful of federal troops and perhaps twenty Seminoles were killed. After the three-year war, 240 more Seminoles were removed to Indian Territory, with fewer than 200 Seminoles now remaining in Florida.

In 1856, a treaty was negotiated between the Seminoles and the Creeks. The treaty provided the Seminoles with their own land and government, thus protecting the Seminoles in Indian Territory from Creek domination. An independent Seminole tribal government, responsible for enforcing its own laws, was organized beginning in 1859. The future looked brighter. Unfortunately, the Seminoles' efforts at improving their life in Indian Territory was interrupted by the Civil War.

With the onset of the Civil War, federal troops that had been stationed in forts around Seminole territory were removed to protect the eastern states. Confederate forces soon took control of several of the abandoned forts. Whereas the federal government had virtually abandoned Indian Territory, the Confederates were willing to embrace the Indians. In 1861, a Confederate delegation negotiated a treaty with the Seminoles, promising better treatment than they had received thus far from the federal government. The principal chief, John Jumper, and twelve band *mekkos* endorsed it. A faction of the tribe, led by Billy Bowlegs and John Chupko, refused to sign, however. They and their followers and almost all of the Seminole freedmen left Seminole territory and went north to Kansas, enduring great hardship along the way. Once in Kansas, these Seminoles, along with other loyal Indians from Indian Territory, enlisted in the Union Army. Jumper organized a Seminole battalion for the

Confederate Army. All Seminoles endured the extreme difficulties of the war: homes and property were destroyed; many
Seminoles became refugees; sickness and starvation were
widespread; casualties and destruction were great. Unfortunately, the difficulties did not end with the war. Seminoles
who had remained loyal to the federal government expected
some reward for their pro-Union efforts but were assigned the
same fate as those who had sided with the Confederates (with
the exception of $50,000 divided among the loyalists for losses
sustained during the war). The northern and southern Seminole factions did not immediately reconcile their differences.
For a time the tribe supported two principal chiefs: John
Jumper for the southern Seminoles and John Chupko for the
northern Seminoles.

In 1866, the Seminoles signed a new treaty with the federal
government. In this treaty the Seminoles pledged permanent
loyalty to and peace with the United States. The treaty also stip-
ulated that the Seminoles would relinquish a portion of their
land (2,169,080 acres of western land were sold, and 200,000
acres were purchased), abolish slavery, and incorporate freedmen as full tribal members. After 1866, the Seminoles and
freedmen shared their government, their schools, and their
land.

By 1868, the war-scattered Seminoles had settled into their
new homelands, later known as the Seminole Nation (roughly,
the present Seminole County), beginning their longest period
of relative stability. Their national constitutional government
was reorganized. Wewoka was selected as the capital, and a
council house was erected there. The tribal government
included a principal chief, a second chief (each elected by a
popular vote every four years), and a council of forty-two
members made up of the band mekko and two others from
each of the fourteen bands (two of which were freedmen
bands). The bands represented in the constitution should be
viewed as an extension of the preexisting *etvlwv* system and
not as a direct continuation of the *etvlwvlke*. The bands repre-

sented in the new government were regionally defined, and the elected band representatives did not necessarily manage ceremonial ground activities. The traditional bands continued to operate the ceremonial Stomp grounds and to function socially and politically (although in an increasingly diminished role). The council was divided into legislative and judicial departments. Laws were enforced by tribal police, called lighthorsemen. This was the beginning of two parallel forms of Oklahoma Seminole social organization: the official government was concerned primarily with external relations, whereas internal relations were structured by the Stomp grounds and churches.

Just as the Seminoles were adjusting to their new self-rule on their own land, still another disruption arose: in 1893, Congress created the Dawes Commission to negotiate the dissolution of the Five Civilized Tribes. The movement to dissolve Indian governments came from two motivations. The ever-growing, non-Indian settlements surrounding the Indian nations required additional lands. The other motivation, more benevolent if not naive, was the recognition that there was a tremendous inequity of land distribution among Indians. The wealthy, well-informed minority of leaders controlled vast amounts of land, whereas the uneducated majority had access to very little land.

By 1898, the actions of the Dawes Commission had been incorporated into the Curtis Act: all tribal governments, including Seminole, were to be abolished on March 4, 1906; Indians were to become citizens of the United States in 1901; all civil and criminal cases were moved from tribal to U.S. jurisdiction; the Seminoles were brought under U.S. laws; and tribal funds were managed by the Department of Interior. Later that year, a Seminole roll was begun. In 1906 the roll was closed, and the allotment process was well under way. The 3,119 Seminoles enrolled (more than 900 of these were freedmen) received an average of 120 acres each (Chaney 1928:77). In 1907, when Oklahoma became a state, the Seminole homelands became Seminole County. County government replaced tribal government. However, because the allotment process moved slower than expected, Congress enacted a law providing for the continuation of a truncated form of tribal government to manage tribal affairs until all of the Dawes Commission tasks were completed. These tasks were still being processed into the late 1960s, when the tribe reorganized. Up until that reorganization, tribal chairmen were appointed by the president of the United States. In the 1930s the Seminoles revived the offices of chiefs and council members to represent the tribe.

Statehood was particularly hard on the Seminole freedmen. The Oklahoma State constitution segregated blacks from Indians and whites. Laws were enacted that created segregated schools, transportation, and even bathrooms. The tribal structure and the political function that had held the Seminoles and the freedmen together were dissolved; social ostracism and racist laws drove them apart.

In the period from statehood to World War II the Seminoles enjoyed peace and stability. Most of the Seminoles participated in subsistence agriculture. Corn, peanuts, rice, sweet potatoes, white potatoes, pumpkins, and watermelons were the main food crops. Many Seminoles raised tobacco for personal use. Cotton and sorghum were cultivated as cash crops. Trapping beaver, raccoons, otters, and possum increased family incomes. Hunting and fishing supplemented hogs, chickens, and cattle as meat sources. An Anglo contemporary, Superior Court Judge C. G. Cutlip (quoted in Chaney 1928:104), described the Seminoles: "They are strictly a communal people as they were in the past. When one has plenty, all the rest belonging to that particular clan participate in the fortune of the fortunate." In her history of the Seminoles, Chaney (1928:85) provided details: "When the crops were being planted and cultivated, it was the custom of the town governor [band *mekko* of] (Tulwamiccoge) to call out the men of the town who would go to a certain field and work the crop. The next day another field was visited and until in this way all the crops of the neighborhood were properly cared for." Older Seminoles today recall such cooperation from their childhood.

Seminole County experienced dramatic growth during the years 1920–50. Vast fields of oil were exploited—billions of barrels were pumped in and around Seminole County. Although $25 million of oil royalties were distributed to the Seminoles during the 1920s alone (Chaney 1928:119), it mostly went to only a few tribal members. "With the full blood Indians, the revenue is paid to an Indian Agent who gives each a regular income. The principal is held in trust" (Chaney 1928:120). Much oil money was being circulated, yet it had very little impact on the long-term welfare of the majority of the Seminoles.

World War II marked another point of change for the Seminole community. Many Seminole men and women served in the military, particularly in Oklahoma's Forty-fifth Infantry. Few veterans returned to agricultural employment, since the growing postwar economy provided alternate employment. Many Seminoles began to participate more directly in the Anglo economy.

The period of Seminole history following the war may be characterized as attempts to restore much of the Seminole self-rule that was lost at statehood. The heart of the New Deal Indian Program for Oklahoma Indians was the 1936 Oklahoma Indian Welfare Act (OIWA), adapted from the Indian Reorganization Act of 1934 specifically to address the special legal status of Oklahoma Indians. Among the Seminoles, the OIWA instituted several programs designed to restore tribal legal identity and to organize the tribe for common welfare. Reorganization was accomplished through a federal charter as a local cooperative association.

In 1946, the Indian Claims Commission was organized to resolve and abolish all Indian claims to land and to litigate wrongs suffered. In the first five years, 588 claims were filed, some of which were Seminole claims. After years of litigation, in 1976 the Seminoles were awarded $16 million for the Florida land sales. The money did not go to the tribe immediately, however, since it had not yet been decided how the money was to be split between the Oklahoma Seminoles and the Florida Seminoles (descendants of those Seminoles who refused to remove to Indian Territory in the early nineteenth century). In 1991, Congress passed legislation that awarded 75 percent of the funds to the Oklahoma Seminoles and 25 percent to the Florida Seminoles. Meanwhile, the $16 million awarded in 1976 had not been left idle during the wait for disbursement. Interest dividends had increased the amount to $52 million by 1991. Of that sum, $38 million went to the Oklahoma Seminoles, and some of that money was distributed to tribal members in 1992. The balance remains with the tribe to be used for housing, health care, food aid, and education benefits.

The freedmen received no benefits from the settlement. Since statehood, the status of freedmen has been controversial. Statehood laws placed freedmen with other blacks of Oklahoma; that is, they were segregated from Indians and whites. The recent history of the Seminoles and the freedmen is, therefore, not a shared history. When Seminole tribal government was reestablished in the 1960s, freedmen were included in the organization of the government, and freedmen hold six seats on the present Seminole council, yet many Seminoles resent their inclusion. Many oppose freedmen receiving any tribal benefits. Part of that resentment is fueled by the 1976 Bureau of Indian Affairs (BIA) ruling that excluded freedmen from receiving any of the 1976 Florida land settlement. The BIA reasoned that since the freedmen were not recognized as Seminoles until the 1866 treaty, they were not entitled to compensation for actions taken in 1823. Some Seminoles have interpreted that ruling to mean that freedmen should receive no tribal benefits. The freedmen, however, are presently pursuing a class-action lawsuit against the tribe to secure benefits.

In 1952, the Voluntary Relocation Program was implemented by the BIA. This program was designed to offer financial assistance and limited social services to tribal members who were willing to relocate to industrial centers such as Chicago, Denver, Los Angeles, Oakland, San Francisco, and St. Louis. The idea was to provide opportunities for self-support and, perhaps, total assimilation. The program provided transportation and moving expenses to one of the participating cities, housing, health insurance, clothing and furniture allowances, and training. More than twenty thousand Indians participated in the first five years, many of these Seminoles. However, there was a high return rate—tribal members moved back to the Indian communities—and the program was abandoned.

In 1975, the Indian Self-Determination and Educational Assistance Act, in conjunction with a series of other related congressional acts designed to allow tribes to administer programs previously provided by the federal government, went into effect. This led to the formation of the Seminole Nation of Oklahoma. This constitutional government was based on the pre-statehood organization of a principal chief and an assistant chief, both elected to four-year terms, and a council of forty-two representatives, three from each of the reorganized bands.

The Seminole Nation today administers programs designed to assist tribal members, programs such as Headstart, food assistance, employment and training for youth, native craft development, health care, scholarships, job skills training, and industrial development. Many tribal members criticize the Seminole government as inefficient, corrupt, and greedy. Older members especially complain that the tribe "should do more for its people." Not surprisingly, one chairman was ousted in 1982 for failing to perform his responsibilities. Another chairman was recently indicted for misuse of funds.

Today, there are about 11,000 people registered with the tribe; 6,400 live in Oklahoma. Of these, 3,800 live in the tribal jurisdiction statistical area, which includes most of Seminole County. Of these, 23 percent speak Mvskoke; 35 percent have poverty status; 18 percent are unemployed. Most Seminoles find employment in manufacturing or service. Less than 3 percent farm. The median income per household is less than

$15,000 annually. Only 56 percent of Seminoles over twenty-five years of age have a high school degree. Many young Seminoles choose to leave the county in search of employment. The second-largest concentration of Seminoles is in Oklahoma City (the largest is in Seminole County).[6]

This book focuses on those Seminoles who participate in the Seminole Baptist church. Participants reflect the demographic spectrum. At any given church function there is a mix of infants, toddlers, children, adolescents, young adults, adults, and elderly. Virtually all members about fifty years of age and older are fluent in Mvskoke; most of their children and grandchildren are not.

Many of the members are retired and are living on Social Security. Several are living on pensions and disability checks. As children, most of these members grew up practicing subsistence farming. Since World War II, the Seminoles have participated directly in the larger economy as laborers, truck drivers, oil hands, domestics, day-care providers, and other various service personnel. Younger members today are employed in such positions throughout the area. Several are employed and living in Oklahoma City, about forty miles northwest of Seminole County.

For most of their lives, members have been enmeshed in the Seminole community. Primary relations are with other Seminole/Creek people. There are, of course, non-Indian acquaintances, but in most instances Seminoles choose to associate with other Seminole/Creek people. At virtually all of the gatherings and occasions I attended (formal and informal), I was the only non-Indian present.

Yet the need for various services forces Seminoles to interact with non-Seminoles. Public education is one of those services. Seminoles are generally very supportive of education. Young parents view participation in the Head Start program as an imperative. I have been in several homes where grandparents or parents were assisting their grandchildren or children with homework. School athletics, particularly football, are actively supported by many Seminole Baptists (the exception occurs when athletics interfere with church responsibilities). Church members are well aware of high school football schedules and team standings, which are often a focus of conversation. This local team pride is also extended to include vocal support of the Dallas Cowboys professional football team and the University of Oklahoma Sooners.

Other service needs—such as groceries, auto repairs, post office boxes, barbers, cafes—also place Seminoles in direct interaction with non-Seminoles. In my observations, such encounters generally show very cordial relations between Seminoles and non-Seminoles. As in many small towns, service personnel are on a first-name basis with their customers.

Adequate, if inconvenient, health service is provided by two local Indian clinics. One is in Shawnee, Oklahoma, just west of Seminole County. The other, more convenient clinic is in Ada, Oklahoma, just south of Seminole County.

All members' homes that I entered had a television. Most had telephones. One had an exterior satellite dish and a VCR. One pastor had a police radio scanner that he used to monitor local happenings. The Seminoles that I met were well-versed in current affairs—local and national. Most discussions of news and politics usually included a moral judgment.

In many ways the Seminoles are like their rural, working-class, non-Seminole neighbors. Their homes are relatively small and old. Daily activities revolve around employment, home maintenance, and domestic duties. Their primary differences involve their Indian ethnicity and their concomitant social and cultural interactions.

CHAPTER 3

Christianity among the Seminoles

The Seminoles' adoption of Christianity was gradual.[1] Seminoles, like many other natives, distrusted Anglos and their foreign ways. Band leaders perceived missionaries as rivals, believing them to undermine the band members' loyalties. Christianity was therefore resisted, and Seminole converts to Christianity were viewed with suspicion. James Factor, said to be the first Seminole converted to the Baptist faith, was removed from his position on the Seminole council in 1860 because he had been "bewitched" by the Baptist missionary. It is not surprising, then, that freedmen—who were already only marginally Seminole—were the earliest converts to the Christian faith.[2] Christianized freedmen often served as translators for Anglo missionaries, mimicking the gestures and inflections of the preachers whom they were interpreting. It was not until after the general disruption of Seminole autonomy (economic and political) and the undermining of customary authority and practice that Christianity became a vital force within the Seminole community.

The first Seminole mission was Oak Ridge Presbyterian, begun in 1848. The mission was sponsored by the Presbyterian Foreign Mission Board. The board appointed Rev. John Lilley and his wife, Mary Anne, to establish a mission school. In 1849 they opened the Oak Ridge school and church. The Lilleys were assisted by an eastern-educated native teacher and preacher named John Bemo. Bemo was himself Seminole.

Success came slowly for the missionaries. In the 1856–57 school year they had only twenty-six students, nineteen of whom were Seminole. The Presbyterians, however, were encouraged by the small advances that were being made among the Seminoles. In 1856, the Lilleys and Bemo were joined by an additional missionary, Rev. J. R. Ramsey, sent to establish another school.

Ramsey's interpreter was a freedman named Robert Johnson. Ramsey (1857) wrote about his interpreter: "He spoke Seminole language with great fluency and most warm and energetic. . . . But still he is an African and he will have African ways and will try to lead our people into such things as having frequent fasts followed by feasts, great camp meetings, observing Christmas and sitting up all night singing." Ramsey complained that since he was forced to use an interpreter, he was at the interpreter's mercy. Since the early interpreters were mostly all freedmen, the latter had great influence in shaping the Seminole churches.

In 1857, the Presbyterians were optimistic about the future of their missions, particularly because of the conversion of the Seminole principal chief John Jumper. That optimism was not long-lived, however. The Presbyterian mission monopoly ended in 1857, when the Indian Missions Board of the Southern Baptist church sent Rev. Joseph Samuel Murrow from Georgia. After a brief stint among the Creeks, Murrow established a Seminole church in 1860 on the new Seminole reservation. The church would later be known as Ash Creek Church. One of Murrow's earliest converts was the Presbyterian native preacher John Bemo. The vexed Lilley vehemently accused Murrow of "using every device to persuade the Indians to leave the Presbyterians and join the new group" (Lancaster 1994:107). Murrow was indeed highly successful. Much of that success, however, may have been due to the times and the attitudes leading to the Civil War.

During the war, most of the Seminoles sided with the South, although a minority of Union loyalists went north into Kansas. The national Presbyterian church was abolitionist; the Baptist stand on slavery was less defined. Murrow, the Baptist missionary, was a southerner from Georgia. The Presbyterian Seminoles sided with the North or converted to the Baptist faith, whereas Baptist Seminoles sided with the South. It was at the beginning of the war that the principal chief John Jumper converted from the Presbyterian church to join Murrow's Baptists. The chaplain of the federal forces stationed at Fort Gibson observed, "The then principal chief, John Jumper, went off to the Baptists, and took all that part of the church that went South, with him; this was much to be regretted; he was among the most promising fruits of the mission" (Grimes 1870:39). Jumper cited theological reasons for his move to the Baptist church. Jumper was baptized by John Bemo, initiating a lifelong friendship between the two.

During the war Jumper became a ranking officer in the Confederate Army. He recommended Murrow for the position of Confederate Indian agent. Murrow was given that appointment in 1862 and continued to lead worship services for the southern Seminoles throughout the duration of the war.

In the years following the war, denominational boundaries continued to reflect the North-South cleavage. Presbyterian missions appealed to the northern Seminoles, and the Baptists attracted those Seminoles who had supported the Confederacy.

Presbyterian mission work, suspended by the war, resumed when the northern refugees returned to Indian Territory. By 1868 the Presbyterians had four mission schools, all sponsored by the Presbyterian Foreign Mission Board. In 1873, David Constant and his wife, Antoinette, were called to begin a mission school in Wewoka. Although only three pupils attended the first day of classes, enrollment had reached fifty by 1876. Today at least two Seminole Presbyterian churches are active; however, the church services mostly follow an Anglo Presbyterian pattern.

Two interesting differences marked the Presbyterians and the Baptists. First, the Presbyterians expected a strict following of the Sabbath—members were not to perform any work on

Sundays. Band chiefs, however, expected the Presbyterian Seminoles to do their community garden work on Sundays, just like everyone else. Presbyterian missionaries viewed this as violating the Sabbath. Baptists, in contrast, were considered lax, since they allowed members to behave the same on Sunday as on any other day. The other difference was the selection of leadership personnel. Whereas the Presbyterians relied on specially trained outside missionaries, the Baptists relied on the more effective strategy of using native preachers. This was particularly true after the Civil War.

One of the most prominent of these preachers was the principal chief John Jumper. Jumper was ordained as a Baptist clergyman in 1865. He was described as "a noble specimen of an Indian man . . . 6' 4" in height and weighs 255 pounds. His features indicate fair intelligence and strong will and yet great benevolence" (Dr. G. J. Johnson 1875, quoted in Foreman 1951:146). He was "zealous for Christ, and at present is the chief prop of the Baptist church among the Seminoles, and believed to be a true man of God" (Grimes 1870:39). Jumper retired from tribal office in 1877, dedicating himself full-time to the ministry. Jumper's zealousness and his success as a native preacher and pastor are attested to by the fact that a church he built, Spring Church, is extant today.

The Spring Church cornerstone says that the church was founded in 1850. That date is unlikely, considering that the first Baptist missionary did not arrive among the Seminoles until 1857. However, Spring Church is recognized as the first of the Seminole Baptist churches. It was described in 1875: "The new house of worship built by the Seminoles is in the grove near to Brother Jumper's residence and is a well constructed frame 25' x 35' on the ground with two stories, the lower for the purposes of week day and Sunday School and the upper floor for public worship; cost $1000.00. Provided with a small bell hung on a pole frame outside the house set up by being fastened to the trees" (Johnson 1875, quoted in Foreman 1951:146). In terminology parallel to that of the *etvlwvlke*, Seminole Baptists today note that Spring Church is the "mother" of all the Seminole Baptist churches. All other Seminole Baptist churches are considered "daughters," or "granddaughters," of Spring Church.

First located near present-day Lexington, Spring Church was later moved to its current location near Sasakwa. Murrow (quoted in Foreman 1951:147) described a Spring Church meeting:

> It is a beautiful site, and when it first came in view with its well constructed eating arbors in a square around the large preaching arbor, all covered with hay, the white tents and covered wagons—the whole covering some ten acres of ground or more, it was a beautiful site. But few visitors from other Nations were present, but the attendance from all parts of this Nation was large, and the services were good. . . . At the all-night meeting last night the colored people became so enthused that they formed a large procession and marched around the encampment singing and clapping their hands. It was a wild and weird scene . . . yet there was a charm and solemnity about it that forbad condemnation.

The arbors have since been replaced with permanent camp houses, and Spring Church still attracts many participants to its services. Spring Church is the largest contemporary Seminole church. It does, however, have a large non-Indian membership.

Other mission efforts were attempted by the Catholics and the Methodists, but these did not enjoy the success of the Presbyterians and the Baptists. A Catholic mission began before the Civil War, but there were few converts, and the mission effort was abandoned. The Methodists were more successful. Hitchiti Church, originally a church for Hitchiti-speaking Seminoles, was established in 1857. The church had been in Creek country, on the north side of the North Canadian River. In 1870, the church moved south to its present location in northern Seminole County.

Mission efforts included the building of boarding schools for Seminole students. The Presbyterians were the first to establish schools. In 1866, Seminole Mission was built north of Wewoka, the Seminole capital. Soon after, an additional three district schools were built around Wewoka. Mekusukey Academy for boys was built in 1870, southwest of the town of Seminole. In 1889, control of the academy was turned over to the Presbyterians. The school was relocated to a new building south of Wewoka in 1893. The U.S. government took control of Mekusukey Academy in 1900 and maintained control until the academy closed in 1930.

A female academy was built by the Methodist Episcopal church in 1880. Known originally as Sasakwa Female Academy, named after the neighboring town, the school was abandoned by the Methodists in 1885. The school headmaster explained:

> I found that the largest part of the school body belonged to either the Baptist church or the Presbyterian, and that the Methodist church, South, which had sent me, had no footing whatever. I felt that the proper thing for us to do as a church was to retire from this school, and ask the Baptists to take charge of it and so I advised the authorities of our church. I further advised that we attempt no missionary efforts among the Seminoles, but to leave the whole field to the Baptists and the Presbyterians as both of these churches had a strong hold among the Seminoles and both were doing good work. (Methvin 1937)

In 1887, control of the school was taken up by the Seminoles. A Baptist, W. P. Blake, was then hired by Chief John Jumper to run the school. In 1892 the school was moved just south of the Seminole capital of Wewoka. The new school was christened Emahaka (named for the Seminole word meaning "the place of teaching"). At statehood in 1907, Emahaka consolidated with Mekusukey. This was the last Seminole boarding school, and after it closed in 1930, Seminole students attended the local public schools or a more distant boarding school such as Chilacco near Ponca City.

With the general paucity of records regarding church participation throughout the history of Oklahoma missions, data regarding participation is necessarily generalized. However, three annual reports from Mekusukey Academy—for the years 1919, 1920, and 1921—have survived.[3] During those years, student enrollment was reported at 151, 149, and 134, respectively. Averaging the three years shows that 42 percent were reported as Baptist, 17 percent Presbyterian, 14 percent Methodist, and 27 percent other. The contemporary situation reflects similar relative success of the various denominations.

At statehood, the once amicable relationship between Seminoles and freedmen was strained, and in many instances relations ceased. The split was evident in the churches as well. At statehood, Seminole churches became strictly Seminole, and freedmen churches likewise segregated into black churches. One Baptist church, located near Maud, is considered to be a freedmen's church. Opala (1980:22) reports another one, Thomas Town Church, located south of Wewoka and founded in 1867. Today there is no interaction between freedmen churches and Seminole Baptist churches. Freedmen churches are not in the Fourth Sunday rotation (see chapter 6 for a description of the Fourth Sunday rotation).

Beginning around the turn of the century, the loss of political autonomy with allotment and later with Oklahoma statehood moved the Seminoles toward fuller participation in the Anglo world. It was during this period that Christian churches, previously negligible in numbers and consequence, sprang up throughout the Seminole territory.

Members today fondly recall the church meetings of their childhood as truly community affairs. They speak of traveling in horse-drawn wagons, carting a family and a weekend's worth of food, and camping in transit. One deacon described how his father would slaughter a hog for every Big Meeting, much to his mother's dismay. A description of one meeting from that era has survived: "In coming together for these camp meetings they bring their provisions, food and bedding and live for the duration of the meeting in their camp houses. Some of these camp houses are luxurious bungalows. Several hundred Indians, both Christian and non-Christians, often attend these camp meetings. These are all fed three times each day, provisions being furnished by the church members and their friends" (Phelps 1937:114). Churches were becoming the primary social and political institution for the Seminole community.[4]

Many churches were built near Stomp grounds, offering an alternative social and ceremonial expression. Eufaula, Green Leaf, Mekusukey, and Arbeka Churches were all established near Stomp grounds of those names. Some church members claim that churches were originally affiliated with the *etvlwvlke*, as were the ceremonial grounds (one deacon used the word *etvlwv* to refer to church gatherings). Such origins are logical and likely. However, in his kinship study, Spoehr (1942:106) denied the coincidence between churches and Stomp grounds: "Today the various church organizations are more vigorous [than Stomp grounds] and probably represent the most vital form of integration, apart from the family, that the Seminole possess. Though the church has taken over a number of features of the Square ground, the clan system has no role, nor does the church coincide with the old town community. The church group is not a closely knit territorial unit; its members are a scattered rural population and suffer from the loose integration which such rurality imparts." No doubt the membership was scattered as Spoehr observed; however, many members of the same church belonged to the same band. For example, today one church has a majority of members belonging to the Tvsekayv Haco band (one of the Eufaula bands), whereas a neighboring church has a majority of members belonging to the Ceyahv band. Members will attend the churches of their parents even though they live closer to another Seminole Baptist church.

Perhaps had Spoehr inquired as to the band affiliations of members, rather than the location of their residences, he may have reached a different conclusion. More important, Spoehr failed to recognize the sociopolitical structures and functions that the churches fulfilled and that had once belonged to the *etvlwvlke*. Curiously, Spoehr also asserted that the clan system had no role in the churches. Yet though clanship perhaps does not have the influence it once had, it does define many social relationships. I have already reported that church members are well aware of their clan affiliation and will address clan members with the proper designations and respect.

There are fourteen Seminole Baptist churches today, but the number is relatively fluid. In the same way that *etvlwvlke*, or bands, experienced regular fission and fusion, so too did—and do—the churches. When churches grow too large, a "daughter" splits off and a new church is started. At times some internal conflict between members drives a split. If this occurs, the fledgling church is not viewed as a daughter but rather "came up on its own." Presently two Seminole Baptist churches, not counted among the fourteen extant ones, have "come up on their own." Time will tell if they are accepted into the church system. If a church's membership diminishes to the extent that it cannot provide enough "workers" to "fulfill the work," members will disband and join a more viable church. Seminole Baptists today recall at least three such churches that are no longer active.

As noted earlier, other Christian denominations, in addition to the Baptists, have a history and presence among the Seminoles. Their success, however, has been overshadowed by the success of the Baptists. What accounts for the Baptist success? Ignoring any perceived ideological and metaphysical differences between the denominations, we can identify at least three empirical aspects of the Baptist tradition that made it attractive to the Seminoles. First, Baptist churches have a high degree of congregational autonomy. Churches have the freedom to develop, govern, and maintain their own organization of the faith. The Seminoles used this autonomy to structure their churches in ways novel to the Baptist tradition: they structured the churches in ways similar, if not identical, to their preexisting *etvlwvlke* (this will be described in detail in chapter 5). The majority of Seminole Baptist churches today are independent; that is, they choose not to affiliate with a larger, governing church body or assembly. As a result of this independent status, there has not been regular reporting of church statistics such as attendance figures or even the number of churches. One organization that does have some Seminole participation is the Muskogee-Seminole-Wichita Association, affiliated with the Southern Baptist Convention. Only three Seminole churches, Spring Church being one of them, are members of the association. Many members of the independent churches have no desire to associate with such a larger body. One pastor reasoned that belonging to a larger body "always includes strings. They want to give us money, but then they'll expect something back later." Those Seminole churches that are a part of the association have adopted a more Anglo model of organization. The independent Seminole churches, on the other hand, associating primarily with other independent churches, are modeled along a preexisting Seminole model, as will be described in the following chapters. Second, Baptist congregations can select and train their own pastors—church leaders do not need to attend a seminary and receive their training from outsiders. Even before the turn of the century, the Baptist mission approach gave way to native-directed churches. Pastors come out of the local community, where they have been enculturated into the social group and where their behavior had been observed for years. Pastors are required to be fluent in English and Mvskoke—to be fully enmeshed in the Seminole traditions and life. It is the local congregation that ordains pastors for service, not some other, higher authority.[5] Third, Baptists are by definition creedless, allowing for wide interpretations of the faith. They are not bound by official dogma imposing itself from outside the community; individuals as well as congregations are allowed a level of interpretation of their beliefs and their scriptures. Again, this will be discussed more fully in the next chapter. These three aspects allowed congregations (often the core of which was people from the same tribal band) to equip and call their own pastors and leaders and to organize according to a structure of their own choosing. Seminole Baptist congregations enjoy great control over organization, rituals, beliefs, and leadership.

Although the Baptist persuasion continues to dominate, Presbyterian and Methodist presence remains among the Seminoles. Individuals claiming membership in Presbyterian churches are regularly found participating in the Seminole Baptist churches, and three Methodist churches are in the Fourth Sunday rotation (described in chapter 6).

A rather significant development occurred in the first part of the present century: churches and Stomp grounds became mutually exclusive competitors. Before that time, the two groups had at least a tacit cooperation. Hadley ([1935] 1987:140) observed the change:

> There is at the present time a division among the Oklahoma Seminoles between the church people and a large group known as the Stomp ground people. The present cleavage is of recent origin. As late as 1912, I am told, the two groups were present at Christian camp meetings and Stomp dance feasts, the old Green Corn festivals. In each case the visiting group did not participate but was simply a friendly onlooker. This is no longer the case. The Christians do not camp at the dances, and the Stomp dance people do not attend church camp meetings as a group, although individuals of either group do visit each other's ceremonies.

Both groups expected loyalty. This competition might be viewed as each claiming to be the genuine expression of Seminole identity. Today, the two groups are officially exclusive. Church leaders, particularly, condemn participation in Stomp grounds activities, calling the dances "devil worship." Stomp grounds participants berate church members for leaving the grounds at midnight and for "dusting themselves off" as they leave (to eliminate any evidence of having been at the grounds). Some individuals do, however, participate in both church and Stomp grounds activities.

As for the descendants of the "unconquered" Seminoles who never removed to Indian Territory, Florida Seminole Baptist churches, having arisen under different circumstances, do not resemble Oklahoma Seminole Baptist churches. According to Oklahoma Seminole Baptists who have visited Florida, their southern kinsmen did not develop a Fourth Sunday rotation system, nor does the organizational structure of these churches resemble that of the native system. The Florida churches are described by those Oklahoma Seminole Baptists who have visited them as "modern," meaning that they strongly resemble Anglo Baptist churches in structure and organization.

The congregation that is the focus of this book is called "Eufaula Church."[6] Eufaula is located in southern Seminole County. Members of Eufaula Church trace their history to the Seminole Baptist Spring Church. Eufaula is a daughter of Spring Church. Members concur that Eufaula is "more than 100 years ago."[7] The head deacon and the minister of Eufaula agreed that the church was named after the Stomp grounds of the same name. Members of Eufaula recount eleven pastors who have served the congregation. Most of these pastors have descendants who are members of Eufaula Church today.

As noted, the historical Oklahoma Seminoles were organized around their ceremonial or religious structure in units called *etvlwvlke*. Finding themselves necessarily participating in a foreign sociopolitical economy, many Seminoles, not surprisingly, thought it expedient to adapt their sociopolitical structure in ways that were acceptable to the dominant Anglo authorities. One acceptable option came to them through the Baptist missionaries.

CHAPTER 4

Beliefs

A basic component of any religion is its system of beliefs. This chapter addresses the connection between contemporary Christian beliefs and traditional Seminole elements. The following characterization of Seminole Baptist beliefs is by no means comprehensive but rather is intended to expose the reader to the "soul" of the people whose social life will be described in detail in the next chapters.

The Seminole Baptists' beliefs compose a unique system developed from the intersection of two vastly different, yet compatible, traditions. Within the Seminole Baptist community, historical indigenous religious symbols were extended, renamed, and redefined to supply interpretations that reinforced traditional categories of meaning while adapting to changing social conditions. The cultural innovations that became institutionalized as the Seminole Baptist churches are creative, deliberate adaptations of traditional beliefs and practices, adaptations made to ensure community survival. Thus, contemporary religious beliefs among the Seminole Baptists are an interesting extension of historical beliefs and symbols that form a locally meaningful system.

In any church denomination—or in any individual congregation, for that matter—there is similarity of beliefs while at the same time there is an acceptable level of variation. This is no less true for the Seminole Baptist churches. One older pastor said that people are like watches. Given two or more watches, a person will see two or more times, each one being a little different. So it is, he said, with people's understanding of spiritual things. These differences are most pronounced in a comparison of the theology expressed by the leadership and that expressed by the laity. Whereas the laity tend to express their beliefs using broad strokes of dualism, justice, and either/or choices, many of the leaders are willing to wrestle with nuance, exception, and paradox and have developed some rather sophisticated theology.

Some pastors and ministers are, of course, better (more *rational*, in a Weberian sense)[1] theologians than others. None of the leaders that I encountered were seminary trained. Their theology, be it developed or not, was acquired in the field—within the Seminole Baptist community. This parochial training does not preclude rational theology, however. I was regularly engaged in theological discussions with pastors and other leaders. Often their theology revealed not only a great depth of understanding of the human situation but also pragmatic wisdom and versatile systematics. Many preachers have command of a great variety of biblical images and are able to articulate them within the current context.

It must be stressed that the Seminole Baptists' belief system is not one simply taken in toto from overbearing missionaries; rather, it is a system adapted to and incorporated into their whole lifeway. Their expression of the Christian faith is uniquely Seminole. Biblical images are interpreted in ways that affirm traditional Seminole values and attitudes. The biblical stories and images have been embraced by the Seminoles: the images are communicated not as foreign but rather as very much Seminole, interpreted along lines meaningful to the community. Their faith regularly moved me to introspection. I found myself on more than one occasion thinking of the words of Agrippa: "almost thou persuadest me."[2] Christian beliefs and practices were introduced to the Seminoles as a foreign culture, yet many Christian elements have been incorporated into the Seminole life and worldview. It is unproductive, if not impossible, to distinguish aboriginal beliefs from introduced beliefs. However, there is a historical, aboriginal precedence to many of the beliefs articulated by Seminole Baptists; at the same time, introduced Christian elements permeate all aspects of their belief system. Christian elements are also found among the non-Christian Stomp grounds Seminoles as well. It is common to hear prayers addressed to Jesus at the contemporary Stomp grounds.[3]

During my first fieldwork interview I asked a deacon to tell me words that I might hear in church, so that I could begin learning them. The first word he gave was *Hesaketv emese*. He said, "It means *Jesus Christ*." Swanton (1928b:481), Adair (1930:111), Swan (1856:269), and Hawkins (1980:325) all record this word, *Hesaketv emese*, as the historical Mvskoke name for the principal deity; it is translated as "the breath master" or "the giver and taker of breath." Bartram (1928:391) referred to "the Great Spirit, the giver and taker away of the breath of life," clearly a translation of the Mvskoke name for the deity. Interestingly, a Mvskoke transliteration of the name "Jesus," *Cesvs*, is available for contemporary Seminoles to use, but except in some songs, it is rarely heard. Virtually all prayers begin with *Hesaketv emese*, and *Hesaketv emese* is exclusively used for "Jesus" or "Jesus Christ" when translating from a biblical text into Mvskoke. The identification of Jesus Christ with *Hesaketv emese* is a significant extension of a traditional symbol. The initial use of *Hesaketv emese* by the historical Seminole Baptists reinforced a traditional category of meaning while adapting to the changing social condition. Its ongoing use connects users to this past and continues to help define the Seminoles as an ethnic group.

Other Mvskoke names that the Seminole Baptists use for the principal deity include *Epofvnkv* ("the one above us"), *Epohfastv* ("the one who cares for us"), and *Pocase Cesvs* ("lord," or "owner," "Jesus"). Swanton (1928b:481) intimates that *Epofvnkv* is perhaps the most ancient address for the deity. One elderly pastor I spoke with echoed this sentiment and stated that the "old people" (meaning the preceding generations) rarely used *Hesaketv emese* and almost exclusively used the term *Epofvnkv*. The pastor explained that the address *Hesaketv emese* was not commonly used because it was "too sacred to speak" and that *Epofvnkv* was used as a respectful substitute. One deacon, while relating the various names for the deity, stated that *Epohfastv* was used only at the Stomp grounds and not in church. However, this term can be heard regularly in church as an address to the deity. The historical titles for addressing the deity were presumably not used in the same sense that they are today. Biblical and Anglo influence has no doubt helped shape Seminole images of *Hesaketv emese*. Swanton (1928b: 481–83) describes a less defined, umbrella characterization of the deities among the historical Seminoles and Creeks. The idea of *Hesaketv emese* as a single creator, for example, appears to be a Christian innovation.[4]

As Christians, the Seminole Baptists profess the person Jesus Christ. When speaking in English, they address the deity *Hesaketv emese* as "Jesus," "Jesus Christ," "the Creator," "the heavenly Father," or "God." When speaking Mvskoke, they seldom use the transliteration *Cesvs*.[5] As was noted above, Jesus Christ is often associated directly with *Hesaketv emese*, or God. When I attempted to probe this association and how it is communicated in sermons, I found a much more complicated understanding. Actually, it would be inaccurate to speak of "an" understanding, as if it were monolithic. There are, rather, diverse understandings. Sometimes Jesus is spoken of as *Hesaketv emese* (i.e., one and the same); at other times he is spoken of as a human man. One pastor told me: "As I see it, Jesus was with God, but God loved us so much that he sent Jesus to die for our sins. Jesus was a man." Jesus is spoken of as the "son of God," the "Savior," "our brother," and "Lord." This mixed presentation of Jesus is perhaps to be expected. Other Christian denominations have wrestled with the human-divine aspects of Jesus for centuries. Many Western Christians explain the enigma with the notion of Trinity (which is no explanation but is rather itself a mystery reified). Certainly, few Christians anywhere could articulate the notion of Trinity in any logical sense, yet most Western, mainline denominations would at least point to the notion of Trinity when attempting to characterize God. Among the Seminole Baptists, the doctrine of Trinity is not expressed. Rather, God, Jesus, and the Holy Spirit are portrayed as separate entities, each with characteristic tasks and traits. One pastor explained:

I changed my prayers about three, four years ago, and I believe I got a better results. I don't push it, and I don't preach it. But you got to find your own way in this spiritual life. I used to say "God"—I'd start out with "God," or "Lord," or "My Father."[6] But I got to studying that Bible where Jesus said, "Anything you need, ask me and I will ask my father." He's our moderator. He asks us to ask him, then he would ask his father. See, here's God . . . and here's Jesus. I would go around Jesus [to] go to a higher authority. I made the parable of the Governor of Oklahoma. You don't go direct to him; you have to go through some channels to get to the Governor and then tell him what I'm there for. Then he'll think a little bit, then he'll say to "come on in." That's the same way with God and Jesus. He gave us his son to give us thoughts through spirit upon his heart. He's our moderator; he's a lawyer. He's so obedient unto his father even unto death. God's going to listen to him. That's why he put him in charge of salvation and all that's in there. I've been going around Jesus, and I used to go direct to God. Seems like a lot of things didn't happen that should have happened but it didn't. I got to studying that Bible. That's what I was talking about, you have to go to the deep root to find out, through prayers and fasting. So I come to find out to my satisfaction that I was leaving out the main ingredient, the main thing. Jesus is our lawyer and our moderator. I say Jesus, then I go from there, and ask your father to forgive me, and ask the father to bless us for our needs. I got better results from that. I don't push it, I may be wrong, see, but that's to my satisfaction. That's what I was talking about growing in spirit—that you have to find a way through his spirit.

Although the specific nature of the relationship between Jesus and *Hesaketv emese* is difficult to characterize consistently, it is probably accurate to generalize that all Seminole Baptists would agree that the death and resurrection of Jesus Christ was an all-important event to which they regularly point. They would speak of Jesus as Savior, meaning the one who will save them from an afterlife of suffering in hell and will bring them to an afterlife of bliss in heaven. The saving graces of Jesus come to an individual when he or she "accepts Jesus as their Lord and Savior" and "has faith in him." The verb "faith" in Mvskoke is *vkvsvmetv* ("to believe, agree, or praise"). The term is used in a similar manner as is our word "believe": I believe it's going to rain; I don't believe you. In the Seminole Baptist churches, *vkvsvmetv* is used in a way very close to that of Anglo Baptists: as a feeling of commitment to Christ.

When describing the attributes of the deity, Seminole Baptists most often use familiar biblical, Christian images (God is the creator and sustainer of the universe; God is spirit; God is omniscient, omnipotent, and omnipresent). The Genesis creation account is the only creation story that I have heard among the church people. When I explicitly inquired about the creation accounts recorded in Swanton (1928b:487–88), I found no one familiar with them or any other nonbiblical myths.

One theme that continues to be rehearsed is the "power" of God. A pastor expressed it well when he said: "God is the creator of all. Everything that *is* comes from God. God works bad things to show people his power. People think that they are powerful. God works tornadoes and floods. We pray for rains when it's dry, all so that God can reveal his power. He is the one with the power. We can't do it ourselves. These things happen so that we will come to God. I fear God, that's why I seek to please him. I always examine myself. God can make

us sick or make us well, he will reveal hidden things to us."
God is understood as exercising power to draw people to God.
That power may be expressed positively (for example,
answering prayers) or negatively (for example, bringing sickness or confounding plans). A deacon explained: "God created
our spirits; they come from God, and he wants them back. The
only way that he'll get them back is if we make him number
one in our lives." When we "make him number one," a right
relationship is established with the deity, and blessings follow,
both in this life and in the next.

Many Seminole Baptists express a dualistic understanding
of things spiritual, the two forces being God and God's adver-
sary, *Estenekricv* ("the one who burns or harms people,"
glossed in English as "the devil" "or "Satan"), also called *Este
vnrvpv* ("one who opposes"). God is viewed as the source of
goodness, health, blessing, and success; Satan is the source of
evil, sickness and death, curse, and failure. A person is understood to align himself or herself, intentionally or unintention-
ally, as an agent of one of these forces. Swan (1856:269–70)
records a historical belief in a "bad spirit." He wrote: "The bad
spirit is styled Stefuts Asego, which signifies the devil, or rather
sorcerer. . . . They believe, also, that the bad spirit dwells a
great way off, in some dismal swamp, which is full of galling
briars, and that he is commonly half starved, having no game,
or bear's oil in all his territories." Swanton (1928b:485) expresses
doubt regarding the aboriginality of this belief, attributing it
instead to Christian influences. He does, however, concede the
"primitive character" of a "kind of dualism based on the
opposing activities of the good and bad spirits." The dualism
expressed within the Seminole Baptist churches, then, may be
characterized as an extension of the traditional belief. A
contemporary notion of the activities of Satan is described by
a pastor: "Like Job says, the bad comes and the devil tries to
get us to turn from God. He's always there tempting us. He
tempted Jesus when he was in the wilderness fasting, telling
him to turn the stone into bread. That old Satan is trying to turn

us from God. He's always there tempting us. In the end days we'll see hard times. We'll see all sorts of things that we've never seen, like water monsters with two heads and any number of horns. We haven't seen such things yet, but we will see them with our own eyes." Satan is portrayed as a powerful, supernatural antagonist who seeks to keep people from God. Satan uses various temptations and enticements to accomplish this end. Those who make God "number one in their lives" are promised a life after death in a *hvlwe tvlofv* ("high town," glossed in English as "heaven") of bliss. Those who succumb to Satan's temptations and "turn from God" are threatened with an afterlife of suffering in *totkvrakko* ("big fire," glossed in English as "hell").

There is strong evidence of an aboriginal notion of an afterlife in which good and bad people are separated. Swan (1856:269–70) reported, "They believe there is a state of future existence, and that according to the tenor to their lives, they shall here after be rewarded with the privilege of hunting in the realm of the Master of Breath, or of becoming Seminoles in the regions of the old sorcerers." Swanton (1928b:481) attributes this belief to Christian influence. He does, however, support the aboriginal notion of a separation "of very bad people" to "dark regions of the west" after death and adds that a "world above was thought to be the realm of departed souls as well as the dwelling place of many supernatural beings" (Swanton 1928b:480). Bartram (1928:391) wrote:

> They believe in a future state, where the spirit exists, which they call the world of spirits, where they enjoy different degrees of tranquility or comfort, agreeably to their life spent here: a person who in his life has been an industrious hunter, provided well for his family, an intrepid and active warrior, just, upright, and done all the good he could, will, they say, in the world of spirits, live in a warm, pleasant country, where are expansive, green, flowery savannas and high forests, watered with rivers of pure waters, replenished with deer, and every species of game;

a serene, unclouded and peaceful sky; in short, where there is fullness of pleasure uninterrupted.

Hawkins (1980:325) recorded a 1799 interview he had with Efau Haujo, *mekko* of Tookaubatche. Hawkins inquired about the Indian belief in a future existence. Efau Haujo responded, "The old notion among us is, that when we die the poyauficchau [*poyvfekcv*] (spirit) goes the way of the sun, to the west, and there joins its family and friends who went before it." Hawkins went on to ask if there was a belief in a future state of reward and punishment. Efau Haujo answered, "We have an opinion that those who have behaved well are taken under the care of Essaugetuh Emissee [*Hesaketv emese*] and assisted, and that those who have behaved ill, are left there to shift for themselves; and that there is no other punishment." But these historical beliefs were not identical to contemporary Seminole Baptist notions of afterlife, heaven and hell, and reward and punishment. Modern beliefs reveal a marked Western-Christian understanding.

Contemporary Seminole Baptists describe heaven in biblical images taken primarily from the book of Revelations (e.g., "streets paved with gold," "no suffering," "no sickness"). But many of the Mvskoke hymns also speak of heaven. One particularly interesting Mvskoke hymn, "Mapohicvt Em Afackakuses" ("How Happy Are They"),[7] speaks of a "third heaven." A pastor once preached a sermon explicating this hymn and explaining what was meant by the three heavens. He said the first is the immediate level of the blue sky; the second is the level of sun and moon and stars; and the third is true heaven where the faithful are in the presence of *Hesaketv emese* ("God").

Many of the interesting and unique aspects of Seminole beliefs regard the notion of *poyvfekcv* ("spirit" or "soul"). Swanton (1928b:489) described the concept in general terms. Although the description is lengthy, it is worth quoting in whole, for it provides a necessary foundation for understanding an important aspect of the Seminole Baptist belief of many Seminoles today:

According to the idea of the southern Indians, something of the supernatural attached to every created thing, every animal, plant, stone, stick, body of water, geographical feature, and even to objects which man himself had made. While these things did, indeed, have certain characteristic appearances and activities which were "natural"—that is, the things normally expected from them—they owed these to a certain impression made upon them in the beginning of things, or at least at some time in the distant past, and it was not to be assumed that they were all the powers which such beings and objects—or, assuming the Indian point of view, we might say simply beings—possessed. The expected might give way at any moment to the unexpected. In such cases the thing itself might exert power in its own right or it might be a medium of power from another being. It might manifest this power at one particular time to one particular person, it might have the faculty of exerting its power constantly, or its power might be brought out from it by the observance of certain regulations. In such cases the response might be an infallible result of performing the regulations, or the charm might be capable of exercising a modicum of volition.

The "power" that Swanton describes is identified by many Seminoles as *poyvfekcv* ("spirit").

The notion of *poyvfekcv* is broad and multifaceted. Every living thing (and some nonliving things, stones for example) contains *poyvfekcv*. *Poyvfekcv* is everlasting, existing even after death. It is the *poyvfekcv* of the Christian that is believed to spend eternity in heaven or hell. Seminoles say that human beings have *hesaketv* ("breath" or "life") and *poyvfekcv* ("spirit" or "soul"). At death the *poyvfekcv* continues to live. Many Seminoles I asked said that they believe that everything living has both *hesaketv* and *poyvfekcv* and that their *poyvfekcv* also continues to live after death. Bartram (1928:27) described this notion, prevalent among the Creeks in his day. He noted: "A pattern or spiritual likeness of everything living, as well as inanimate, exists in another world." Many Seminoles believe that at death, *hesaketv* ends and the person's *poyvfekcv* spends eternity in heaven or hell. Others do not distinguish between human *hesaketv* and *poyvfekcv*: both are eternal. There is some disagreement regarding nonhuman life. Some say that all living things have *hesaketv*, since that is life, but not *poyvfekcv*, which they consider a uniquely human attribute. Most agree that all natural (i.e., not manmade) things, living things especially, have both *hesaketv* and *poyvfekcv*.

Seminole Baptists believe that some people have the ability to manipulate nonhuman *poyvfekcv* for benefit or for ill. Moreover, this "something of the supernatural" avails itself to certain individuals: although all people may recognize the potential, some people are believed to have regular access to the supernatural power. These people may speak to wild animals, expecting them to speak back; they may gather natural objects (plants, feathers, minerals), carefully singing medicine songs, so that the efficacy of the spirit is maintained and these objects are implored to provide benefit. A person who is recognized as having the ability to influence and manipulate *poyvfekcv* is called *heles hayv* ("medicine maker"), *kerrv* ("knower"), and *porrv* ("witch"). Each of these three has a characteristic way of using or influencing *poyvfekcv*.

The *heles hayv*, usually glossed in English as "doctor," uses botanicals and "medicine songs" primarily to effect bodily healing.[8] The *poyvfekcv* of the plant is directed to assist the ailing individual. The *heles hayv* may also be retained to restore a broken marriage, exorcise ghosts, counter the bad medicine of an enemy, win court cases, or change one's luck. This doctor may prescribe "black drink" (the principal medicine of the Stomp grounds), "whole body cleansing" (during a new moon, at midnight, in a creek or stream), a sweat bath, "bleeding" (the patient is cut with a piece of glass, and the source of the malady, usually a hair or a weblike blood clot, is sucked out), and the like. Swanton (1928b:620) described the historical *heles hayv*, or "high priest," as the one "who communicated the necessary spiritual qualities to the medicines at the annual busk, had general charge of the public health, protected all from ghosts, and so on."

One *heles hayv* I interviewed stated that he has been practicing for twenty-one years. He keeps records on each of his patients: name and address, reason for coming to him (ailment and symptoms), his diagnosis and prescribed treatment. Over sixteen hundred patients are listed in his journals. To work his treatments, this *heles hayv* collects various natural objects (feathers, herbs, and stones, each with its own *poyvfekcv* useful to accomplish particular ends). When collecting these objects, the *heles hayv* kneels before the object, facing east, and prays to it. He asks that it would cure the ailment or perform the task. The object is placed on a white kerchief, and medicine songs are sung, then he blows on the objects. They are then infused with *heleswv* ("medicine"). When songs are sung correctly, the medicine takes effect. If songs are sung incorrectly, the *heles hayv* must sing the song backward—word order is reversed. The song is then sung again—correctly. The *heles hayv* said: "It is God that makes the medicine work through me. If the songs are sung correctly, then God hears and works. If the songs are incorrect, then God doesn't hear them—it's like so much wind." However, when an ailment is properly diagnosed and the correct medicine song is properly sung over the correct medicine object, then the desired end will occur.

The ability of the *heles hayv* is usually attributed to God, yet the individual must cultivate and develop the talent. One pastor put it this way: "God is the creator. He has all the power in heaven and earth and even under the earth. There aren't many Indian doctors left who know all the sicknesses. Most of the old-timers have died and taken their knowledge with them. But I would say that it is a talent that God has given them: they know the herbs and medicines and the songs." Young *heles hayvlke* often learn their medicine songs from an established *heles hayv* (who is often a relative). Few, if any, *heles hayvlke* today have the knowledge and the abilities of those in the previous generations, yet many Seminoles, Christian or not, make use of their services.

The *kerrv* might best be characterized as a clairvoyant. He or she is called on to diagnose ailments, locate lost objects, and foretell the future. Swanton (1928b:615) described the role of the *kerrv* as a "prophet" and "diagnostician . . . he could foretell death, sickness, or crime." Again, the contemporary positions, found also in the Stomp grounds, have historical precedence. Sometimes a pastor, minister, or deacon may also be a *heles hayv* or a *kerrv*. In other instances the *kerrv* is simply a floor member (layperson). The ability of the *kerrv* to perform appears to be the result of his or her own *poyvfekcv*. Though not directly manipulating *poyvfekcv*, the *kerrv* taps into the realm of the spiritual to perform the function. The natural abilities (a person simply has them or does not have them—they are not learned) of the *kerrv* are recognized by the community. The *kerrv* will continue in that role as long as he or she is effective. The most effective *kerrv* are said to be young, male celibates.

Swanton (1928b:631) wrote, "The great powers which doctors and graduates of the native schools generally enjoyed, while in theory capable of being exerted for the good of the community and the individuals composing it, might equally well be perverted to their injury or destruction." A person who uses the powers in this way is called a *porrv* ("witch," this person may be male or female). Swanton (1928b:632) quotes Gen. E. A. Hitchcock, reporting that these witches "can take the form of owls and fly about at night and at day return home in the form of women and men; that they can take the heart and the spirit out of living men and cause their death; that they can cripple people by shooting rags or blood into their legs through a reed or out of their mouths." Such activities of witches are frequently reported today in and around the Seminole churches. One pastor explained: "Those who do witchcraft also have that talent from God, but they go the devil's way. Sometimes they will leave medicine at church grounds because they're jealous. They do that witchcraft because maybe they don't get too many visitors at their church and we do." Those *porrv* who transform into owls are called *'stekene* ("Great-horned owl," "witch"). They are said to fly about, working their mischief. Many members place specially prepared feathers in their homes above their doors to protect themselves from *'stekene* that may be flying about. These feathers will "flutter and flap around like a bird in flight, making all sorts of racket" to warn of the 'stekene's presence. Specific incidences of alleged witchcraft and the social consequences will be described in chapter 7.

A person's *poyvfekcv* is believed to be independent of the body. It is understood as the true self, and it is what gives a body life and animation. The separation of the *poyvfekcv* from the body can be temporary. A minister explained: "When you're deep asleep, at about midnight, your *poyvfekcv* leaves your body and wanders. Your body is dead. Your spirit goes to places where your mind directs it: It may be to another place in the house, or anywhere. You know that your spirit has left because you don't know anything that happened around you while you slept. Your *vpuetskv* ('dreams') are memories of what your spirit was doing while your body was left in bed."[9] The separation of *poyvfekcv* from the body becomes permanent at death,[10] yet this soul may still be near.

Many Seminole Baptists understand that when a person dies, the *poyvfekcv* goes to the *poyvfekcv enfekupkv* ("spiritual resting place," "paradise") to await judgment. One pastor elaborated on the notion of paradise:

> Well, to me—there's a lot of interpretation in there—but to me, when a person dies, the paradise is heaven too, you know. The Bible states that. Because Paul stated that, "I don't know if there's a second or third heaven." Well, he's talking about this paradise, the waiting place. He's in comfort. He's not suffering, he's in comfort. He's just waiting for that great day to come to pass. He'll have to stand before the judgment seat of Christ, though, regardless, because if his name is on the book of life, he's going in. But the place he's going to put us in is no cemetery, no bereavement.

Clearly this paradise is not a purgatory that needs to be worked through, such as the "soul's journey" described by Swanton (1928b:513); rather, this is a holding place for the soul while it awaits judgment. The pastor continued: "And paradise is a heaven—it's hard to understand. But to me it's still a heaven, but he hadn't got to that last place yet. But he's still in comfort, not in torment."

Seminole Baptists believe that the *poyvfekcv* is free to leave and return to paradise while awaiting judgment.[11] It is reasoned that the *poyvfekcv* desires to be near its former loved ones as well as its own body. Several Seminoles described how they had heard noises in their houses, noises that they attribute to recently deceased family members returning to their homes.[12] The movement of the *poyvfekcv* between paradise and earth accounts for the construction of a grave house, or *cokuce* ("little house"), over a grave. These wooden structures (see figure 1), resembling miniature frame houses, are built soon after burial. They are erected to provide a place of comfort for the spirit as it returns to be near its former body. These grave houses are usually not maintained and are left to ruin, since it is reasoned that in the time it takes for the houses to fall, the spirits cease returning to the body, and the comfort of the house is no longer necessary.

Although there was considerable variety in the burial customs of the historical Seminoles and Creeks (Swanton 1928a:388–98), the practice of erecting grave houses and the custom of placing objects with the deceased are ancient. In former times, items that represented favorites of the deceased were placed within the *cokuce*. Swanton (1928a:390), Bartram (1928:403), Romans (quoted in Swanton 1928a:392), and Swan (1856:270) all record the placement of objects in Seminole and Creek graves: guns, bows and arrows, pipes, clothes, and "every other useful thing he had been possessed of" (Adair 1930:191). Seminole church people today still place objects with the body; such objects were significant to the deceased: a jar of food, a pack of cigarettes, a change of clothes. Nowadays,

Fig. 1. Grave houses. Photo by author.

these items are usually placed within the casket before burial. I was told this change took place because the *cokuce* were being broken into by vandals or thieves and the items were being removed.

The Seminole Baptists' continuation of this practice represents an adaptation that occurred in a culturally meaningful manner. It is not surprising, then, that some of their practices are not meaningful to people outside of the community. A Seminole pastor told me that an Anglo Baptist preacher attending an Indian funeral asked why the objects were placed in the grave and argued, "The fella's dead; he can't eat the food or smoke the cigarettes." The Seminole pastor responded: "White people place flowers all around each other's graves. When the dead white man sits up to smell the flowers, the dead Indian will be right behind him eating the food and smoking the cigarettes."

When a body is buried, it is always oriented east-west, with the deceased's head placed to the west. This appears to be an ancient custom for southeastern peoples in general and for

Seminoles in particular (Swanton 1928a:390). Swanton (1928a: 395) states that the deceased is faced east "because that quarter is associated with the renewal of life." The motivation for this custom is now spoken of in Christian terms by the Seminole Baptists. A pastor related: "So we got kind of a belief that God will come from the East. When people are buried, then, they always put the head west, facing east. His eyes would be looking east. He's dead. He's through with this world. They're through. Nothing here for them on this earth. His body's going back to dust. But when we're alive, when we sleep, we put our head east. Dead people put their head west."[13] Thus as the deceased body sits up to meet Christ, it will be facing east. Again, the burial practices are drawn from Seminole history, yet they are reinterpreted. Traditional symbols are given new meaning.

In some ways Seminole Baptists are similar to other Baptists. Among Seminole Baptists, just as among non-Seminole Baptists, the King James Version of the Bible is regarded as authoritative. The book is referred to and described as "the Word of God." But I have never witnessed discussions or sermons regarding its inerrancy, as are often heard in or around many rural Anglo Baptist churches. The book is simply accepted as authoritative. The issue of Christ's virgin birth, so often a touchstone of orthodoxy among Anglo Baptists, is absent from Seminole theological discussions. In fact, I have never heard contentious discussions or theological "hair-splitting." There is, rather, the cooperative venture that emphasizes shared dimensions of the interpretations of the faith. Theological discussions generally focus on personal Christian responsibility and salvation.

Unlike many other Baptists, few Seminole laypeople bring Bibles with them to church. In fact, carrying a Bible at the church grounds marks one as a pastor or minister. Others who bring Bibles carry pocket testaments, but this practice is usually limited to deacons or women's leaders. At church gatherings, the leaders communicate the authoritative words and the interpretations of scriptures.

As in all other Christian churches, Seminole Baptists practice water baptism. The ritual is viewed as an initiation into the Christian community and as a "washing away" of past sins. Most Seminole churches do not have an indoor baptistery, so baptisms are performed in a local pond or river. Baptisms are performed in spite of inclement weather. Deacons speak, somewhat fondly, of chipping holes in a frozen pond to perform a baptism. It should be noted that "going to the water," or bathing for ceremonial cleansing, is an important element of the Green Corn Festival. This bathing immediately precedes the breaking of the ritual fast (see Swanton 1928b:553, 603–5; Howard 1984:121, 143–44). This similarity between "going to the water" and baptism is fortuitous only. It does not reflect direct borrowing, yet the precedence of ritual immersion in water no doubt made the Christian practice of baptism understandable. Again, the aboriginal form was similar, yet the meaning of the Christian practice is vastly different.

From the above description of Seminole Baptist beliefs, it should be evident that within the Seminole Baptist community, historical religious symbols were extended, renamed, and redefined to provide interpretations and a meaning system that reinforce traditional categories of meaning while adapting to a changing social and political context. Religious beliefs among the Seminole Baptists are an extension of historical Seminole beliefs and symbols, placed in the context of a Christianity unique to Seminole Baptists. Changes in and extensions of beliefs have been attributed to assimilation and acculturation. Yet such a characterization ignores the verity that cultural innovations are creative and deliberate vehicles of community survival. One pastor, commenting on the historical beliefs of the Seminoles, said: "The old people used to say that even before the white men and the Bible arrived, the Indians knew *Epohfastv* ['the one above']. They always knew God. They were a witness for God to the white man as they showed love to the *Mayflower* travelers, teaching them how to plant corn and how to celebrate Thanksgiving. They had love for the *Mayflower* people." The past is continually being reinterpreted to make meaningful the present situation. Seminole Baptists recognize that their ancestors had different practices, yet they feel a spiritual affinity. Although some of that "kindred spirit" is justified, other elements are less so, but certainly there is a connection.

Thus religious beliefs, like all other aspects of culture, are continually being modified, reinterpreted, refined, and adapted to fit the current situation. One afternoon while I was visiting a pastor in his home, he told this wonderful narrative, blending native and biblical images:

When we're out in the woods, fasting and praying, we need to remember our objective: the cross of Christ. We need to press on toward that goal. I keep him in my mind. The cross is at the top of a hill; we are on the path to it. As we walk, *sokhv hvtke* ["white pig," or "possum"], *wotko* ["raccoon"], *cetto* ["snake"], and *locv* ["turtle"] will cross our path, but we can't become distracted. Those are temptations trying to keep us from our goal. You need to fast and pray and make a parable within yourself and visualize it and use it . . . [to] compare yourself that you're on that road and a lot of these temptations are coming your way. I will not turn from them. I will keep going; I want to see Jesus, the path going up to Calvary's mountain.

The snake is your enemy.[14] He was the first one to enter into the Garden of Eden, and he caused that woman to sin. See, the snake is Satan. That snake will cross your path.

And *kono* ["skunk"], you're scared of him because he smells. He'll cross your path.

Yaha ["wolf"], you're afraid of him, he might attack you. The wolf's howl will scare you. You know the Bible speaks of the wolf in sheep's clothes, he's a deceiver. Evil spirits, Satan, will try to hinder you cause you're on that path that Jesus laid and you're going to Jesus. Any little thing can hinder you.

Locv ["turtle"] is humble and slow, and he'll cross your path.[15] He's slow and he can't hurt you, and you're going up to heaven slowly cause you still got that breath in your life. He's encouraging you.

The possum pouts, he's leaving pouting.[16] A lot of Christian people in church who have leaders or something they don't like jump up and walk out. They're all pouting. When you walk up on *sokhv hvtke*, he'll growl at you and try to scare you, but he'll fall over like he's dead. I'll compare it to a Christian person. A Christian person is not supposed to pout, we know that. If a Christian pouts and quits church, [it is] like he's playing dead. You're playing dead when you're out of fellowship; that death's liable to get you. You know a possum will pout, and that makes them dogs that much worse, and they'll sure-enough get him. Or if he pouts on the road, he's liable to get run over. Same way with a Christian. If you're out of fellowship or quit church, you're like that possum. You're playing dead, and it's liable to come to pass.

Opv ["barred owl"] watches.[17] He's always on the alert. The Christian always has to be on the alert. The owl has a vision at night, he can see in the dark. Even in the dark, before Christ, we are in the light. And God will bestow upon your heart where you can see the dark side of life through fasting and the prayer.

A lot of things will try to hinder you, at the same time you're going up the hill kind of slow to see Jesus. Keep a going. Keep a going. Visualize that in your mind. When you get to that cross, pray try to see blood dripping. Eventually you'll go to crying. Then you'll know, and you're satisfied, and you're happy, then he'll hear your prayers.

In this account, the attributes of animals that Seminoles recognize are used as a parable to interpret Christian life. This narrative was told to provide focus for the solitary Christian devotion out in the woods, fasting and seeking an encounter with the divine (a practice that has native precedence, see Swanton 1928b:619). In this narrative, local animals are teachers. Animals were frequent actors in native Seminole narratives. They often had lessons to teach, advice to give, and examples to follow (or avoid). On more than one occasion I have heard Seminole Baptists speak to animals and wait for replies. Animals may be messengers of God. In the above narrative the animals are teaching a Christian message: remain faithful. This blending of cultural traditions is typical of the Seminole Baptist beliefs.

This brief characterization of the beliefs of Seminole Baptists should show that their Christian faith developed from the unique intersection of two vastly different cultural traditions. Within the historical Seminole community, indigenous religious symbols and meanings were extended, allowing a meaningful response to the changing world. Christian symbols and meanings were adapted as they were adopted. The belief system that developed is not the simple result of acculturation and assimilation. Rather, Seminole Baptist beliefs developed within a historical context as an adaptive response to changing social and economic conditions. The resulting belief system is an aspect of a Christianity that is uniquely Seminole. But beliefs are only one aspect of a religion. How those beliefs are expressed is another. In the following chapters, additional beliefs will be discussed in the social context in which they occur, for it is this dimension of the belief system that must be emphasized—how beliefs are enacted and used in the social world of the community.

CHAPTER 5

The Church Setting

The primary location of Seminole Baptist social situations is the various church grounds scattered throughout Seminole and Hughes Counties in south-central Oklahoma (see figure 2). For many Seminoles, these churches have become the primary social institution, just as the historical *evlwvlke* were for their ancestors. It is at these grounds that church members gather, strategically exposing their social faces to other members and thus regulating and integrating their moral community. Church gatherings are both cultural events (activities bounded in place and time around buildings, ritual accoutrements, and situational proprieties) and social gatherings (focused and unfocused interactions that effectively engender social processes).

Most of the fourteen Seminole Baptist churches today are in remote, rural settings placed among stands of blackjack oak or, less commonly, amid pasturelands. Two churches are just outside city limits, but they nevertheless retain a feeling of isolation. Central to each of the Seminole Baptist compounds, often called the "grounds" in parallel with the modern ceremonial Stomp grounds, is the *mekusvpkvcoko* ("prayer house"), the church building (see figure 3). These buildings are quite similar to those of rural Anglo churches. Most are white clapboard structures and include a bell-tower steeple. Some church houses have a brick facade; others are made of concrete blocks. Seminole churches differ from Anglo rural churches in

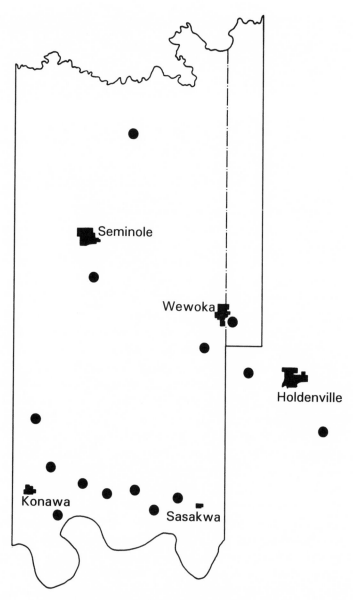

Fig. 2.   Map of Seminole County and adjacent area showing the
location of fourteen Seminole Baptist churches, represented by dots.
Map by Christine Schultz.

Fig. 3.   A typical Seminole church and arbor. Photo by author.

the region, however, in three ways: the ring of camp houses surrounding the building, the interior arrangements of the building, and the arbor attached to the church building (see figure 4).

Camp houses serve as temporary residences during meeting weekends (see figure 5). Between three and twenty *'stehvpo* ("person's camps"), or camp houses, surround each Seminole church. Camp houses are separated from the church building by an encircling road. These houses vary in shape and size. They are simple and unfinished inside (with wall studs exposed), but they have all the necessary furnishings for cooking and sleeping. Most are small, with three or four rooms. Few have running water and toilets. Most have electricity and are heated with propane. Several have wood-burning cookstoves. They all have large, roughly constructed tables on which community meals or "refreshments" are served and eaten. Although some of the houses are permanently inhabited, the majority remain vacant for most of the month.[1]

Fig. 4.   *Eufaula Church. Photo by author.*

Fig. 5.   *A camp house, with the church arbor visible in the right background. Photo by author.*

Fig. 6.   A deacon standing in the men's prayer ground. Photo by author.

Scattered behind the camp houses are *cokuce* ("little houses"), or outhouses. Only a few of the grounds have modern toilets. Most of the compounds include a "prayer grounds," a clearing in the surrounding woods with two parallel benches, approximately ten feet apart, where participants can go to pray (see figure 6). One part of the prayer grounds is designated for the men and another for the women. The deacons and ministers gather here to collect their thoughts and appoint workers before the services.[2] The women's leaders frequent their prayer grounds less regularly. In the past these grounds were where older women would instruct the younger women in things spiritual. Cemeteries are located on or adjacent to many church compounds, and grave houses are commonly seen standing (see figure 7).

The church houses are rectangular, the length oriented east-west (see figure 8). The entrance doors face east.[3] All Seminole churches are oriented this way. Church house interiors reveal a characteristic arrangement of furnishings (see figures 9 and

Fig. 7.   A Seminole cemetery with grave houses. Photo by author.

10). *Obliketv cvpko* ("long chairs"), or pews, are arranged around the perimeter of the church, the bulk of them placed in multiple rows along the northern and southern walls. The pews along the southern wall are reserved for the men, the ones along the northern wall for the women.[4] The pews along the eastern wall are for the *mapohicvlke* ("listeners"). These are the nonbelievers, "sinners," or others who choose not to participate fully. A single row of pews on a raised platform along the western wall are for the pastor, ministers,[5] and women's leaders.

Just in front of the leaders' pews is the *oherkenaketv* ("to preach on"), or pulpit. The pulpit is a wooden podium from which sermons are delivered. A small, wooden table is found along a wall or in front of the pulpit. This is the Communion table, which is placed in the center of the sanctuary during Communion meetings to hold the Communion elements. During non-Communion meetings the *obliktv merkv* ("mercy seat"), a short wooden bench, sits in the center of the sanctuary between the men's and women's pews. Its use is described in

Fig. 8. Diagram of church and camp houses. Drawing by Christine Schultz.

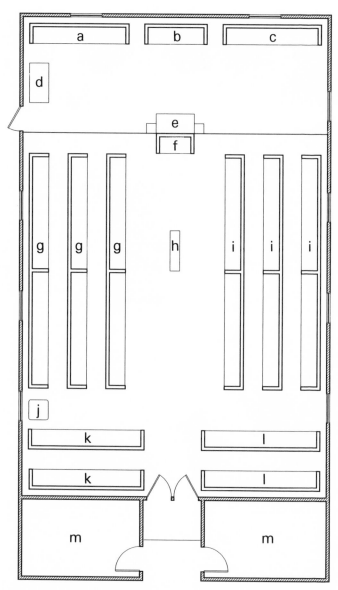

Fig. 9. *Typical Seminole Baptist church interior: (a) ministers' pew; (b) pastor's pew; (c) women's leaders' pew; (d) Communion Table; (e) pulpit; (f) deacons' pew; (g) men believers' pews; (h) mercy seat; (i) women believers' pews; (j) table holding water bucket and offering baskets; (k) men listeners' pews; (l) women's listeners' pews; (m) sacristies. Drawing by Jimmy Dunlop.*

*Fig. 10.   Church interior, from the visitors' section looking west.
Photo by author.*

the next chapter. Two of the churches have a baptistery—a permanent, indoor pool in which participants are immersed during the ritual of baptism.

On the eastern wall there is usually a hat rack, where the men hang their hats during the meetings. The rack also holds a cow-horn (*wakvyvpe* or *pofketv*, "cow-horn" or "to blow"), which is sometimes used instead of the bell to signal the beginning of the service.[6] Along the southern or western wall, a small table supports a water bucket and ladle that serve as a drinking fountain. This bucket is filled with drinking water from the outside well before each service. Near the water bucket hang baskets that are set out at the appropriate time during the service to collect the offerings. A calendar is hung in view of the sections for the women's leaders and the men's leaders. These are consulted often to verify the meeting dates of various churches. Some churches have kerosene lamps hung on the walls to provide light during power outages. Commonly, framed photographs picture past deacons, ministers, women's leaders, and pastors. A few churches have pianos, though they are seldom used. Religious artworks, such as crucifixes and tapestries or prints depicting biblical events, are quite common.

Outside under the attached arbor, the pews and benches are arranged in the same pattern as described above. The arbor is a pavilion-like structure consisting of a shingled roof, suspended by rough timber or masonry columns, under which services are held during the hot days of summer. Winds blowing through the trees keep the participants moderately comfortable even when the temperature rises above 100°. Swanton (1928a:191) noted that "some of the open-air features of the old ceremonial grounds have been preserved in the Indian churches of modern times." He was referring to these arbors.

The church grounds resemble the "old ceremonial grounds," as well as the contemporary ceremonial grounds (now usually referred to as the "Stomp grounds"), in several ways. In the ceremonial grounds (both historical and contemporary), the ceremonial center is the fire. Opler (1972:14) reports, "The use of a common fire, the use of a common hearth, is the symbol of unity for these people—a beautiful and poetic conception." For the churches, this center and symbol of unity has become the Communion table. As one moves from that center, the resemblance continues. At the ceremonial grounds a region is set off around the fire by a berm that has been raised by repeated raking of the grounds during preparations. Within that region arbors (usually four), containing benches, are placed at the cardinal directions facing the center (fire) and are reserved for participants (see Swanton 1928a:276–96 and Howard 1984:112 for figures illustrating the various historical Seminole grounds). The churches also have four regions of pews, oriented along the cardinal directions, facing the center (the Communion table). At the ceremonial grounds the ritual leaders usually occupy the westernmost arbor. At the churches the leaders sit in the westernmost pews. Similarly, visitors or the uninitiated sit in the easternmost arbor at the ceremonial grounds and in the easternmost pews in the churches. As at the church grounds, camp houses also ring the Stomp grounds. The camp houses of the Stomp grounds are usually less substantial than those located at church grounds, however. Most of the Stomp grounds camp houses are pavilion-like, with unenclosed roofs and dirt floors. Yet their placement and use are analogous to those of the church camp houses.

These similarities remain hidden from many of the participants. Ironically, discussions of similarities often entail describing the ceremonial grounds as "like a church," rather than understanding churches as being laid out similarly to the preexisting grounds. One reason the similarities go unnoticed, or are viewed as coincidental, is that the church members have developed Christian explanations for the layout. Consider the orientation of the church building. One pastor explained: "Just like the Wise men came from the east seeking Jesus, so do we. That's why [in] all the Indian churches the doors always face the east. The church faces east. But that's the reason, that Christ, when he was born in the manger, the Wise Men out of the east came and seen him, and the sun comes from the east when it rises, and it's our belief that Christ, when he comes, he'll be coming from the east. That's why all the Indian churches' doors face east." Rather than acknowledging the direct extension of the historical placement of the ceremonial arbors and personnel, church members have developed meaningful interpretations to fit the changed circumstances.

The custom of separating participants into different regions of the church is recognized by the Seminole Baptists as being foreign to non-Seminoles. Yet the practice is defended not by pointing to the historical Seminole custom of ritual separation by sex, clan, and adulthood but rather by using Christian terms. One pastor explained:

White people have accused us of separating people down here. You know, like sinners back here, and men on one side and women on one side. But they don't understand. What we're doing—that's a church ordinance. It's not scripturally, I guess, but that's a church ordinance. You take a man and woman sitting together, man and wife, they'll go to whispering. They'll go to talking. They're separating them. And when girls and boys sit together, they'll go to talking and this and that, and they're going to distract a preacher, or somebody else might want to hear sitting close to them. That's the only reason they separate boys from girls and men from boys. And then Christian people—we want to recognize who are the Christians and who is not. It's to benefit all to preach to the lost. So the Christian people—they are already saved, so I don't care anything about them. I mean, don't get me wrong—they already made it. I'm not trying to talk to them. I'm trying to win souls right here. And these Christian people are helping them. And they want them to be together in their prayers and they want them to be together in their songs so that one music will be coming from one place. If some of them sing up there and some of them back here, they going to get their songs going this way. The leaders—that's how we recognize them—you walk in the church—all the preachers sitting up there—you know they're preachers. You don't even know the people, you don't [know] what church they come out of. But they're the preachers. The women leaders, they sit in the front, you know they're leaders. They're capable of leading the songs and prayers if called upon. That's how you recognize them. It's for a good purpose, but I been asked by a lot of white people why we keep them separate like that. It looks to them like we're judging them here, separating them. I tell them no, that's not the idea. I said we do separate them on account of they go to talking to each other and they annoying the preacher and they annoying the person that want to hear the preacher on account of their whispering and talking and giggling and this and that. So we try to keep that under control. That's where the pastor comes in. He's got to put it over to them, to keep this quiet, because the Spirit comes and goes, the Bible says. The Spirit might be here, and the preacher's hot and the song is good. We might could win a soul, but they back there talking, going in and out, causing disturbance. They're going to distract this man's mind, and he might not know what to do. He might want to go outside and see what that commotion's going on or he wants to go up and maybe accept Christ. He don't know what to do. He's a sinner and he'll still be a sinner when it's over.

Thus the separation of various participants is maintained to avoid unnecessary distraction, to ensure the nonbeliever every opportunity to hear the gospel message. Only after I had been in the community for over a year did I hear an additional explanation of the separation of the sexes. A deacon explained that the custom of separating men from women comes from the historical belief that a woman's menstrual period would "weaken the men" (see Swanton 1928a:359 for a similar historical accounting). He reasoned that the contaminating aspect of menstruation could be carried by the wind, and since the prevailing winds in central Oklahoma are from south to north, the women's seats are downwind of the men's. The deacon stated that in the old days, women (and children) were not allowed anywhere near the men's area. This was especially true for the ceremonial grounds. The separation of menstruating women is particularly pronounced at the Stomp grounds. In the churches these restrictions have become lax.

Clearly, the physical layout of the church compounds is a direct extension of the historical ceremonial Stomp grounds tradition; but the adaptation of the grounds tradition extends beyond the physical compound. There is also a direct connection between the traditional organizational structure and the organizational structure of the Seminole Baptist church system.

The Seminole Baptist organizational structure is built around ordained[7] positions of leadership. These positions are pastor, minister, layman, exhorter, deacon, and women's leader. Members who do not hold leadership positions are called "floor members." All members of the same congregation, whether leaders or not, are called *coko vtekkike* ("inside the house"), or "members." Many of the church leadership positions are similar to the historical Seminole political and ceremonial leadership positions and appear to be direct extensions of those aboriginal positions.

The pastor, or *ohliketv ohlikv* [8] ("the sitter who sits in the chair"), is the public leader of an individual congregation. The pastor "chairs," or directs, the various gatherings of a congregation. The role of the pastor was explained by a deacon: "The pastor is the head of the church, the head of the flock. He makes sure the church stands in order. The name for pastor is *ohliktv ohlikv*. It means 'chair' and 'sits.' It's kind of funny to think of it that way, that's what the pastor does anyway, he's the chair person, in other words." An elderly pastor described the role of the pastor as that of a servant of the congregation rather than its master:

> The job is . . . I'd sure like to explain that to you—a lot of people—a lot of Indians don't understand it. A pastor's job . . . a lot of pastors think that they got there to . . . just let me put it this way . . . they think they ruling the whole church. In other words, he thinks he's the boss. But it's not the purpose of that. The pastor's job is to watch his flock and strengthen them and encourage them. The pastor of the church, the chairman—he knows each and every person. And when they elect—vote and get this pastor in, his job is to watch his flock. Don't let 'em— lose 'em—in other words, we call it—we use that word—lose 'em—not for them to go to other denominations, or we won't give them membership if they're gonna go to other denominations. The pastor have to know all of these things. And being a minister, a deacon—those what I call an office job—they cannot put their wives or husband away, and get remarried and hold this office job because the Bible's agin it—divorce and so forth. The pastor, he's got to be—he's got to walk that chalk line. He have to tell all of the church ordinances. He's got to look at it in the Bible, see what's going to happen.

The image of shepherd is useful. The pastor is to provide spiritual and emotional care for his congregation's members. He must also know "each and every person" and not "lose 'em." The pastor watches his flock, pointing out inappropriate behavior when necessary and, most important, keeping the members in the fold.

Although the pastor is considered the "head of the flock," his authority within the congregation is far from absolute. Pastors have great influence over their members but not ultimate control over the congregation. It is the floor members who appoint and support the person as pastor. A pastor warns: "Then the kind of thing that a pastor's got to watch, and if he's not really taking care of his flock, the floor members—the ones that put him up there—and the floor members got the authority to get him off—they'd have to have a legitimate excuse, though, like through his sickness, let's let him rest for three months or six months. And then we might reinstate him. But whichever way the Lord leads, that'll be the thing." Thus the accountability between a pastor and his congregation is mutual. Just as the pastor is to evaluate the behavior of his members, so the congregation evaluates the behavior of its pastor. The congregation exerts considerable social pressure on the pastor to keep him "on the chalk like." Such might be expected, considering that the pastor, more than any other member, regularly represents the congregational face within the larger Seminole Baptist community. As a result, his behavior is closely monitored and judged. (In chapter 7, I will provide an example of how a congregation selects and supports its pastor and how it removes that support when such action is deemed necessary for the maintenance of the congregation's face.)

Usually there is only one pastor for a congregation. If for some reason (e.g., poor health or other employment) an individual cannot adequately fulfill his obligations, a congregation may appoint another individual to serve as his assistant. This person is called *ohliketv vpoktv* ("chair twin"). The term was translated for me by one holding the position: "It means kind of like a twin or one is next to him. The easiest way to explain it would be, next to the pastor. But we call it an assistant pastor. *Ohliketv vpoktv*, that means you're with him all the time or you're together all the time, or something like that." The role of assistant pastor is virtually identical to that of pastor; the duties and obligations are shared between them. Only one person serves as the actual chair of a particular gathering, however. If the "twin" is present at the gathering, his role is likely to be that of minister, as described below.

Pastors are often appointed for life, but many churches have recently begun appointing them for only a one-year term, so that each year the pastor comes up for reinstallment. One deacon lamented: "It used to—it'd be lifetime pastor, the older bunch. But now, I think they usually give him a year or two years." The move to shorter appointments may be the result of congregational instabilities caused by more and more members participating in the Anglo economy. Shorter appointments also give the floor members much more control over the behavior of the pastor. The process of annual installation allows members to remove, relatively easily, pastors who fail to meet expectations or to reinstall a pastor, thereby affirming his performance. This may represent a shift in power from the pastor to the floor members.

The pastor serves a function similar to that of the historical Stomp grounds *mekko*. Swan (1856:279) stated, "Miccos [*mekkos*] are counselors and orators." Bartram (1928:389) observed that the *mekko* "is loved, esteemed and reverenced, although he associates, eats, and drinks with them in common as another man; his dress is the same, and a stranger could not distinguish the king's habitation from that of any other citizen. . . . Their micco seems to them the representative of Providence or the Great Spirit, whom they acknowledge to preside over and influence their councils and public proceedings . . . he presides . . . in their councils. . . and even here his voice in regard to business in hand, is regarded no more than any other chief's or senator's." Such descriptions aptly characterize the role of Seminole Baptist pastors: the pastors are the orators, the counselors, and the ones who oversee the churches, along the lines of the historical *mekko*, who oversaw the *etvlwvlke*. But the pastor, who once had virtually the same authority as the historical *mekko*, who was also appointed for life, now has much less power.

The next ordained position, ranking just below pastor, is the minister, or *erkenakv* ("one who speaks, or preaches"). His primary obligation is to serve as the preacher during gatherings. The pastor chairs or directs a meeting; the minister is called on "to deliver the message," or preach a sermon. The minister's role is that of speaker. In a way similar to that of the historical *henehv* ("second chief") and the *vsemponvkv* ("speaker"), who made "long talks" and spoke on behalf of the *mekko* (Swanton 1928a:295–96), the minister speaks for the pastor on behalf of his flock. A person must first be ordained as a minister before being considered for the position of pastor. All pastors are thus ordained as ministers; however, not all ministers are pastors. A congregation usually has only one pastor but will likely have multiple ministers.

A man never goes directly from the status of floor member to that of minister. He must undergo a training process, with each phase of the process involving a new status. When a man demonstrates leadership potential, he may be ordained into the position of *vcahnv* ("one who exhorts"), or exhorter. A deacon described this role: "The exhorter is the pastor's helper. He looks after the members and exhorts to them—tells them what to do and what not to do as Christians. If he sees somebody doing something, why, he has the right to correct us. He does it in a good way, you know. When he corrects somebody, feelings may be hurt, or they'll get mad, that's the chance you'll have to take; that's why they have a lot of prayers to do that work."

After successfully fulfilling the role of exhorter, the person may move on to the next phase of his training. He would then be ordained as "layman."[9] A deacon, making the distinction between the exhorter and the layman, said: "A layman has a little more knowledge and experience than an exhorter. It's the faith and belief that you have in you that's the main thing. The layman is almost a minister." When the status of minister is reached, the person usually maintains that status for life.

In recent years the more usual route for a person to go from floor member to minister is to be ordained as a "trainee." After a time (usually several years), he is ordained as a minister. The ordination as exhorter and layman is becoming less common. In my fieldwork, I never encountered a person in the position of exhorter or layman; I was only told about people who had filled those positions in the past. Men going through the training to become ministers were always referred to as "trainees." This contraction in the number of kinds of leaders is likely the result of the diminishing number of members. There are simply fewer personnel available to serve as leaders. Several Seminole Baptist congregations have so few partici-pants that all of the members hold leadership positions.

The *coko vfastv* ("one who takes care of the house"), or deacon, has a less spiritual role than the pastors and ministers. His position is identified with a cane, which he is to have always in his possession.[10] One deacon spoke about the symbol of his cane and about his role: "The cane symbolizes that we are deacons and that we're in charge of the church. We're like janitors and everything. We do this and that, and carry on all the time. That's the way it's been since way back. We sit people, we turn the bench, we help out the church pastor and do whatever he says to do. Of course, we usually know what to do, so we just carry on. The most deacons we've had is five. There's supposed to be seven, that's the old way. That's the pattern we try to follow." Deacons also go through a training period. During this time they are called "deacon trainees." They are ordained into the trainee position and are given a cane at that time, as a sign of their status. Deacons maintain the church property, pay bills, sweep floors, cut grass, and do other chores to keep the church grounds in order. During a gathering, their task is to greet and seat all visitors, regulate the heat and lights, collect the offering, and oversee the logistics of the gathering.

The minister at Eufaula explained that the historical title of *tvstvnvke* means "deacon." The word *tvstvnvke* is usually translated as "warrior"; however, one can see the logic in extending this term to the church deacons. Swanton (1928a:297–98) reported that the *tvstvnvleke* "were also the native police . . . they carried out the decisions of the miko . . . and they punished any one who failed to obey the laws and regulations of the council or who failed to attend the annual busk. When matters of great importance were to be discussed they were called over to the Chief's bed to take party in the deliberations; on other occasions matters were sent over to them to be ferreted out." The deacons similarly assist the leaders, providing oversight and order. The Eufaula minister added: "In the same way that the Stomp grounds has workers, so does the church. The *mekko* is like pastor; *emponvkv* is like the ministers, who are the 'spokesmen for Christ'; and the *tvstvnvke* is like the deacon." At contemporary Stomp grounds, the *tvstvnvke*, also called the *envprvlv* ("the loaner or one who hands out" but given the English gloss "stickman"), directs activities and selects leaders for the dances. Howard (1984:129) refers to these men as *impuhata cukoafasta* (*empohetv coko vfastv*, "one who cares for the house and is listened to"), which he translates as "deacon." The "house" that the stickmen oversee is the *coko rakko* ("big house"), which is one of the native terms for the Stomp grounds. Like the church deacon, this position is marked with a cane.

Two adjunct positions, or roles, found in many of the Seminole Baptist churches are *heles hayv* ("medicine maker") and *kerrv* ("knower")—positions that were described in the previous chapter. Not each church has people performing these two roles, but men fulfilling these roles are known to members within each of the churches should their services be required.

There is only one leadership category for women. This role is called *hoktake enhomathoyv* ("front woman"), or women's leader. Sometimes the term *hoktake seme'yvpvyv* is used for this position. This term implies a leader pulling a rope from which the followers are led—"like how the mother duck gets her little ones to line up and follow her." The women's leaders function almost like a female deacon. They are to make sure that camps are open and that adequate food is prepared and served for refreshments. These women also oversee the spiritual training of younger women, admonishing and encouraging them. One of the women's leaders—usually the oldest and most experienced of the group—is recognized as having seniority over the others. There is not a special title for this position. The authority of the women's leaders is almost exclusively over other women. However, the senior women's leader has the authority to publicly chastise the pastor, should she deem it necessary. She does this only in extreme occasions. (An example is provided in chapter 7.) The ideal number of women's leaders in a congregation is seven. Participants speak of this full complement being met in the previous generation, but only rarely today does a church have the ideal number of women's leaders.

The women's leaders go through a training period. A pastor noted: "They have to be found through fasting and prayer too. They just go through the same procedure as a deacon or minister. We read the scripture to them and install them as a Woman Leader." The women's leader with the least seniority is known as the *seme'yvpvyv hvce*, or "tail of the women's leaders." She is the one who must always "be moving about, doing what had to be done, like a servant." This is considered an aspect of her training.

The term for women's leader, *hoktake enhomathoyv*, or *hoktake seme'yvpvyv*, does not appear in Swanton (1928a, 1928b). No female leadership titles are recorded, but occasionally a woman served as "chief" (Swanton 1928b:696, 700). The more typical public leadership authority of the "chief" appears to be similarly restricted to other women (Swanton 1928b:528).

Other, nonordained positions are the *mekusapkvcoko cokvhayv* ("house of prayer book maker"), or church secretary, and the *mekusapkvcoko tokanap vfastv* ("one who cares for church money"), or church treasurer. The church secretary, who is usually also a women's leader, records minutes (if deemed necessary) at the church business meetings and is responsible for written correspondence between churches. The church treasurer, who is usually also a deacon, is responsible for paying bills and overseeing the church's money.

Leaders are chosen from within the congregation and by the congregation. A pastor explained: "The worker, they have to elect him from the floor—floor members—they're the ones that make us ministers, make us deacons, make us pastors. They'll fast and fast and pray and pray till they all with one accord come to say, 'Well, Jack will be the pastor.' That's how we're supposed to install a worker." Unlike the clergy in Anglo Baptist churches, the leadership is trained within the local community and serves within the local community. The contrast between the Anglo process and the Seminole process was noted by a pastor:

> See, white people, they can go to seminary and automatically they'll license them when they graduate and later on they can ordain him. Indians won't do that. They go through fasting and prayers. You know, Jesus in his teachings—said time and again—said these kinds of things don't come but by fasting and prayer. Lot of people don't believe in fasting. But Indians do. They're strict on that. Too many young people think that just because they go to seminary they should be a pastor. It ain't so. We don't know him. He didn't grow up around us. We don't know if he's easily angered, or jealous. We need to know our pastors.

The local community has the authority to select and train its pastors directly—pastors are generally selected out of the congregations in which they will serve. This responsibility is carefully fulfilled. Again, the pastor represents the congregation to the community. A congregation's face may be enhanced or damaged by the behavior of its pastor.

When a position needs to be filled, the members follow a formal process for selecting an individual. The process for selecting a deacon was described by a member:

> The pastor is the one that have to approve so whatever the congregation decides—said, "Let's look for a deacon—let us fast and look for a deacon," through the Spirit. The pastor have to announce that to the congregation, "So this is what the deacons have want of and you floor members will agree to that. If you do let it be known by raising our right hand." They'll have a secretary, *cokv hayv*, sitting there and she'll write down everything. And then through this congregation, they'll fast and pray. Maybe once a month the pastor will ask "Have you all found a deacon?" Some of them might say, "Yes." They won't name him, till the time comes when the pastor says, "You all name him." And it might rock on maybe six months. We have a time getting an officer like that, though. We try to all come to one conclusion, with one mind, you know—they want the same person. And when it finally comes to majority—say maybe seven out of ten want this person, well, then the church will take action. We'll say, "Well, the majority want this person." We gonna leave it to you to decide, if we could go ahead and ordained him. But they'll have to set a date for that ordination, later on. That's when we put him on trial basis—see if he's got the qualifications, see if he can do the work. Then later we'll ordain him.

Ministers are similarly selected; however, an "ordination board" made up of area ministers often is appointed to identify a minister from the local congregation for the local congregation. The process was described by a pastor: "The church selects an ordination board of ministers. They gather at the home church or wherever the ordination is going to take place. Then they select a chairman of the board, ordination board, usually one of the ministers who is more knowledgeable or experienced in that line of work. Among themselves they select a leader of the ordination board." Congregations are ostensibly autonomous, yet the employment of an ordination board, made up of pastors and ministers from sister Seminole Baptist churches, attests to the importance of the larger community—congregations are constituent units of the larger Seminole community. The appointment of a minister trainee by an ordination board represents an additional level of control by the community to ensure integrity (shared expectations and behaviors) within the larger Seminole Baptist community. The pastor continued: "And the way that's done is we decide on it and come together on it. We start fasting and praying on that. Once a week with our fellow co-workers, or any time individually, it's up to you. Usually you don't have to have a board, just a pastor, to have authority to promote an exhorter to a layman." Members recognize that the final authority for selecting leaders is the local congregation. The local congregation decides which of its own will represent its congregational face in this very public role.

The position of pastor incorporates a certain social prestige for the holder. It is often, however, a thankless job. Pastors receive only nominal financial reward for the position (often less than $50 per month), yet they are held responsible for the smooth operation of the congregation. Many men are reluctant to serve in the position yet will agree to serve when the members select him. A deacon explained: "Some pastors serve a year, then the church has to reinstate him or let him go. Maybe he don't want it. In most cases when they offer him the job, like that, they usually go ahead and do it, carry it out. You're not supposed to decide such things by yourself. It's supposed to be the church that decides that." Some men find that the social prestige of the position of pastor is worth pursuing, and at times several men will tacitly campaign for the single position. (One such episode is described in chapter 7.)

Many participants view the leadership positions hierarchically, with the expectation that when a role is successfully performed, it will lead to promotion to the next level of service. When I asked this deacon if he thought he would be promoted to exhorter, he responded:

> I really don't know. I've often thought about that, though, but some ministers preach "once a deacon always a deacon." I'm studying on it. The way it is if you don't have many workers at your church, like at our church, if the church asks you to do something, it's hard to turn them down if you're qualified. I don't know if I'm qualified for that work. They may take me as a trainee. I wouldn't say no, I don't know if I'm qualified. If the church says I am, I'd have to pray on it. If I don't say "no," I'll probably get stronger. It's just like anything else—experience is the best teacher as they say. Seems like if you've been in a church for a while, and you've got the know-how, you're going to eventually be a deacon or a minister. That's the old-timers' view and it seems right. That's the way it should be, I guess.

It is the "church"—that is, the congregation or immediate social group—that selects, trains, and appoints people to serve as leaders within the community.

It is difficult, although possible, for individuals to move membership from one congregation to another. In the rare occasion that a leader (pastor, minister, deacon, or women's leader) leaves his or her home congregation to join another, he or she leaves the position behind—the leadership credentials, as it were, remain with the home congregation. It is the local community that gives the status, and it is the local congregation that can withdraw it. A pastor described what happens when a leader seeks to leave his own congregation:

> If he's a Baptist and he wants his membership to go to Presbyterian or Methodist or something, we won't let him out. But if he's going to another Baptist, yes, we'll let him out. And if he's an all-day minister, a deacon, or a woman leader, we'll hold that job because this church give it to him. If he's going to another

church, we'll hold this, but biggest part of the time we used to send a recommendation, written, saying that his standing with this church was good. He was a minister, but we gave it to him, so it would be up to you to give that back to him or whichever you wish. . . . If he goes off and then he comes back, they'll write us the same way or let us know the same way and they'll leave it up to us that he's going back to his own church. And then we'll have to let him ride for thirty days, sixty, some of them got different ruling, you know, different church order. Whenever the time comes, you think, well, let's just reinstall him cause he's got ordination. He did go yon and back. They've reinstalled him. They call it love, you know, cause they trying to—they don't want to take anything away from him that God gave him.

A deacon provided an example of how this actually works:

I'll tell you about what happened in our church. It was some time ago. *Cesse* ("Mouse," in this case a nickname) and his wife were not at Eufaula where they are now. They went to a Presbyterian church. Anyways, after twelve years they found *Cesse* as an exhorter and layman, and then minister. I think he did a little pastoring there. They got to where they didn't get along too good there, and *Cesse* said he had the urge to come back to Eufaula, and we always welcome back anyone who wants to come back. They can rededicate, or in their case, they became members. We have to accept them on the bottom rung, in other words on the bottom, and work their way back up. That's what *Cesse* did. He was an exhorter for a while and then a layman, and now he's minister. That's the way it is with women too. His wife used to be pretty experienced in that other work, but they had to do it all over when they came back to our church. I think she was a women's leader over there.

Switching congregations is discouraged and is quite costly. One can see the functional sense of this strategy. It would be

counterproductive for the larger community to have constituent units competing for the same members. Instead, a mechanism has been established to promote cooperation among the
congregations, namely the Fourth Sunday Meeting rotation,
described in the next chapter.

The local congregation identifies, trains, and supports individuals to serve in the leadership roles. Able individuals are
carefully chosen to ensure that the ideals of the community
(both the local congregation and the larger Seminole Baptist
community) are represented by the person fulfilling the role.
For although leaders serve within the local congregation, they
nevertheless represent the congregation's face—that is, its
public image—to the larger Seminole community. Mechanisms
are in place (e.g., appeal to individual and congregational face,
and attendant sanctions) to ensure that the leaders fulfill the
ideals of the community. (Examples of the implementation of
these mechanisms are described in chapter 7.)

The Seminole Baptist community has institutionalized leadership positions and roles. These positions—pastor, minister,
deacon, and women's leader—show a close correlation to the
historical native leadership positions of the *etvlwvlke*, or bands.
As has been shown, the historical native positions and their
contemporary Christian correlates function in similar structural
ways. This is not surprising, considering that the churches are
a direct extension of these historical sociopolitical groups that
served as a basic organizational unit of the Seminole people.
Leadership positions in the churches function at a structural
level to organize the social life of congregational gatherings. In
addition, such a position offers prestige and enhancement of
the holder's face while also obligating the holder to certain
behavioral expectations. In the next chapter I will describe the
primary social occasions at which these leaders perform their
roles.

CHAPTER 6

"Fulfilling the Work"
at Church Gatherings

The Seminole Baptist church system is organized around three
primary social situations, or occasions: weekly Prayer Meetings,
Fourth Sunday Meetings, and Big (or Communion) Meetings. It
may be useful to think of these three occasions as concentric
circles making up the structure of Seminole Baptist social life:
Prayer Meetings form the central circle; next are Fourth Sunday
Meetings; and the outside ring comprises Big Meetings. The
innermost circle, composed of Prayer Meetings, represents the
most intimate or private region of the social interaction. Participants are bound to regular, weekly interactions of congregational life. It is at this level that most of the interpersonal
conflict arises and is resolved. The next circle, composed of
Fourth Sunday Meetings, broadens the interaction. Multiple
congregations within the system extend their concerns to
include the larger community. At this level, congregational face
is exposed to the larger community. The outside ring, composed of Big Meetings, represents the furthest-reaching interactions. The whole Seminole Baptist community is celebrated
and affirmed; unity and oneness is the theme. Within these
ever-widening circles, individuals, as members of particular
congregations and as members of the larger Seminole Baptist
community, encounter other individuals. At each of these
levels, individual faces are exposed to risk. The larger Seminole
Baptist community can, therefore, regulate private and congregational conduct to ensure community continuity.

The first occasions to be discussed are Prayer Meetings, which occur weekly at each church grounds. The primary participants in Prayer Meetings are members of the host congregation; few visitors attend. Attendance at Prayer Meetings is relatively light: Eufaula's Prayer Meetings number between 6 and 30 participants, with a usual attendance of about 12.[1]

Fourth Sunday Meetings occur once every four weeks at each church grounds. Individual congregations host Fourth Sunday Meetings in a cooperative rotation with other Seminole Baptist churches. Attendance at Fourth Sunday Meetings is usually between 25 and 80. At Eufaula's Fourth Sunday Meetings the attendance is usually about 35. Most participants at a Fourth Sunday Meeting are visitors to the host congregation (that is, Seminole Baptists who are members of other churches in the rotation).

Last are Big Meetings, which center around the sacrament of Communion. Big Meetings occur in most congregations four times annually. At least one church, however, hosts eight Big Meetings each year. Big Meetings enjoy the largest attendance of all the occasions: between 30 and 125. At Eufaula's Big Meetings the attendance is usually around 45. Like the participants at Fourth Sunday Meetings, most of the participants at Big Meetings are visitors.

Since the Prayer Meeting format serves as the pattern (with significant exceptions described below) for all the social occasions of the Seminole Baptist churches, it will be discussed first.

Prayer Meetings

Each week members of Seminole Baptist churches gather for a *Mekusvpkv Nere* ("Prayer Night"), or as it is glossed in English, Prayer Meeting. Some of the congregations have Prayer Meetings on Friday evenings, others on Wednesday nights. The meetings begin about 7:30 P.M. and usually conclude around 11:00 P.M.

Participants begin to gather for church meetings about an hour before the scheduled beginning time. The first to arrive are usually the deacons, who make sure that the facilities are presentable and operable, that the furnishings are in place, that the heat or fans are on, and so forth. It is from such tasks that the deacon gets his name, *coko vfvstv* ("carer of the house").

As other members and visitors arrive, they greet each other by shaking hands and saying "*Ecca*" ("Hello") and "*'Stonko*" ("How are you?"). Following greetings, the participants cluster, usually according to gender, to converse with each other. The mood is usually light, with much laughter and catching up on news.

Thirty minutes before the service is to begin, the deacon rings first bell. When the bell is rung, all those present stop their talking and break eye contact with each other. A member explained: "When the deacon rings the bell, he is praying. We need to respect that and not interrupt him." The bell is rung about a dozen times.[2] When he is finished ringing the bell, conversation begins again where it left off. People continue to arrive and greet those who are already there. A few churches do not have bells; instead, a horn fashioned from a hollow cow-horn is blown to signal the beginning of the meeting.[3]

In the interval between first and second bells the deacons assemble for a brief meeting to coordinate tasks for the upcoming service. One deacon noted: "Usually the menfolks get together, we get our heads together, our ideas together, and have a prayer before the service. We talk to the Lord and ask the Lord to help and guide us through the services. And whoever we know is going to preach, why, we ask him [the Lord] for the ideas and the right kind of words to say, and ideas like that before we start."

This deacons' meeting begins with the head deacon leading a song and a prayer and then speaking words of encouragement to the other deacons present. Often another deacon will lead an additional song and prayer and speak words of encouragement. The purpose of this meeting is to appoint workers for the service immediately following. By the time of this meeting, the deacons have a fairly good idea of who is in attendance, so speakers and other workers (e.g., who will turn the mercy seat during the invitation, who will count the offering) are chosen. One deacon reports the result of this meeting to the *ohliketv ohlikv* ("the sitter who sits on the chair"), that is, the pastor.

As the service is about to begin, the head deacon invites those present to take their seats. Members sit in their appointed seats, and visitors are assigned seats by the deacons.[4] The deacons exert great care in seating visitors to ensure that no one is offended—that their face receives proper recognition. Ministers and pastors must be seated at the western end; visitors are given the "best seats" along the front rows. On the rare occasion that an unknown person enters the church, the pastor or a deacon will inquire into his or her identity to make sure that the person's social face is given proper recognition.[5] After all are seated, the deacon rings the bell for a second time.

During the ringing of the bell, the pastor begins singing a prayer song; others follow his lead and join in the singing. Prayer songs are sung a cappella and in unison. Foot tapping emphasizes accents and rhythms. The songs are reminiscent of spirituals: they have a mournful, plainsong-quality that might be characterized as chant. Most of these songs speak of current hard times being replaced by an eternal life of well-being. One song that often begins meetings is "Vnokeckvt Omecicen."

> *Vnokeckvt omecicen hvlwe tvlofvn apeyakvres.*
> *Vnokeckvt omecicen hvlwe tvlofvn apeyakvres.*
> ("On account of love we are going to heaven.")

> *Mekusapvlke omvlkvskat hvlwe tvlofvn apeyakvres.*
> *Mekusapvlke omvlkvskat hvlwe tvlofvn apeyakvres.*
> ("All of you People Who Pray are going to heaven.")

> *Pomerkenvkvlke omvlkvskat hvlwe tvlofvn apeyakvres.*
> *Pomerkenvkvlke omvlkvskat hvlwe tvlofvn apeyakvres.*
> ("Our preachers are going to heaven.")

Purvhvlke omvlkvskat hvlwe tvlofvn apeyakvres.
Purvhvlke omvlkvskat hvlwe tvlofvn apeyakvres.
("Our fathers are going to heaven.")

Hopuetake omvlkvskat hvlwe tvlofvn apeyakvres.
Hopuetake omvlkvskat hvlwe tvlofvn apeyakvres.
("Our children are going to heaven.")

Eyasketvt omecicen hvlwe tvlofvn apeyakvres.
Eyasketvt omecicen hvlwe tvlofvn apeyakvres.
("On account of humility we are going to heaven.")[6]

While the last verse is being sung, the pastor stands and, by raising his hands, invites the congregation to rise with him. Before the end of the song (during the final chorus), the participants slowly turn, first to face the east and then to face their pews. When the song is completed, the pastor says *"Eman"* ("Amen"), and all kneel to pray. The pastor begins by invoking *Hesaketv emese* ("Maker of breath"), *Porke Epohfastv* ("Our Father, the One Who Cares for Us"), *Porke Epofvnkv* (Our Father, the One above Us"), or *Pocase Cesvs* ("Our Lord Jesus"). The members respond, *"Eman,"* then all people begin praying out loud, simultaneously and independently.

The individual prayers, of course, vary greatly. Early in my field experience, before I understood any Mvskoke, I inquired as to the content of the prayers. A pastor responded:

Well, most of them pray for some soul to be saved. Some soul might rededicate their lives. And some just pray for the preacher to deliver the message. But it always winds up together in our prayers. You listen to them and understand them. I notice they all come together with one conclusion. They all praying for the same things. But the way they used to tell us to pray back yonder in my day, when you go to church—you been praying out here in the country at home. When you come to a place— church, you should come together—what I call refreshment of our works, bring our works together, praising the Lord. You been praying all this and talking to God, telling him what you need, and this and that and this and that. When you come to church always pray for some soul to be saved. And to be with the minister when he delivers the message, that they might come—I'm bound to use that word "hot." I mean, you know, you just feel warm and you want to preach. Words will come to you just a flying.

Those who are the first to complete their prayers listen to the prayers still being spoken, demonstrating their approval and agreement by saying "*Eman*" at appropriate places. The one who leads the prayer is usually the last one praying. He concludes his prayer with "*Nak omvlkat cenpohayet cenke ofen hayes*" ("What all we ask we place in your hands") or "*Cesvs enhocefcat ofen respoyis*" ("In Jesus' name I end this"); then all those present join him with "*Eman*" and return to their seats.

Immediately someone else (usually, but not always, a deacon) leads a song and then a prayer in the same fashion just described. A prayer song often sung is "Yvmv Estemerketvn."

Yvmv estemerketvn tehoyvnvyof, tehoyvnvyof, tehoyvnvyof, Cesvs vpakares.
("Here to suffer as I pass through, I pass through, I pass through, I'll be with Jesus.")

Erkenakvlket yican hecvkes, Erkenakvlket yican hecvkes, Erkenakvlket yican hecvkes, Cesvs vpakares.
("The preachers they see come, The preachers they see come, The preachers they see come, I'll see Jesus.")

Mekusvpvlket yican hecvkes, Mekusvpvlket yican hecvkes, Mekusvpvlket yican hecvkes, Cesvs vpakares.
("The People Who Pray they see come, The People Who Pray they see come, The People Who Pray they see come, I'll see Jesus.")

Emestvlket yican hecvkes, Emestvlket yican hecvkes, Emestvlket yican hecvkes, Cesvs vpakares.
("Their people they see come, Their people they see come, Their people they see come, I'll see Jesus.")

Elkv Hvccen tehoyvnvyof, tehoyvnvyof, tehoyvnvyof, Cesvs vpakares.
("Death Creek I'll pass through, I'll pass through, I'll pass through, I'll see Jesus.")[7]

The prayers, filled with imagery and formal language, are spoken with great eloquence. The following is one such prayer spoken by a deacon:

[Translated from Mvskoke:]
Giver and Taker of Life and Breath, Master, Our Father. You are most powerful; you will live forever! Your name is sacred.

Here on earth your power is over all things. Your word which has come to us is to be here always. When all that is, from this earth to the heavens, passes away your word will live on as you have decreed.

Your prophecies are fulfilled; the word is fulfilled. Therefore on this day is Friday Night Prayer Meeting—your name is here. You have gathered your children together in this place. You continue to be merciful to us. We gather, we pray, we praise you in all things, glorifying you, and believing in you completely.

Your name is most holy. You rule over all things. You will live forever.

In your goodness we have promised to labor always, but our work becomes burdened by worldly cares and is slack at times. However, you continue to be merciful to us. Because you continue to give us another day we have returned this day mindful of you. We do the work, the holy work of confessing your word.

We believe that your mercy will be with all of your children who learn. Keep giving your mercy upon the one who says "I hope not to stand in want of learning." Our work this day is that one may learn, that through the Spirit one will live, that we might all live. And through your continued blessings the local preacher has once again returned to labor with us so that we may be prepared. By your blessings, many works are done, although we strive in imperfection.

[The prayer continues in English:]

Father we praise your name, and all that you have given us on this day, Father. We thank you for the food and shelter and clothing that you have given us. These are for the physical needs, Father, but as we gather this evening to eat the spiritual food, and drink the water, the everlasting water, the water that you say, "You drink of this water, you will never thirst no more," Father. As we come together, we are thankful for the visitor that we have today, and all the workers, brothers and sister, wherever they may be, and the ones that aren't here, Father, may your blessings be upon them also. And Father, we want to remember the ones that are sick, the ones that are physically handicapped, Father we pray that you be with them also. Help us Father, in every way. May we grow stronger in thy grace. And we come before you to ask that your blessings be upon this church, upon all of the workers that are working today and other times that we come in here. The others that aren't here, Father, just give them the help and the strength to come and gather with us and we'll all worship together, Father. As we go on to the services may your blessings be upon us. We pray that you'll bless our pastor and our minister, our brothers and sisters and also our visitor. And all that are here on the church ground, even our children, Father. We ask this in thy holy name, the Father and the Son and the Spirit, we pray. Amen.

Three or four prayer songs and prayers are led by various members. Specific individuals are not appointed to lead these songs and prayers; rather, one simply begins a song, and the rest of the congregation follows.

The service continues with another prayer song. The following is an example:

Hvlwen heckv ofvn, hvlwen heckv ofvn, hvlwen heckv ofvn. Hesaketv emese.
("I'll be born in heaven, born in heaven, born in heaven. Maker of Breath.")

Pomerkenvkvlke mekusvpvkes, Pomerkenvkvlke ayemahes hvlwe tvlofv mimvn.
("Our preachers they pray, our preachers press on there in heaven.")

Mekusvpvlke mekusvpvkes, Mekusvpvlke ayemahes hvlwe tvlofv mimvn.
("The People Who Pray they pray, The People Who Pray press on there in heaven.")

Cvrvhvlke mekusvpvkes, Cvrvhvlke ayemahes hvlwe tvlofv mimvn.
("Older brothers pray, older brothers press on there in heaven.")

Cvcustvke mekusvpvkes, Cvcustvke ayemahes hvlwe tvlofv mimvn.
("Younger brothers pray, younger brothers press on there in heaven.")[8]

After the third or fourth prayer song, the pastor stands at the pulpit for a "devotional reading," consisting of a formal welcome to those present, a scripture reading, and a short homily explicating the text. A typical devotional reading is introduced as follows: "It is good that we could gather together once again. We have another day. You and I didn't know if we were going to make it. We only had a hope that we would be here tonight to fulfill the work. God has provided that you and I should be here. Some are not here, but God knows their excuse. We're going to go ahead and fulfill the service." If there are visiting ministers or other visitors present, they are acknowledged and greeted by the pastor and their home congregations are noted. Visiting other congregations is referred to as "helping out" that congregation and is viewed as a positive and necessary action.

At the pulpit the pastor reads a passage from scripture. This passage is read from the King James Version of the Bible and then is translated into Mvskoke. Those pastors who are literate in Mvskoke will read the same pericope from the Mvskoke-language Bible.[9] At the conclusion of the devotion, the pastor announces the number and order of the preaching and when invitations will be extended. The pastor usually concludes this section by asking the congregation to rise for a song and prayer. Unlike the other prayer songs, where a person volunteers to lead, this song and prayer are led by a person assigned by the pastor. The pastor appoints a visitor, if present, to offer the song and prayer for the preacher's message. At the beginning of the song, the first preacher takes a seat next to the pastor behind the pulpit.

At a few of the churches, one Prayer Meeting each month is designated as a *Soletawv Mekusvpkv* ("Soldier's Prayer"), or "Service for the Armed Forces." The Prayer Meeting format is maintained but includes a recognition of Seminoles in the armed forces and a song and prayer for them. This addition occurs either immediately after the pastor's devotional reading or in lieu of it. The pastor at Eufaula lead this segment as follows:

It is good that we could be here today. God has provided you and I tonight one more time to blend our voice in song and prayer. First of all tonight, on a special Friday night like this, we got Armed Service that happens to be tonight. You all might have a relative or a friend or whoever you know. It is for you and I, for our protection, that they're over there now. You know they like to be home same as you and I. They know how the country is now here and there, and they have to be on the lookout for you and I so we could be out of danger. We'll have a song and a prayer for the armed services, and after that we'll have another song and a prayer, and then we'll hear the message. But I'll give opportunity a little short time to mention some of your friends or some person you know in the armed service. I know we feel like we have some in the reserves too, they could call any time. You can name the person you know, maybe your buddies, I'll give you all a short time to mention friends of yours maybe in some kind of the armed forces. . . . [Here the pastor sat down, and various members stood and named friends or relatives currently serving in the armed services. After all had been given the opportunity to speak, the pastor continued.] You and I don't know any boys that's in a running war, still they are protecting you and I. So we're going to have a prayer to fulfill that and also we're going to listen to the message and after the message is through we're going to give an invitation. Someone will lead us in a song prayer as we all stand.

Individuals are named, their locations and duties reported. Some members will announce that although they do not know anyone personally who is presently serving, it is a good thing to remember those serving and to offer prayers on their behalf.

Whether the Prayer Meeting is for soldiers or not, the service continues with a song. A popular song is "Heleluyvn."

Heleluyvn yvhikares, hele, heleluyvn,
Heleluyvn yvhikares, hele, heleluyvn.
("I will sing hallelujah, hale, hallelujah.")

Purahvlket mimvn vpokes hele, heleluyvn.
("Our fathers are dwelling there hale, hallelujah.")

Puwvntaket mimvn vpokes hele, heleluyvn.
("Our sisters are dwelling there hale, hallelujah.")

Vkvsamvlket mimvn vpokes hele, heleluyvn.
("Believers are dwelling there hale, hallelujah.")

Emestvlket mimvn vpokes hele, heleluyvn.
("His people are dwelling there hale, hallelujah.")

Pometvlvvlket mimvn vpokes hele, heleluyvn.
("The Bands are dwelling there hale, hallelujah.")[10]

At the conclusion of the song, people again turn and kneel in prayer. The prayers at this time are spoken on behalf of the preachers—that their message will be heard, that God's spirit will speak through the preacher, and that, most important, some one will be saved after hearing the message. Here is one such prayer offered in English by a young member of Sand Creek Church:

Our most gracious heavenly Father. Father, we thank you again for this time and this opportunity that you have given us. As we gather here in this house we pray that you would bless each and every one of us, and that your blessings would be upon the pastor of this church. Father, we ask that you would bless all the brothers and sisters in Christ that are here. And as we go into this service tonight we just pray that you would let your will be done in this service. We're all knowing that without you we can do nothing. And Father, you have gathered us into this house, and as we go forth into this service tonight we just pray that the Holy Spirit will abide in each and every one of us. As we sing these songs, making a joyful noise unto you, and as we go into the words of God tonight, Lord, we pray that you would bless the ministers as they bring these words forth that some soul may come forth to get saved tonight, Father. We know that we are just on borrowed time tonight, but we just pray that those who are without Christ would take heed to these words tonight, that they will just look up to you as their personal Savior tonight while the time is available. Father, we just ask you to bless the pastor as he watches over his flock and that you will be with all the visiting churches that take part in the services tonight, that you will just work with each and every one and that your Holy Spirit will work within this house tonight. Father, we just pray and ask all this in Jesus' name. Amen.

After the prayer is spoken and the congregation returns to their seats, the appointed preacher leads a song. During the last verse he stands at the pulpit, and at the conclusion of the song he begins his message. These sermons usually last about forty minutes.[11] The following is an example of a typical sermon:

It is good to be back once again in the house of the Lord. It is a great blessing that he has given unto you and I that we can fellowship with one another. The Lord has been merciful to us and he made it possible for you and I that we could come together in fellowship in the Lord and rejoice tonight. You know this may be the last time for one of us. We hear this time after time, and pay no thoughts to it. Though I'm sure there are many that are out in the world that have had not thoughts of this though they have heard it. There are many that have been called out. But today through the love of the Lord he gave you and I the privilege that we could come together.

[Reading from the Bible:] And Jesus had spoke in parables unto a great multitude. You know the same day (Matthew 13:1–23). . . . You know this reading that you and I is talking about, he told his disciples when they asked him why he spoke to the multitude in parables. Jesus answered them and told the disciples, "because it is given to you to know the mysteries." And God reveals to those disciples and he also reveals to you and I, and we believe in the spirit of God and he reveals things to you and I, the things that he had revealed to his disciples.

There are some that would laugh to see the things, the mysteries, of the kingdom of heaven today, that would laugh to see what God reveals. God reveals things. And if you pray over this and if you think about this, God can reveal these things to you. You'll know if these things were accomplished or not by the spirit of God, what he lays upon your heart, he reveals these things.

I heard an old minister preach at High Springs. I always believe in the elders, when they pray to God, God had revealed to them the things that are going to happen and the things that's going to take place, that's beyond, that's from today that you and I see, that's been fulfilled, the things that had been predicted that's going to happen. I see these things that are taking place. I know that all of our elderlies, because I had an uncle and he talked to me about these things. He said the coming of the Lord is near, he said it's more closer than it used to be. No one knows the time he's going to come, but he gives a sign that you and I have seen and heard. But all these things we are forgetting.

This is what I was talking about the elderlies, they see things through fasting and through prayer God revealed to them the things that was going to take place. Even though they didn't know how to read a Bible. And God had showed them the things that was going to be taking place today, by prayer, this is how they knew, you know they knew the things that was going to happen. Because as I had said, I talked with one of the elderlies of Sand Creek you know he had told me many things that was gong to take place, that was going to happen and just a little before he passed away I seen these things that he had predicted was going to happen, take place.

You know this is how God reveals to you and I if we believe and if we trust him. He shows us things that's going to come, come before, these things take place. You know this is true. God can reveal these things. This is why he was speaking to his disciples. Because he said it is given to you to know the mysteries of the kingdom of heaven. And there is many that do not have it and this is why the parables have been written, that you and I can be able to understand what he's talking about.

You know that the seed that was sown was to you and I the words that is being preached is what was sown into a man, into his heart. So when you hear the message and do not understand the word that has been presented, the wicked one is Satan, the wicked one comes to take the word that has been presented, he takes it away from you and this is how Satan works. You know when you hear he removes it from you, he don't want you to understand the ways of the Lord. There are some that receive the word of God in their heart, but due to no root in these words that you had sown in your heart, even though you had accepted the Lord with joy, due to no root, and Satan comes and takes all these things away from you through trial and persecution.

Jesus was the sower, and when he had planted these words in your heart Satan comes along and when he comes along with the care of the things that are in this world, he puts it before you. He brings all these things upon you. When the cares of the world come upon you, you start backing away from the things that the Lord had given unto you. And it chokes up the word that had been planted in your heart. You know it takes prayers, it takes a lot of prayers to believe, to have that faith in the Lord.

Satan is a deceiver, he's a liar. But when we begin to serve the Lord he knows our weakness, this is where Satan comes and put many things before you. When all these things the trials and temptation that comes upon you start backing away from the Lord Jesus Christ.

You know Jesus tells us to be patient and to wait and all things that are needful in you life the Lord is willing to give to you. But it may be through trials that things that are needful in your life may come. It may not come right when it's needful, but the Bible tells us that he says I know your needs, and I will provide all things, but you and I have to believe, we have to believe in the Lord. You know there's times that when something that is needful in your life come upon you it gets hard to trust in the Lord. Sometimes it makes you wonder why, why are these things so. But Jesus knows best for you and I. You know that through the trials and temptations that come upon you if you don't heed to the world, he'll strengthen you that you can stand the things that's happening in your daily walks of life. It takes trust to overcome the things that are in the world.

You know this parable that we had read it also is speaking to you and I as a servant of the Lord, that even though we say that we serve the Lord, there are many times we rebel against the things that you and I are being taught. We hear these words, but still yet we do not hear because the Bible tells us that our ears are dumb. That's why this message that was written to you and I and to those that are back out in the world today.

You know many times as a servant of the Lord we have a tendency of backtalking one another. We say things about a brother or a sister. You know that Satan is a deceiver. He makes us talk about one another. You know it's hard to control the tongue. This tongue can save you. Either that or this tongue can lose your soul. It depends on how you and I are going to choose to walk. You know it's sure hard to follow the commandments that the Lord Jesus had given to you and I. It's hard to follow them if you try to do it fleshly, but if we follow him by the spirit of what is being revealed, what is being revealed to you and I, if we live by that you and I are going to make it. But if we try to live by this by flesh we're going to lose our soul. This is why Jesus tells you don't let no one deceive you.

The things that are needful out there in that world Jesus can give you. You don't have to do nothing, just serve the Lord Jesus Christ, live in his commandment the best you know how, and he's going to take you home. But what Satan brings before you and I all of that is going to come to an end. And when it comes to an end there is going to be a great suffering, and this is why Jesus is calling you, this is why Jesus gave you this privilege to be here tonight. Tonight pray to Jesus and he'll help you overcome Satan. As we stand we're going to give an invitation.

Sermons typically begin with the expression of gratitude for the opportunity to "gather together to blend our voices in song and prayer," to be in "fellowship with each other," and to "fulfill the work." A selected passage from the Bible is read, usually in both English and Mvskoke, and the sermon continues with an explication of the chosen text. Anecdotes and examples are used to support the texts. Often the "elderlies," respected ancestors, are pointed to as worthy examples of living out the faith. The underlying worldview expressed in sermons is highly dualistic. Dichotomies are presented—good and evil, heaven and hell, spirit and flesh, Jesus and Satan—and the virtues and dangers of each are expounded. The difficulties of everyday life are acknowledged. Members are encouraged to "carry on," to "do the best you can," to "resist temptation and the lusts of the flesh," and to "trust that God will take you to a better place [heaven] in the end." Members are encouraged to assist and support each other and to control themselves. In each sermon, at least implicitly but usually explicitly, listeners are reminded of the threat of hell and the promise of heaven. A fundamental goal of each sermon is to move the listener to introspection: "How do I measure up?"

Following the message, the speaker extends an "invitation," or in Mvskoke, *ohhoyketv* ("to call"), for anyone "who doesn't know Christ, and wants to rededicate[12] their lives, be baptized or become a church member" to come forward and make that desire public. In the center of the sanctuary is a bench that is normally oriented along an east-west line. This bench is called the *ohliketv merkv* ("mercy seat").[13] During the invitation, a deacon turns the mercy seat to orient it along a north-south line. A song is being sung during this time, and the congregation stands at the invitation.

Many times no one responds to the invitation, and the service goes on. If, however, a person "feels led" to respond to the invitation, that person comes and sits on the mercy seat. Should this occur, the minister approaches the individual at the seat and shakes his or her hand. The minister then returns to his place behind the pulpit, the congregation is seated, and the pastor comes forward to preside over this segment of the service.

The pastor approaches the seated person and asks for a "statement" regarding the purpose of his or her coming forward. Stated reasons are most often prayer requests or rededication. After the pastor has heard the statement, he announces it to the congregation. The deacon is then called on to ask the person questions of clarification or challenge. After the questions are suitably answered, the pastor calls on the congregation to "give witness to the rededication by raising your right hand." This is not viewed as a vote but rather as an acknowledgment of the person's statement and a witness to the stated intent. A deacon explained the process:

> Well, when they come back like that usually the minister of the church or the pastor will go to the one who is going to rededicate and ask them to state their reason for coming up and the one who's going to rededicate will present their case to the pastor, then the pastor usually repeats what the candidate says. He then says it's up to the church now to accept, or reject, or what. That's when the deacon stands up and is asked if he has any objections, or questions to ask. Usually we don't have any questions to ask. For anyone who wants to rededicate, they know their reasons for coming up for confessing their thoughts to the Lord. What they are in need of is a witness. So I make a motion that we are his witness. And I'll ask for a motion and a second. Usually the other deacon seconds. And that's all it is. That's the orderly procedures. Then the members raise their hand. It's like a vote, but they're witnessing to the one who's coming back to church. And when they come up, their asking for witnesses to rededicate their life. That's what we're there for, to witness somebody's rededication and to receive someone who's coming back. You're going to support them in their church work, that's why you raised your hand.

At this point the deacon leads a song, and all members rise. The pastor shakes the seated person's hand again, then steps aside. The ministers approach the mercy seat and shake the hand of the seated individual. The deacon then ushers all of the male members out of their pews, one row at a time, and up to shake the hand of the seated person. The men are followed by the women's leaders and lastly by the women members and guests. Many of the people have words of encouragement (e.g., "God bless you" or "I'll pray for you"), which they whisper to the person as they shake his or her hand. When all have shaken the seated person's hand, the person is escorted by the deacon to shake the hands of everyone unable to stand (those in wheelchairs or the elderly who have difficulty getting out of their seats). When all have been greeted, the person is restored to his or her place, the mercy seat is turned back, and the service continues, usually with an additional speaker presenting a message, followed by another invitation sequence as described above.

Following the last invitation, an additional song is sung and an offering is taken. A deacon turns the mercy seat, and a hand-woven offering basket is placed on the center of the bench. A song is sung, led by anyone. After everyone has been given the opportunity to approach the bench and leave an offering, the basket is taken up by a deacon and the offering is counted in the sacristy. The offering total is announced when the pastor solicits announcements. The Prayer Meeting collection ranges from $17 to $60, most often being around $25. This money is used to pay church grounds expenses such as electricity and propane.

When the offering song is over, the pastor stands at the pulpit to make announcements and to solicit announcements from others present. These announcements usually concern upcoming church meetings or events. Often visitors will stand and voice their gratitude for the opportunity to be present and the "wonderful message" and conclude with an open invitation for all those present to come to the next Fourth Sunday Meeting of the visitor's church.

One of the final announcements is an invitation for all those present to partake of refreshments following the dismissal.

With announcements completed, a final song, a prayer song for healing, is sung. The pastor appoints a leader, most often a women's leader, for this task. The pastor invites all those present to name those kin and friends who are sick and who should be prayed for. Then the final song is sung, ending with a prayer for the sick just mentioned.

After the song, a man (usually a visiting minister who presented a message) concludes the service with a blessing and dismissal. This is a prayer that he alone speaks. It is a prayer of thanks and a request for continued blessings. After this dismissal, all of the people shake hands with all of the others. Members will say to the visitors, "*Mvto, ralalvkvs!*" ("Thank you, come again!"). Informal chatting takes place, again usually divided along gender lines.

When the hosts and hostesses serving the refreshments are prepared, they announce to the deacon to gather the people in. The deacon says "*hompvks ci!*" ("Come and eat!"). The deacon also appoints a person, usually a visitor, to "bless the table." This visitor, who speaks a prayer and is the first to eat, usually sits at the head of the table.

All of the participants who stay for refreshments (most of those who were at the gathering and sometimes other family members who have been present but did not participate in the gathering) assemble at a camp house for a meal. Each of these camp houses has a long wooden table with benches on both sides. Men sit on one side and women on the other. Visitors are fed first, and male members sit with them as long as there are seats. The food is set out in bowls and plates, which are passed around for people to serve themselves. Typically served are red beans and rice, black-eyed peas, pumpkin, fried chicken, chicken and dumplings, boiled meat, *tosina*,[14] *vpvske nerkv*,[15] fry bread, *taklik kvmokse*,[16] *vpvtvkv*,[17] *catv hakv*,[18] *tvfvmpuce*,[19] *pvrkowvfken*,[20] raisin pie, fried pies, cakes, and always a jar of *sofke*.[21] Tea, coffee, and soft drinks are also served. Since there is no running water in most of the camp houses, a bucket of fresh water and a dipping ladle are always available.

The abundant food is prepared by women members. Swanton (1928a:312) observed at a gathering, "The women are charged with the duty of preparing the necessary food and drink for the assembly." The same holds true today. I once heard a young woman ask an elder why the men never helped with the food preparation. The elder woman responded, "We haven't heard about women's lib out here."

There is always plenty to eat, and the hosts constantly urge the guests to eat more. The mood around the table is festive and light. Many jokes are told and recent biographies detailed.

Discussion of Prayer Meetings

Prayer Meetings are social occasions at which members are brought face to face, providing opportunities for impression management, or face work. Events are managed according to culturally defined situational proprieties, and individuals maintain or enhance their faces and effect the desired social outcomes. Members of the churches interact with each other weekly during these occasions, exposing their social faces to the local community. Appeal to face at such occasions is one of the instruments of social maintenance in the Seminole community.

Prayer Meetings begin with the informal greetings of members and visitors: handshakes and pleasantries. Even these quotidian actions are avenues of face work. Goffman (1967:41) notes the function of such routine greetings at social occasions: "Greetings provide a way of showing that a relationship is still what it was at the termination of the previous co-participation, and, typically, that this relationship involves sufficient suppression of hostility for the participants temporarily to drop their guards and talk." Since some of the participants (visitors from other congregations) may not have seen each other for weeks or months, greetings establish a basis for picking up mutual interaction where it was last left off. Host church leaders are expected to greet each person in attendance and shake his or her hand. Many nonleaders and visitors will also greet participants as they arrive or will make the rounds and greet each of those who arrived previously. Some people, however, greet only those around them. Considering that participants are expected to greet each other, people could strategically manipulate this expectation by withholding the greeting. I never witnessed this, however.

What can be manipulated is one's conversation partner. The informal conversation in Prayer Meetings and at other social occasions is a locus of face work. Participants consciously and unconsciously appeal to face-guiding conduct in regard to talk. Goffman (1967:36) notes:

> Once engaged in conversation, he must demand only the amount of attention that is an appropriate expression of his relative social worth. Undue lulls come to be potential signs of having nothing in common, or of being insufficiently self-possessed to create something to say, and hence must be avoided. Similarly, interruptions and inattentiveness may convey disrespect and must be avoided unless the implied disrespect is an accepted part of the relationship. A surface agreement must be maintained by means of discretion and white lies, also that the assumption of mutual approval will not be discredited.

Although participants in conversations risk their face, the risk is relatively low. There is little to be gained within these small enclaves, and most people simply seek to get through the occasion without disrupting relationships. Certainly there is a strategic consideration in the selection of which person or enclave one chooses to (or not to) converse with. Specific examples will be discussed in chapter 7.

Ringing the bell announces the formal beginning of Prayer Meetings. As the bell chimes, a prayer song is begun. Singing songs and speaking prayers is considered by participants to be one of the principal reasons for gathering. Singing and praying form a portion of the *vtotkv* ("work") that must be "fulfilled" during a gathering. The ostensible purpose for gathering is to "fulfill the work," that is, to perform the segments of the worship service, particularly the invitation to "get saved." Fulfilling the work is viewed as pleasing to God. When people lead a song or a prayer, or lead some other aspect of the gathering, they are *vtotkv esfaceces* ("fulfilling the work"). Thus during a service, most men are eager to lead songs and prayers, since that is one of the "works" of such gatherings.

Eagerness to lead songs and prayers is considered an admirable trait. Leading songs and prayers is, therefore, one way a person can enhance face during a gathering. Often several people will attempt to lead a song simultaneously. When this happens, the less aggressive one will quit singing and will follow the remaining leader. There is a built-in mechanism to prevent overzealous participants from leading all of the songs. Since people speak of being "led by the Spirit" to lead a song and a prayer, an overly anxious leader faces being criticized for not following the urging of the Spirit and for simply "wanting to hear his own voice and not the Spirit's."

There is also a threat attached to the notion of work. During one message, a visiting minister told how he had failed to keep his wartime promise to remain faithful to God. After arriving stateside, he "followed the ways of the world and stopped coming to church." Soon after, two of his brothers, a sister, and his mother died in one year's time. He blamed this on the fact that he had not kept his promise to become a worker for the Lord; it is taught that dire consequences follow from slacking one's duties. Several preachers have been heard to say, "Sometimes God moves that way to wake you up." Whether through promise or threat, the divine imperative to "fulfill the work" obligates members into face-to-face interaction.[22] Once members are engaged with other members, the mechanism of face ensures the integration and maintenance of the social unit.

The sermon sequence usually begins with an expression of appreciation for the opportunity to gather. Although the community requires participation, people are directed to view it as a privilege. Visitors to the gathering are acknowledged. The visitor's face and the face of his or her congregation are thereby publicly enhanced. The sermon and the invitation sequence may be characterized as the focus of this gathering—both for the participants and for our understanding of the gathering. For participants, the hope of "saving a soul" is the prime motivation for the occasion itself. Supplication for a soul's salvation is the theme of every prayer, and preachers use sermons to cajole, threaten, and bribe listeners to "get saved." In these aspects one can see most clearly the social function of the occasions, namely, local social unit or congregational integration and maintenance.

The decision to accept the invitation is intensely personal, and individuals have varying motivations to "go forward." Certainly the emotions are genuine, actual tears are shed, and remorse is felt. Yet to be understood, these decisions must be analyzed within the larger social context. At the invitation, individual participants come forward to initiate, acknowledge, or maintain their place within the congregation. The invitation must be viewed from the level of the individual as well as from the level of the larger community: individual motivations are explained by enhancement of face, whereas the larger community is motivated by social function. Social occasions function as defining institutions for the community, and a person's social identity is intrinsically associated with participation in such social occasions.

A participant in the Seminole Baptist church system must make a public declaration of the desire to fully integrate into the church community. This act is spoken of in various terms: "coming to Christ," "being born again," "getting saved," "accepting Christ," and so on. The person, on making this declaration, is expected to participate fully in the church community: regularly attend the gatherings, behave in an acceptable manner, and support the efforts of the church community. The outward sign of this commitment to the church community is baptism. Baptism might also be characterized as a ritual of initiation into the community.[23] Immediately after the baptism, the convert is coached on proper behavior, is assigned a specific seat in the sanctuary, and pledges to behave in a manner consistent with the church community's expectations.[24] Only twice during my field experience did a participant come forward to "make a decision." One was a child, the niece of a member; the other was the adopted daughter of a women's leader. Both these decisions occurred at Prayer Meetings and were accompanied by requests for baptism, performed the following morning.

More often, however, people "fall away" from their promised behavior and must "rededicate themselves to the Lord." Rededication provides the opportunity to "cleanse the heart before witnesses during a church service." A pastor explained the role of rededication: "When you rededicate, then you're in good standing. You can rededicate as often as you want to. Some guys rededicate every week. You can't overdo it. You could sit on that bench every day. That's admitting your faults to the Lord, you know. We need to know that they're serving the Lord and they can go up when they need to. It's up to them. And I know when I need to rededicate. . . . We don't put on a shirt and wear it forever. We take a bath. We need to put on clean clothes. It's the same way with faith. Faith gets old." In Goffman's terminology, rededication is a means of corrective face work. Rededication is a means of publicly confessing faults that have led to interpersonal conflict; it is a public statement of a promise to change behavior. The rededication process is highly ritualized (conventionalized). In my field experience I never witnessed the process as a direct response to specific offenses. Rather, the confession or statement was usually very general: "worldly behavior,"[25] "living in the world," "anger," "failed my Lord." As the above statement of the pastor explains, a person is directed to examine his or her heart at every gathering and to determine if there is some sin, some offense, that needs to be confessed and repented of. A properly socialized person is sensitive to his or her failure to live up to the expectations of the community. Participants at church gatherings are interminably urged to ask themselves: "How am I doing?" "Is my commitment genuine?" "Is my faith as strong as it should be?" "Am I fulfilling the expectations of my community?" Sermons are filled with directives to examine oneself, and participants are agitated into doubt about the sincerity of their commitment to the Lord.

When a person is so moved to publicly admit improprieties, the local community listens to the statement and witnesses his or her intent; then, one by one, each participant shakes the person's hand and offers encouragement. In this way the penitent is assured by his or her social group that the relationship with them has not experienced irreparable damage and that the person's face is still worthy of being supported by the community.

Those people who remain steadfast, who are not easily turned, are considered *hunnemahetv* ("to be heavy"). A pastor described how some converts are given to steadfastness while others easily drift: "When you baptize a person, some of them just walk real light. Can't hardly tell they're walking. Thems the kind I've noticed in my time that they ain't going to stay with it. Those that walk heavy, I mean they're just heavy, them the kind that gonna stick with it. They might fall out for two-three days or a week, but they'll be right back." To remain "heavy" is a difficult task. To assist the converts, many members obtain specially prepared pebbles from a *heles hayv* ("medicine maker"). These tiny stones are carried in a wallet or purse or are worn in a small pouch tied around the neck, providing supernatural assistance to remain faithful and steadfast.[26]

The effect (social function) of "getting saved" is initiation and integration into the Seminole Baptist community. A person makes "a decision" to "come to Christ." With that decision comes certain expectations in behavior, most notably regular participation in church gatherings. It is within these gatherings, or social occasions, that a person is socialized into the Seminole Baptist community. The effect of rededication is reintegration into that community or, at least, a reassurance of one's place within the community. If a member fails to fulfill the behavior expectations of the congregation or church community, rededication is the vehicle for reintegration. Of course, participants would express this differently, yet they would recognize the fact that church membership obligates participation in the church community (the "work" must be fulfilled). Community is maintained only by the face-to-face interaction of its members. The obligatory nature of social occasions ensures that the interaction occurs regularly.

All participants in a social occasion risk face and have an opportunity to enhance face. Preachers, whether pastors or ministers, particularly expose and risk face every time they deliver a message. This is an intrinsic aspect of the preacher's role, and it may be what attracts some men to aspire to the position. One of the responsibilities of the preacher is to point out (often explicitly) behaviors that need to be changed. A pastor explained: "To the one that is not consecrated, he's got to preach on consecration. And maybe he's got one in there that is, ahhh, a gossip, he's got to preach on obedience, not to gossip. He does that when no visitors just his members there, you know. He's supposed to do that. That's the right procedure for a pastor." Occasionally the preacher will name an individual and their sin as an example to the rest of the congregation. In one message the pastor said: "Look at Roy's backsliding as an illustration. Roy came forward and promised to follow Jesus, but he lied about his promise." This does not seem too strong of a reproach until one considers that Roy was present during this message. Speakers often ask, "Is there something in your life that needs straightening out?" Challenges such as these are quite risky, yet preachers are expected to take such social risks for the integrity of their congregations. A preacher must be a sensitive diagnostician to discern whom and when to challenge. When listeners "come under his preaching," that is, when they come forward at the invitation, the preacher's face is greatly enhanced. Conversely, a preacher may also be subject to reproach if no one responds to his invitation. Members will criticize speakers whose messages fail to meet expectations: "He said the word of God is quick and active, but it sure took *him* a long time to say it"; "I couldn't keep awake and I fell asleep"; "I was afraid I'd fall out of my seat"; "He killed our spirit." One man noted, "He sure quoted a lot of scriptures." Another replied "Yes, but he was showing off his knowledge, not the Spirit."

In all of the Seminole Baptist churches, even those that do not host special services for the armed forces, veterans or people serving in the military are highly esteemed. Often visitors will choose to attend a Prayer Meeting because it includes the service for the armed forces. Churches that host these services are commended by members of other churches. Additionally, various churches host special Veteran's Day services in which people with military experience are honored. During the special services for the military, the pastor urges the congregation to "remember that those in the service are there to protect us. They are defending freedom, our freedom to worship as we see fit." Such service is recognized as valuable, if not imperative, for the Seminole community as well as for the whole nation. This motivation may be enough to justify the continued recognition of those who are serving or have served in the armed forces; however, there may be an additional reason. The armed forces are one of the few vehicles that Seminole young people have for economic advancement. Thirty-five percent of Seminole men are veterans.[27] Such employment, of course, takes the members out of the community. The services for the armed forces are a way of keeping these members "in mind" during their absence and therefore, in a symbolic sense, still within the community. Veterans are also honored during Seminole Stomp grounds activities. Considering the number of veterans, and the historical warrior tradition and ideology, it is not surprising that veterans are thus honored.

Fourth Sunday Meetings

The next level of social occasions in Seminole Baptist churches is Fourth Sunday Meetings. Whereas Prayer Meetings are the primary social occasion of the local community (individual congregations), Fourth Sunday Meetings form the basis of a cooperative system involving all of the Seminole Baptist churches. Unlike Anglo Baptist churches, which hold services weekly at their facilities, Seminole Baptist churches hold Sunday services at their church grounds once every four Sundays. On the three intervening Sundays, members visit other churches in the rotation. Thus, the majority of people in attendance at any Fourth Sunday Meeting are members of other congregations and are not members of the host congregation. The format of these gatherings is very similar to the Prayer Meeting format previously described, yet the social function of the Fourth Sunday Meeting is much different.

These gatherings are called *Totvlketuce* ("little gatherings"), or in English, "Fourth Sunday Meetings." The meeting weekend is a series of gatherings that begin the Wednesday or Thursday before the actual fourth Sunday and conclude the evening of the fourth Sunday. In the days before modern transportation, members and visitors would travel by horse or wagon to the church grounds and would camp there for the entire weekend. Today people come and go throughout the weekend, and only rarely does someone camp overnight, let alone for the whole weekend.

The focus of the weekend is the gatherings on Sunday. (The other gatherings that make up the weekend will be described below, in the discussion of Big Meetings.) As noted, the Sunday gatherings generally follow the model of Prayer Meetings. Participants arrive and greet each other, the bell rings on two occasions, and the formal gathering commences: a number of prayer songs, prayers, a devotional reading, songs for the minister, one or more messages, invitations, and prayer songs.

The offering procedure is the first notable difference. During the offering, the mercy seat is turned and three offering baskets are placed, in a row, on top. The three baskets collect offerings for different purposes. The north basket is for the "work of the sisters"; the center is for the "church"; and the one on the south is for the "brothers." The money collected in the sisters' basket is distributed by a women's leader to the women who have opened up camp for the meeting. This is used to help defray the costs of providing the food for all of the people gathered. The central basket, for the church, is used to pay for church expenses such as electric bills and propane. The brothers' work is to assist any member who has fallen on hard times. When the need becomes known to the congregation, it is discussed at the monthly business meeting, the decision to help or not to help is made, and if necessary, the amount of the help is determined. If the congregation decides to help, the money is disbursed by the head deacon.

After an additional song and prayer, announcements are given. One of the final announcements is an invitation for all those present to partake of refreshments during the upcoming break. It is stated which camps will be opened, and their locations are announced. Unlike at Prayer Meetings, at Fourth Sunday Meetings multiple camp houses are opened to accommodate the large number of visitors. At this time the deacon passes out slips of paper on which the name of a camp house owner is written; these are given to various visitors, who are thus appointed as "head men." Their duty is to "bless the table," to be the first in line for the food, and to sit at the table head. With announcements completed, an additional song is song. Then one of the ministers who spoke during this portion of the service gives the blessing and dismisses the service for refreshments.

Members and visitors mingle and visit after shaking hands with all those near. After a few moments, the deacon makes his rounds to all of the camp houses that are opened, to see if they are ready to serve. When it has been determined that all is prepared, the deacon rings the church bell, announcing that refreshments are about to be served. Head men go to their appointed houses, and other members and visitors disperse to the various camp houses.

At Prayer Meetings, refreshments end the gathering. During Fourth Sunday Meetings, refreshments provide a break in the formal gatherings. After the meal, while the women are occupied with domestic chores, the men leave the table and gather on the porch area, under the arbor, or at some other comfortable space. Here the visiting continues—relationships are established or maintained. This break lasts about two hours. A first bell signals that services are about to begin again, and a second bell starts the afternoon services.

The format of the afternoon services is identical to that of the morning services: a number of prayer songs followed by prayers, a devotional reading, songs for the minister, one or more messages followed by invitations, and prayer songs. If there is an offering taken, it is a "love offering" for the local pastor. Before the offering, a visitor (having been appointed by the deacons prior to the service) reminds those present of the importance of the pastor's work and appeals to the participants to give generously to support the pastor's work.[28] After additional songs, the pastor announces a break. One of the ministers who spoke during this portion of the service gives the blessing and dismisses the service for "coffee, *sofke*, and sweets."

The camp houses that were opened for lunch refreshments are opened again to serve light refreshments during this break. People generally visit a different camp house from the one at which they ate lunch. Pies and cakes left over from lunch are set on the table, and guests help themselves. Typically a bowl of *sofke* is also eaten. After about thirty minutes, people begin to gather around the arbor, and services are called to begin, with the deacon inviting folks to come in. The bell is rung, and services resume.

The late-afternoon services tend to be the shortest. Three or more prayer songs are sung, the pastor gives a short devotion, and usually not more than one speaker preaches. After the invitation there is another song and the dismissal. Head men are chosen to bless the tables for the evening meal (each camp house has a different head man from the one who fulfilled the work at noon). Guests usually do not attend the same camp house that they did at lunch and during the afternoon break. Visitors, therefore, visit three different camp houses during the day, interacting with a relatively large number of different people.

Many people do not attend all of the services in a given day. People arrive and leave throughout the day. The largest attendance is during the morning service; each of the latter services has progressively fewer participants. Members of the host congregation are expected to attend all of the services, however.

Discussion of Fourth Sunday Meetings

There are more than sixty Seminole/Creek churches in eastern Oklahoma. The fourteen churches identified as Seminole[29] all display a marked similarity in configuration and arrangement. This homogeneity is due, in large part, to the organizational structure of Fourth Sunday Meetings, which obligate members of the larger community to interact regularly with each other. Attendance at any given Fourth Sunday Meeting consists of a majority of visitors. Thus the Fourth Sunday Meeting structure ensures regular and wide interaction among church members in the Seminole community. Face management in church gatherings exposes individuals and congregations (functioning as a constituent social unit) to the regulation of the larger unit of the whole Seminole Baptist community. Participants' level of interaction ensures a high degree of cultural integrity and shared social standards across the larger community. Hence, the larger Seminole Baptist community may be maintained without the whole community gathering periodically to reinforce shared cultural and social standards.

When one participates in the services of another congregation, the person is said to be "helping out"[30] that congregation. During announcements at one Fourth Sunday Meeting, a member of the host congregation, Cedar Creek Church, stood and addressed the seven visitors from Sand Creek Church: "People from Cedar Creek have been helping out Sand Creek, and people from Sand Creek are now helping us out. This is a good thing." This statement was met with a chorus of *"Eman"* ("Amen") from members of both churches. "Helping out" is an obligation of participants in the Fourth Sunday Meeting rotation. Below is a list of the twenty-eight churches that I witnessed interacting with Eufaula in Fourth Sunday Meeting rotation during my field experience.[31]

Seminole	High Spring*	Spring	Sand Creek
Arbeka*	Seminole	Many	Eufaula*
Cedar Creek*	Baptist*	Springs*	Bird Creek*
Wewoka*	Salt Creek*	Cold Springs*	Middle Creek #2*
Nuyaka	Hill Top	Alabama	Rock Springs*
Thewahle	Snake Creek	Koasati	Wetumka
Greenleaf	Trenton	Hutchachuppa	Mekusukey*
	Middle	Okmulgee	
	Creek #1	Little	
	Cedar River	Quarsarty	
	Arbeka		

This list includes all of the churches that members of Eufaula have identified as Seminole (those marked with an asterisk), as well as many Creek churches. Each column represents churches that hold their Fourth Sunday Meetings on the same week. The spellings of these names are taken from a document that participants distribute among themselves.

The Fourth Sunday Meeting rotation schedule necessitates choice, since on a given week there are at least six churches offering a Fourth Sunday Meeting. Participants choose to attend one of those churches. Participants speak of being "led by the

Spirit" when making the decision to attend services. Often several members of the same home congregation will travel together to visit a particular church. Part of the conversation during the Prayer Meeting refreshments is often a discussion of where individuals are planning to attend Sunday services. One deacon voiced the stated ideal: "You need to attend different churches, and not just those where your friends go. We're not supposed to show favoritism." This ideal urges wide interaction between churches. In actual practice, however, members tend to participate in a select group of churches. The interesting question concerns which churches are attended and why.

Geographic proximity may account for some of the choices: churches farthest from one's home congregation are attended less frequently, if at all. The converse, however, does not apply: churches closest to one's home congregation are not necessarily the ones most frequently attended. I will use Eufaula as an example. Members of Eufaula attend services at their own church whenever services are conducted. This means that the other churches offering services on the same Fourth Sunday as Eufaula (those in the first column in the list above) will not be attended by Eufaula members. On the other three Sundays of the rotation, members are free to attend any of those offering services (any of those congregations listed in the other three columns, as well as some thirty other Creek Baptist churches). Ideally, members would alternate their participation equally to include all of those churches in the rotation, but this has not been the case. For example, in the second week of the rotation (represented by the second column), members of Eufaula have attended High Spring, Seminole Baptist, Salt Creek, Hill Top, Snake Creek, Trenton, Middle Creek #1, Cedar River, and Arbeka. The church most frequently attended was High Spring, which is, incidentally, the church geographically closest to Eufaula. The third week of the rotation presents a different picture. The closest church on that week is Cold Springs. This church, however, was only infrequently attended during the study period. The one most frequently attended was Many

Springs, almost four times the distance of Cold Springs. During the fourth week of the rotation, Eufaula members attended, almost exclusively, Sand Creek Eufaula, although two other churches were geographically closer. Geographic proximity may be a factor in the selection process, but it is not the only factor.

Other factors considered in the selection of which of the available churches to attend include the following: where one's kin attend; where those with whom one has enduring social relationships attend; the current status of a congregation's face; and the previously stated ideal of wide participation. As for kin, members do frequent those churches attended by primary family members (siblings and children). Of course this refers to family members who are not members of one's home congregation. In some cases the church attended by primary kin is also where the visitor previously held membership. Many times a marriage will take a person out of one's home congregation and place him or her in the church of the spouse. This is spoken of as "marrying into a church." Yet although kinship is one factor, the churches most frequently attended by Eufaula members (High Spring and Sand Creek Eufaula) are not those with the most primary kin (Bird Creek and Spring).

Another important factor in determining which church of the rotation will be attended is the visitor's enduring social relationships. People visit the churches of friends, those with whom they have enduring social relationships, more often than other churches. This should not be too surprising. Church gatherings provide one of the few regular opportunities for Seminoles to interact socially. Each Fourth Sunday Meeting includes several opportunities for interpersonal interaction and conversation (before and after services, as well as extended time during and after refreshments). Many members choose to attend those churches that provide the opportunity to renew or maintain enduring social relationships.

Another factor that may determine which of the churches will be attended is the social standing of the congregation, or the congregational face. Congregational face is the obligation of individuals toward their immediate social unit (congregation). People manage impressions of self and also impressions reflecting the social worth and intention of their congregation to the larger community. Members represent their congregations, and as a result congregations develop images, or faces, defined in terms of approved social qualities. Some congregations have a very positive social value resulting from successful face enhancement.

A congregation may enhance its face in several ways. The most common way is to schedule special services, most often to hold a revival. Revivals, held annually or semiannually, are a series of meetings, usually a week of evening meetings, led by a visiting, charismatic preacher. Revivals build in a certain amount of success by scheduling different churches to provide devotions for each of the nights of the revival. A congregation may also enhance its face by sponsoring a Gospel Sing. This is a special gathering dedicated to music. A group of members of a visiting congregation come prepared to sing two or three hymns (either in Mvskoke or in English). Often a professional musician or group is brought in to perform. Gospel Sings go late into the night, and the "better ones" will go all night long. Some churches are noted for their consistently successful Gospel Sings. One congregation, Cold Springs, has an annual Gospel Sing that attracts more than two hundred spectators (including some Florida Seminoles and Miccosukees who come up each year for the occasion). Other churches seek to enhance their face by hosting holiday services: the traditionally sacred holidays of Christmas, Second Christmas,[32] and Easter,[33] as well as the secular holidays of Thanksgiving,[34] Halloween,[35] and Veteran's Day.[36] Holiday services generally follow the format of regular meetings, as described below, with the addition of some recognition of the holiday being observed. The larger the attendance during special services, the more the congregation's face is enhanced. Conversely, poor attendance results in diminished face. A congregation must be reasonably assured of success to risk its face. Thus special services, and revivals especially, are spaced carefully (dates are calculated after polling other congregations and their intentions of holding special services).

Large attendance at any service enhances the face of the host congregation. Large attendances are expected during revivals, holiday services, and Big Meetings (described below). During other times, large attendances are the result of fortuity (many visitors happen to select the same church to attend) or of the charisma of the pastor or ministers. The reputations of the pastor and ministers often attract or repel visitors.

The preacher, particularly if he is a pastor, is the public representative of a congregation. He, more than any other member, might be considered the prime carrier of the congregation's face. The behaviors and reputations of the leaders, therefore, are carefully monitored by the members of a congregation. Pastors and ministers are chosen carefully. Congregations prize charismatic preachers—ones who "preach hard words," that is, who chastise listeners and urge repentance and "right living." Particularly dynamic preachers are invited by other congregations to lead revivals. Such an invitation enhances the preacher's, as well as the congregation's, face.

Conversely, some congregations are marginalized by other congregations of the rotation. The reasons are varied, but usually this is the result of some social impropriety of the congregational leaders (accusations of adultery or drunkenness are the most common) or of the fact that the congregation "came up on its own" and therefore is not reckoned as a valid option in the rotation. A congregation's reputation, from the perspective of the whole Seminole Baptist community or that of only a faction of it, thus encourages or discourages attendance, making congregational face an important factor in determining which church of the rotation will be attended on a given Sunday.

Finally, in explaining how churches in the rotation are selected for attendance, one should not discount the influence of the ideal previously stated: that members should "attend different churches." In the discussions concerning which church will be attended, it is not uncommon to hear such statements as "We haven't been to Bird Creek for a while" or "I've been thinking we need to visit Snake Creek." People most often frequent the churches of their kin and friends; however, the directive to "visit around" motivates members in varying degrees to attend congregations not normally visited. Although other factors are perhaps more important, this ideal nevertheless encourages wide interaction among the community members.

I have introduced the concept of congregational face to describe a primary level of orientation situated between individual self-interest or individual face and membership in the larger community. Members of the same congregation interact weekly at Prayer Meetings and through those occasions develop social relationships in which they are dependent on each other to support each other's face. At social gatherings and occasions, individuals manage impressions of themselves and, as members of an immediate social unit, or congregation, must also consider impressions fostered toward that social unit. Impressions are managed at both levels, individual and congregational, to effect desired social outcomes.

The term "congregational face" identifies a concept that is extendable to include other social institutions; congregations are certainly not the only social unit with a level of orientation between individual self-interest on the one hand and the larger community on the other. A similar level of orientation can likely be found in other social settings, among many other gatherings of people. Congregational face might better be understood as "corporate face." This level of face occurs in any social setting, sacred or secular, in which people rely on their immediate social group for endorsement, support, and valuation and therefore manage others' perceptions or impressions of that social unit to enhance that social unit's corporate face vis-à-vis the larger community, thereby enhancing the face of the individual members. Locations of corporate face might include charity groups, clubs, businesses, or sports teams, for example. Corporate face may be found anywhere that an immediate and enduring social group mediates individual behavior for the larger community. In such an application of face, people manage the impressions that others have of them as individuals as well as the impressions that others may have regarding the immediate social group (e.g., the charity group or the club). Congregational face is, then, a type of corporate face.

The Fourth Sunday Meeting rotation broadens the scope of interaction among Seminole Baptists. Whereas Prayer Meetings serve parochial needs (individual and local group interactions), Fourth Sunday Meetings serve the larger community, ensuring shared standards of behavior and expectations as individual and congregational faces are exposed to the larger community. Fourth Sunday Meetings, therefore, situate individuals within the context of the larger community.

Big Meetings

The third primary social occasion is the Big Meeting. These gatherings are referred to by various names: *Tokvlketv rakkat* ("big gathering"); *Uehomecate esketv* ("to drink red whiskey or wine");[37] *Ohhoyvnkv ohhompetv* ("passover table").[38] The English gloss is usually "Big Meeting," although the gathering is also referred to as Communion Meeting or Wine Meeting. Like the Fourth Sunday Meeting weekends, these meeting weekends comprise a series of formalized gatherings or services. The distinctive element of the Big Meeting is the ritual blessing and consumption of bread and wine: the Communion service. The format of the Big Meeting weekend is outlined in appendix B.

The Big Meeting weekend begins on the Thursday evening before the Sunday when the bread and wine is consumed. Thursday's service resembles a regular Prayer Meeting. There are, however, usually a few more visitors in attendance. After refreshments on Thursday night, fasting begins for members of the host congregation. The fast continues until after the *Elvweckv Nettv* ("Fasting day"), or Fasting service, the following morning.

The first bell for the Fasting service is rung at 8:30 A.M. Members begin arriving at about that same time. The male members gather in a camp house, and the female members gather in the sanctuary. As the members gather, they join in informal social and interpersonal conversation. After the second bell (rung at about 9:00 A.M. by a women's leader), the women, who are in the church building, begin a service consisting of songs and prayers and "words of encouragement."[39] The men, seated in the main room of the camp house, gather for songs, words of encouragement, and exhortation.[40] During this very informal gathering, the men are often involved in personal grooming (e.g., paring their fingernails, pulling out their facial hairs with a small broad spring, and combing their hair).

After about an hour and a half, a women's leader rings the bell for a third time and thus signals the men to join the women in the sanctuary. The men enter as the women are singing a song. A prayer, led by the women's leader, follows the song. When the prayer is concluded, the women's leader formally hands over leadership of the service to the pastor. He continues by leading a song and a prayer, followed by a short devotional reading.

The format of this service is distinctive in that the pastor gives short devotional readings after each song and prayer. During this gathering, each male member is expected to lead a song and a prayer. The service is considered incomplete, or unfulfilled, if every male member present does not *vtotkv esfaceces*, or lead a song and a prayer.[41] The service is fulfilled after this is accomplished. Occasionally a male member will have to leave the service before it is concluded, but he will leave only after he has first led a song and a prayer. Having thus fulfilled his work, he is free to go. In this way, local congregational unity is affirmed before the upcoming, public Big Meeting.

At the conclusion of this service, all those present retire to a camp house for informal conversation and breakfast. The service usually concludes around noon, with the visiting around the breakfast table continuing until midafternoon. Most members are not in a hurry to leave and will tarry an hour or two after the meal is finished even though they must return for another service later that evening.

Considering the importance of fasting in pre-Christian Mvskoke life,[42] it is not surprising to find that fasting is an important aspect of Seminole Christianity. Swanton records that a strict fast was held by warriors planning expeditions (1928a:408, 410), by stickball players preparing for games (1928a:457), by all in times of "national distress" (1928b:535), and by those wanting to "avert grievous calamity of sickness" (1928b:535, quoting Bartram). A wilderness fast was also "undergone by those desiring to become doctors or learned men" (Swanton 1928b:546). For contemporary Seminole Baptists, Fasting services are held on the Saturday morning of a Fourth Sunday Meeting weekend and on the Friday morning of a Big Meeting weekend. *Elvwecet* ("fasting") was defined by one pastor as follows: "The word for fasting is *elvwecet*. That means 'make yourself hungry.' That means take everything away from your physical body that would give you comfort. In other words, you kind of punish your body, or something to that effect. You can't drink water, you can't smoke, you can't eat a bite of anything, or chew gum—nothing can touch your mouth, in other words." Fasting is to be done in secret.[43] The purpose of fasting varies, but it involves the desire to either fulfill a work or get supernatural favor. When a person fasts for a Fasting service, the reason is the former. It is often repeated that the elders would fast and pray and receive miraculous assistance: "The older ones that came before us, they used to fast two, three days at a time. It wasn't no problem for them to fast all day. Some of the old-timers would go out in the woods and fast and pray. Sometimes they would see Jesus and speak to him, and God would reveal a lot of things to them. He would reveal a lot of things." The "things" that "God would reveal" included where to find lost items, the ability to read either English or Mvskoke or to speak English, and new songs. Pastors and ministers are to fast for the ability to more effectively communicate their messages. The spiritual benefits of fasting are lauded: "Your songs comes out hot when you're fasting. Your preaching comes out hot. And oh, you got the power behind you when you're fasting. It has happened—it does happen. That fasting is something that a lot of people don't believe in. But most of your Indians really believe in it. And it does happen. I know it does."

While fasting and praying in the woods, a person is likely to have supernatural encounters. One pastor related how when he was in the woods, fasting and praying, he kneeled and noticed that all the sounds of wind and birds stopped. He felt a "presence," which he identified as Jesus. He said that he "felt Christ's breath on the back of his neck." He continued to pray, not turning to look for fear that he would, indeed, see Christ behind him. The pastor said that many times people out fasting and praying will see Jesus and communicate directly with him.

Several members noted that when one is out fasting and praying, snakes will often come. Swanton (1928b:490–95) records several types of supernatural snakes that figure in Creek and Seminole folklore: huge "tie-snakes," which can carry off full-grown horses; "sharp-breasted snakes," which are a foot and a half in diameter and leave a furrow in the ground to record their passing; and massive water-dwelling "horned snakes," which boast deerlike antlers. Once after a service, I heard a young member report to his elders his experience while fasting and praying alone in the woods, as he had been directed. He described how his prayers were continually being interrupted by a "stirring in the grass." He said that the stirring kept coming closer. Finally, the stirring became so disconcerting that he gave up his prayers and began walking back home. He had no sooner begun his walk than he saw the source of the stirring: there on his path was a huge, black snake. Soon the snake slid off the path and was lost in the grass, and the young man hurried home. After his narration, the young man asked the elders what this event meant. One of the elders responded: "Let me ask you a question. Who was it that deceived Eve? What form was he in?" The young man said, "The devil." The elder replied: "That's right, it was the old devil tempting you, and he won. He kept you from praying. Next time you need to stand firm and continue to pray and not be tempted." Another person present related the biblical account of Jesus' wilderness experience (Matthew 4:1–11). Later, a *heles hayv* told me: "If a snake crosses your path, you know it has been sent by an enemy. Before going on, you need to spit[44] on the path that the snake took and turn your hat backwards. The bad medicine is then killed."

I recall the profound effect this interaction had on me as I listened to this account. I began to understand that these Seminole Baptists have not simply taken foreign biblical accounts into their beliefs; rather, the faith that they profess and live by is one that is incorporated into their lifeway through their own culture history. I was struck by how very Seminole this biblical account sounds: Jesus, fasting and praying in the wilderness, is approached by a supernatural serpent and is tempted. The individuals are not simply Baptists who happen to be Seminole; they are Seminoles who have incorporated a version of Christianity into their culture. In that context, the account took on a very Seminole feel: a lone man enters the wilderness, seeking divine guidance; he fasts and prays, then is approached by a supernatural serpent.

While fasting and praying in the woods, people also often hear the voices of the *vculvkvlke* ("elders," "old people," glossed in English as the "elderlies" meaning "deceased ancestors") joined in songs and prayers. These voices provide great encouragement and comfort to those who are fortunate enough to hear them.

Fasting, although done in private, should be considered a corporate endeavor. The sacrifice is made for the sake of the community. All of the members must be in unity in their fasting. It is said among the Seminoles: "One person can hold the church back. One person can keep the church from moving on." This sentiment is especially evident during Big Meeting weekends, when the fasting must be done by all members. Various jokes are heard during Big Meeting weekends about one member tempting another to break the fast by making coffee or bacon or by offering chewing gum. One member joked during the breakfast following the Fasting service, "This breakfast was better than the first one I had this morning." The response of the other members was a playful derision: "No wonder we couldn't get off the ground this morning, you held us back." The membership needs to be "of one accord."

The evening service is a Prayer Meeting with the addition of "testimonies." After giving the devotional reading, the pastor invites members to "give testimony" to their faith. Each person present, beginning with the ministers and deacons, is given the opportunity to stand and give testimony. The following testimony is an example: "*Ohliktv*, my brothers and sisters in Christ: It has been thirty days since I last stood before you to confess my faith. I want you to know that my faith is still the same. If I have offended any of you, I apologize and ask you to forgive me. I covet your prayers. I ask you to pray for me, and I'll pray for you." Each testimony is followed by a round of "*Eman*" from the others present. Testimonies allow individuals to affirm publicly their membership within the community. With the exception of these testimonies, the service format is identical to the Prayer Meeting format previously described.

The Saturday of a Big Meeting weekend continues with a day of services. The first is a Sunrise service, beginning at about 7:00 A.M. There are usually fewer than ten people present at the Sunrise service, a brief service composed of songs and prayers and a brief devotional reading by the pastor. This is followed by a midmorning service beginning at about 9:00 A.M. and an evening service beginning at 7:30 P.M. These two services follow the usual format of songs and prayers, devotional readings, songs and prayers, one or more messages followed by an invitation, additional songs and prayers, and dismissal.

Sunday mornings of Big Meeting weekends begin with a Sunrise service, followed by the usual schedule of a Fourth Sunday Meeting. The highlight of the Big Meeting is the Communion service, which replaces the late-afternoon service of a Fourth Sunday Meeting. The ringing of the bell calls members to the Communion service following the afternoon break. Members are seated together in the front two pews.[45] The ambiance of this service is markedly different from that of the previous services of the day. Participants enter in silence and anticipation. A pastor explained the sacred quality of the Communion service:

> Because God blesses it, it is very, very *acake* ("sacred"). It's more than a symbol, it's more sacred than *heleswv* ("medicine").[46] It went through a lot of prayers. A lot of prayers go into it. It is very, very sacred. I get nervous when I lead a Communion service. Even though I've done this hundreds of times before I still get nervous. Before we serve the bread and wine the ministers and deacons pray over it, "Bless it as your body, bless it as your blood; bless it and make it sacred. Make me worthy to eat your body and drink your blood. Jesus come this sacred moment, bless this bread and bless this wine and make it holy." We're all supposed to pray that way and be of one accord. Jesus wants us to be of one prayer. The old people used to meet throughout the night after a Communion service, just like we have a wake for the dead, they'd stay with the body and blood of Jesus.

While the congregation watches in silence, the deacons prepare the Communion table. The table, normally in front of the pulpit, is brought into the center of the sanctuary. Two deacons carefully place a white lace tablecloth over the Communion table. A chalice and a paten are removed from their case[47] and placed in the center of the table. The bread is placed on the paten, and the chalice is filled with wine from a new bottle. The deacons reverently cover the elements.

The sacramental quality of the Communion service is recognized in the preparation of the elements:

> Jesus talked of watches during the night. There were four of them. The first was from 6:00–9:00 P.M.; the second, 9:00 P.M.–12:00 A.M.; the third, 12:00–3:00 A.M.; and the fourth, from 3:00–6:00 A.M. It is during the fourth watch that the woman leader prepares the communion bread. She must do it while it is still dark, before there are any disturbances, before the birds start singing to distract her. She makes it in quietness. She prays all the while she makes the bread (you can tell if she has been praying or not, if she was distracted the bread will be doughy and thick; if she was praying, then the bread will be thin and break easily). It was before the sunrise that the women came to Jesus' tomb and found it empty. It was the women who came first to the tomb, that's why they prepare the bread. The bread must be made from new flour, you can't use what's left over in your kitchen. A woman goes to the store and buys a little packet of flour, that's what she makes it from. The deacon must be in prayer when he goes to the store to buy the wine. There are lots of prayers in the bread and in the wine, there are a lot of hands in that.

The bread is considered very sacred. It is no ordinary bread. If the preparer makes it correctly (with adequate prayers and humility), the bread will provide a divine blessing to those who partake of it.

After the table is prepared, the deacons are seated and the pastor leads a song and a prayer. Several other songs and prayers are led by the deacons and floor members. The praying is more urgent during the Communion service—many tears are shed as supplications are voiced. The pastor's devotional reading is from one of the New Testament accounts of Communion (such as Luke 22:14–20). His commentary focuses on the solemnity of Communion and the imperative to fulfill this work. The pastor concludes his devotional with an impassioned prayer asking that the congregation be made worthy of the sacrament.

The deacons return to the table after the pastor's prayer and uncover the elements while the congregation sings an appropriate hymn. One such hymn that is commonly sung at this point is "Cesvs Alakvtes":

Cesvs alakvtes, akerricakes, mekusapakes, Hesaketv emesen.
Jesus came, think about it, pray, God.

Porvhkan omates, akerricakes, mekusapakes, Hesaketv emesen.
He came for us, think about it, pray, God.

Eponvkecates, akerricakes, mekusapakes, Hesaketv emesen.
He loves us, think about it, pray, God.

Catv pvlatkvtis, akerricakes, mekusapakes, Hesaketv emesen.
He spilled the blood, think about it, pray, God.[48]

The head deacon breaks the bread into bite-sized pieces, then approaches the pastor with the paten. The pastor takes a piece of bread and eats it. The deacon makes his way to all of the ministers seated up front, offering them each the paten. After the ministers have eaten the bread, the deacon works his way around the men's side, then to the women's leaders, and then to the rest of the women. The deacons are the last to take the bread. When they have eaten it, the paten with the remaining bread is placed back on the table and is covered. Additional songs and prayers follow, such as this one:

Tohweklepkv vnakvn Cesvs cvhuericvs.
Jesus keep me steady near the cross.

Catv fihne vcakat estofis vmwiecvs.
Your blood is flowing sacred, always.

Kalfvle, Kalfvle, mvnsekvsvmares,
Calvary, Calvary, I will brag on it,

Mvt tvpalv herusan safvcketvtares.
I will be happy with it.[49]

While a prayer song is being sung, the chalice is uncovered by the deacons, and it too is offered to the pastor, the ministers, the male floor members, the women's leaders, and the female floor members, who drink from it and then hand it back to the deacons. The deacons are the last to consume the wine. They return the chalice to the table and cover it. While the deacons are covering the elements, the floor members move the pews back against the north and south walls. They do this to provide a large open area around the Communion table.

In this space, all of those in attendance form a single-file circle around the Communion table. The men are on the southern side, the women on the northern; the pastor and ministers are on the west, the listeners on the east. One or more songs are sung. During this portion of the service, the theme of unity is acted out. The pastor enters the edge of the circle and faces the minister who was standing immediately to his right. The pastor shakes his hand, pulls him close, and quietly speaks to him some words of encouragement. The pastor continues in a counterclockwise direction, shaking the hand of each individual within the circle and speaking personal words of encouragement to each one. After the pastor has addressed three or four individuals in this manner, the minister who had been standing next to the pastor enters the edge of the circle and faces the person who was standing immediately to his right, shakes his hand, and speaks words of personal encouragement in the same manner that the pastor had done. After the minister has addressed three or four individuals, the person who had been standing next to the minister enters the edge of the circle and continues the pattern. Eventually all participants enter the circle to shake the hand of, and speak words of encouragement to, every other person in the circle. After a person has made the round, he or she returns to his or her original position in the circle, to be addressed by those still making the round. Each person, therefore, has an active role in addressing others and also a passive role in receiving the address of others. This portion of the service is extremely emotional and moving. Some of the interactions are quite lengthy and personal. Many tears are shed, and there is a feeling of solidarity among the participants. It is not unusual for this portion of the service to last for more than an hour.

When all of the participants have made the round, a final song is sung, and the pastor or a minister speaks the blessing. One song regularly sung as a dismissal at Communion services is "Lord Dismiss Us." It is an ancient song and is sung with great emotion.

Cemekusapeyvte mamusen tem vwahes;
We are praying before you, then we are going to dismiss;

Cenherketvn puwahlvs; mohmet sepuwahecvs.
Your peace we are asking you to distribute; and then we want
   you to dismiss us.

Mohmen yvmv ekvnv enkvpvkakeyofvt,
Someday this earthly life and the land we live in will be separated from us,

Cenliketvn roricet, fekvpetvn puyaces.
In your place we will arrive, and rest will be what we want.[50]

The service concludes with the usual handshakes and members saying to the visitors, "*Mvto, ralalvkvs!*" ("Thank you, come again!"). Informal conversation takes place while the refreshments are being prepared. At the same time, the pews are returned to their usual places.

All of the children who are present on the church grounds gather on the front pew on the men's side. The deacons distribute to them the leftover bread and wine until it is all consumed. A pastor explains: "We give it to the children because Jesus loved the children. We can't just throw it away because it went through a lot of prayers. We give them the bread and the wine so that they'll be blessed. I know some churches don't give it to the children, they bury their leftovers. I think that is more appropriate then throwing it in the trash." Thus the children do not participate in the service but do receive the benefits of the elements after the adult portion of the service is completed. This practice is analogous to the Stomp grounds practice of having children consume "medicine" to receive the blessing of health and strength. In this way, even the youngest member's place in the community is affirmed.

Refreshments are served in the camp houses; afterward, the participants return to their respective homes. Members and visitors depart, having fulfilled their work and affirmed their membership in the community.

Discussion of Big Meetings

The overarching theme during the Big Meeting weekend is *unity*: "We need to be of one accord," "of one mind"; "there should be no conflict"; "we should have only good thoughts"; "we're all supposed to pray that way and be of one accord. Jesus wants us to be of one prayer." The theme is reinforced throughout the services, and the Big Meeting concludes with a ritual of handshaking and supportive encouragement—a demonstration of unity. All baptized members are expected to participate in their congregation's Big Meetings. One pastor stated the ideal, "When we go to drink that wine and eat that bread, well, they want each one to get in their chair, where there was appointed to him. Be like each one getting into their stall." Communion services represent the consummate religious obligation of Seminole Baptists. Communion is viewed as a work that requires complete community cooperation and provides spiritual benefits to the community.

Participation in Communion is a moral imperative. During sermons one will hear warnings such as the following: "We are spiritually dead if we don't take Communion," and "It says in the book, 'If you do not take my body—bread—body, drink my blood—wine—said there's no life in you.'" Not surprising, then, Communion services have the largest attendance of all the Seminole Baptist gatherings.

One reason for the high attendance is, of course, the highly sacred nature of the gathering. Another reason is that the Communion service is considered a gathering of the larger community. In fact, for the Communion "work to be fulfilled," there must be "workers" (ministers and especially deacons) from visiting congregations. Visiting deacons distribute the consecrated bread and wine to the congregation. Ministers are needed to preach throughout the afternoon. As a part of their preparations for a Big Meeting, host congregations often directly request participation from neighboring deacons and ministers. Sharing leaders among congregations hosting Big Meetings exposes the face of these leaders to public sanction. As representatives of their congregations, the leaders also risk their congregations' face as well, since congregational relationships and memberships are exposed to the regulation of the larger community. It is evident, then, that congregations are not strictly autonomous; rather, individual congregations are constituent social units of the larger Seminole Baptist community. It is this larger community that holds participants to standards of conduct that define the shared community.

Because of this wide community involvement and the overarching theme of unity, the Big Meeting is the most important gathering for the larger Seminole Baptist community. The particularly sacred quality of the occasion validates the importance of attending. Members who would be too ill to attend a Prayer Meeting or a Fourth Sunday Meeting will make every effort to be in attendance at a Big Meeting, and the other participants will praise that person's dedication. Big Meetings place a large number of Seminole Baptist members into face-to-face interaction. The obligatory nature of these gatherings, the widespread participation, the overlap of personnel, and the frequency of Big Meetings result in wide interaction among members of various congregations, serving to integrate the entire Seminole Baptist community. Thus, lines of communication stay open, and shared social standards are reinforced. It is unnecessary, as a result, for the Seminole Baptist community as a *whole* to gather periodically.

Comparison of Prayer, Fourth Sunday, and Big Meetings

During the three primary social occasions of the Seminole Baptists—weekly Prayer Meetings, Fourth Sunday Meetings, and Big Meetings—participants are held to standards of conduct, to situational proprieties, that emphasize and interpret the community they share. These occasions structure Seminole Baptist social life. At these occasions one can readily see the interdependence of culture and social interaction. These events are guided by community-specific norms and conventions that organize social interaction. When participants gather to "fulfill the work" of the occasions, they are placed in face-to-face encounters in which their individual and congregational faces are exposed and must be managed. In this way, the community monitors and regulates behavior. Participation in the various occasions is the fundamental vehicle of social integration into the wider Seminole community.

The congregation is the basic level in the Seminole Baptist social organization. It is here that members are initiated into the larger Seminole Baptist community. Most church members will enter into the Seminole Baptist church system via the relatively private Prayer Meetings. The Prayer Meeting, occurring each week, is the primary social gathering of members. It is at Prayer Meetings that the congregation socializes new members, for here members expose their individual social faces. Faces, or social representations of self, are strategically employed during Prayer Meetings to bring about desired social outcomes (either individual or corporate interests). Simply being present at a Prayer Meeting signals one's social identity as a Seminole Baptist.

Social identities are an important element in effecting any social work. Social identities obligate certain social actions—Seminole Baptists are bound to participate in the church's occasions and must be appropriately involved. Social identities also empower social action within the community. Members fulfilling some institutionalized social role, such as pastor, minister, or women's leader, bring into social encounters a certain prestige that influences the outcome. It is also at the level of congregation that most episodes of interpersonal conflict are played out.

Prayer Meetings are often attended exclusively by members of the local congregation. Held weekly, Prayer Meetings are much more intimate than Fourth Sunday Meetings. Sermons, therefore, tend to focus on parochial issues, individuals are often named as examples, behavior is criticized, congregational face is refined (ideal public behavior is promoted), announcements are more personal, and the pre-service and refreshment visiting is of an interpersonal rather than polite nature. Rededications, decisions, and requests for baptism are more frequent in Prayer Meetings than in Fourth Sunday Meetings. Few people come forward during Fourth Sunday Meeting invitations (notable exceptions are discussed in the following chapter).

Fourth Sunday Meetings function to broaden social interaction among members. Three weeks out of each month, members are obligated to interact with other social units. At this level, congregational faces are exposed to the larger Seminole Baptist community. Here participants are held to shared standards of conduct that define their community. The meeting ambiance is more celebrative and sermons are less critical at Fourth Sunday Meetings than at Prayer Meetings.

Of the Seminole Baptist gatherings, Big Meetings have the furthest influence: visiting participants come from many different congregations, and the number of visitors in attendance greatly exceeds the number of members of the host congregation in attendance. Whereas Prayer Meetings are parochial and "private regions," Big Meetings are the most "public," drawing from the largest pool of community members for participation. Big Meetings draw the broadest interaction among the Seminole Baptists. Big Meetings may be the only social occasion where distant acquaintances will interact and where occasionally members of the host congregation will encounter unfamiliar visitors. The required participation of members as well as visitors, and the underlying theme of unity, emphasize the importance of community.

Seminole Baptists represent a traditional community. *Traditional* does not imply unchanging or static; rather, changes are directed in culturally meaningful ways that allow the social group to sustain identity while adapting to changing circumstances. The cultural features that bounded the historical Seminoles have been adapted and modified into the Seminole Baptist church system. Of course, no cultural patterns are duplicated precisely from generation to generation. Instead, what is often called "tradition" undergoes regular modification; specific cultural expressions are negotiated and build upon prior expressions. This is evident for the cultural patterns, or the situational proprieties, of the Seminole Baptist church community.[51] The cultural structures that organize social occasions are continually exposed to reinterpretation and redefinition. Innovations are regularly proposed by members and leaders in an effort to retain congregational vitality and to enhance congregational face. Occasionally, innovations are adopted (although they are usually interpreted as revitalization rather than innovation). The Seminole Baptist community members adapt or construct cultural and social facts as ways of adapting to changes in the conditions of everyday life. Congregations, as an aspect of social organization, are responsive to those changing conditions.

Missionaries have been viewed as the spearhead of assimilation, yet the consequences of their activities were often not what was predicted—indeed, "social engineering" seldom results in what is expected or desired. Church members, praised as being assimilated, were left alone. Even today, an outsider conducting a perfunctory evaluation of the community would likely conclude that Seminole Baptist congregations, though perhaps a little eccentric, appear to be assimilated. However, as I have shown, Seminole Baptists are not assimilated into the dominant Anglo world; instead, the church system has become a vehicle for maintaining a distinct Seminole identity. The historical Seminoles responded to external changes by adapting their traditional forms of social and cultural organization within the limited economic and political options available. Churches were formed in culturally meaningful ways as an adaptation to the existing tradition of religious occasions used for social regulation.

When the Seminoles lived in the Florida region, their social organization was centered around the ceremonial cycle of the *etvlwv* ("band") system. Regular rituals and annual ceremonies provided the occasions for social integration. When the Seminoles were removed to Indian Territory, they brought the *etvlwv* system with them. Ashes from the Florida town fires were carried to Indian Territory. New ceremonial fires were rekindled on top of these, and new band or town centers were established. The transplanted *etvlwv*, however, was used in different ways after removal. American political domination disrupted Seminole life, and band autonomy was compromised. In Indian Territory, the Seminoles were more directly under U.S. political rule. A constitutional government was imposed on the Seminoles, and the *etvlwvlke* experienced a dramatic reduction in political power. External relations, historically fulfilled by the *etvlwvlke*, were directed by the official constitutional government. The bands continued to function internally, however, providing organization among Seminoles. Bands, which continued to sponsor Stomp dances and the Green Corn Festival, were the primary means of community integration into the twentieth century.

Early in this century the churches, which had been a secondary social institution, began to rival the *etvlwvlke*. It is interesting to note that during the 1930s, as the churches were superseding the role of the *etvlwvlke*, Stomp grounds were obligating attendance at their dances. Absent members were fined: excused absences were fined from $1 to $5, and unexcused absences were "fined a steer, or several hogs" (Hadley [1935] 1987:142). Stomp grounds thus obligated attendance, in much the same way as churches do now. By 1950 there were only two active Seminole Stomp grounds (Wright 1951:237), but there were perhaps seventeen Baptist churches, in addition to several Methodist and Presbyterian churches.

Churches may originally have served as a buffer between federal agents and policies bent on assimilation on the one hand and traditional Seminoles struggling to maintain a distinct Seminole identity on the other. Seminole history reveals repeated attempts by Euro-American forces to crush band autonomy and structure. It became increasingly difficult for bands to function—first politically, then socially. Participation in bands and in band activity was officially discouraged by agents of the federal government, and church participation was encouraged. By joining churches, the Seminoles may have given the appearance of accommodation, yet the churches took on a distinctively Seminole configuration. The *etvlwv* socioreligious structure of the historical Seminoles was incorporated into the organization of congregations. Congregations, often founded by people from the same tribal band, took on the function of the historical *etvlwvlke*. Congregational leadership roles were patterned after the *etvlwv* leadership. The layout of church grounds was patterned after the ceremonial grounds even while being rationalized with Christian concepts. Many of the beliefs that informed historical Seminole life are held by dedicated church members today. These are all cultural adaptations that organize social life in traditional ways.

Just as the historical Seminoles came together annually at the Green Corn Festival, or busk, Seminole Baptists come together quarterly at Big Meetings, as a mechanism to unite the larger community. The functional theme of unity was the focus of the historical Green Corn Festival (Swanton 1928b:548–49) and is also the theme of the Big Meeting weekends.[52] Whereas the busk was ceremonially centered around the fire, Big Meetings center around the Communion table and the Communion elements. The social function of both rites is virtually identical: to integrate local constituents into the larger whole.

Seminole Baptists have developed a cultural system that is responsive to their needs for meaning as well as their needs for community organization and maintenance. Face management in these social occasions exposes relationships and congregational memberships to regulation by the larger community. In lieu of formal, centralized social structures, face management during Prayer Meetings, Fourth Sunday Meetings, and Big Meetings provides a mechanism for the integration and maintenance of the Seminole Baptist community.

CHAPTER 7

Social Life at Eufaula

For the participants within the Seminole Baptist churches, the social occasions described in the previous chapter function to integrate their church community. These occasions do this through their obligatory nature: community members are obligated to participate in face-to-face encounters. Social situations provide the stage for face maintenance or face enhancement—that is, face work. Each time community members encounter one another, there is an automatic appeal to face. A socialized community member has deep feelings attached to face, thus making him or her vulnerable to the sanctions of the community. Appeal to face in social occasions within the church system is the dynamic mechanism by which the congregation as a social unit manages conflict and promotes cooperation.

Members speak of the objective of the social occasions as *vtotkv esfaceses* ("fulfilling the work"). Although this statement ostensibly refers to a spiritual work, we may also take it as implying a corresponding social work of the sort described by Goffman (1967). Goffman's (1967:15ff) model proposes two basic kinds of face work: avoidance and corrective. In the avoidance process, a person prevents threats to face by avoiding contacts and interactions in which threats are likely to occur. This approach includes such strategies as actually withdrawing physically from encounters, avoiding expression of damaging information, and using self-deprecation, jokes, or any other strategy for avoiding "making a scene"—or *incident*, in Goffman's terminology. An incident is an event that is "expressively incompatible with the judgements of social worth that are being maintained, and when the event is of the kind that is difficult to overlook" (Goffman 1967:19).

The corrective process is used to counteract previous incidents and therefore to reestablish *ritual equilibrium* between the participants in the social encounter. The set of actions initiated by an acknowledged threat to face, resulting in the reestablishment of equilibrium, Goffman calls a *corrective interchange* (Goffman 1967:19–23). An interchange involves two or more players or teams exchanging four *moves*.

The four moves that make up an interchange (not including the initial misbehavior giving rise to it) are *challenge, offering, acceptance*, and *gratitude*. The challenge is the official call of attention to misbehavior, giving it the accredited status of an incident. In the offering, "a participant, typically the offender, is given a chance to correct for the offense and re-establish the expressive order" (Goffman 1967:20). Effective offerings include attempting "to show that what admittedly appeared to be a threatening expression is really a meaningless event, or an unintentional act, or a joke not meant to be taken seriously, or an unavoidable, 'understandable' product of extenuating circumstances" (Goffman 1967:20). The offender may redefine the offensive act or redefine himself or herself: "I was not myself"; "I have changed now." The offender may offer compensation or penance. But whatever the offender does, his or her actions must prove that the offender and the ritual code that was violated are still "in working order" and must be upheld. When "the person to whom the offering is made can accept it as a satisfactory means of re-establishing the expressive order and the faces supported by this order" (Goffman 1967:22), the third move, acceptance, has been played. The final move in the corrective interchange is gratitude: "The forgiven person conveys a sign of gratitude to those who have given him the indulgence of forgiveness" (Goffman 1967:22). When the four moves are successfully completed, the interchange is complete and equilibrium has been restored.

Conflicting individual agendas regularly result in interpersonal conflict. Social groups must develop strategies for settling such conflict. Participants within the Seminole Baptist churches have institutionalized and conventionalized a version of Goffman's corrective interchange: through sermons, pastors challenge individual or corporate behavior; the "invitation" that follows the sermons allows for penitents (whether they were challenged by the pastor during the sermon or were challenged by any other member in other contexts) to make an offering; the ritual handshake following a rededication is a vehicle for acceptance; and finally, those then restored, at least tacitly, into the fellowship express gratitude by their full participation in the congregational life. This conventionalized corrective process has its limits, however. Offering statements are highly generalized, that is, are usually not in direct response to a specific challenge; rather, the offender says simply, "I have failed my Lord," or "I am backslidden." All participants present during the offering statement are virtually required to accept the offering and approach the penitent to shake his or her hand, whether the offering is considered acceptable or not. This institutionalized interchange has a place, yet it is not the only way that Seminole Baptists use the corrective process, as will be demonstrated below.

From the following characterization of Eufaula's social life, amounting to a recounting of a series of such interchanges, the reader will see that few of the interchanges are neatly concluded. As Goffman (1967:22) admits, "The phases of the corrective process—challenge, offering, acceptance, and thanks—provide a model for interpersonal ritual behavior, but a model that may be departed from in significant ways." In the account below, such departures from the model are significant: challenges are ignored; offerings are judged inadequate or are not extended in the first place; misbehavior continues after a challenge has been issued; a person may not accept a challenge and may withdraw from an encounter in a huff, leaving the offended players floundering. In addition, a single player may be trading moves with several people simultaneously. This may result from a player being involved in multiple interchanges or from moves in a single interchange having different success rates among the different parties involved. One player must calculate actions and manage impressions for optimal benefit. Often a single action has conflicting consequences. Unresolved conflict is, however, costly to the community. The work of the congregation is impeded by unresolved social difficulties, so a motive for resolutions is always before individuals and congregations.

In the social life of Eufaula, interchanges directly involve other members, yet often the actions within the congregation are known around the larger community as well (via overlapping kin and enduring social relationship networks)—that is, beyond the discrete boundaries of the social situation in which they occur. The manner in which interchanges are handled influences the perception of one's congregational face vis-à-vis the larger Seminole Baptist community. Maladroit interchanges within a parish are potential incidents involving the face of the congregation of which the participants are members. Individual self-interests must often be subordinated for the benefit of the congregation as well as the larger community. Occasionally, however, unresolved interpersonal tensions involving a portion of the congregation become a church community incident requiring official attention. Such an incident—or, more accurately, series of incidents—occurred at Eufaula and resulted in the postponement of a Big Meeting.

Incidents engaging congregational face work may also be explicated with Goffman's corrective process model. One of the players (teams) is the particular congregation; the other is a solicitous segment of the larger Seminole Baptist community. The challenge may come from the larger community, but it may also come from within the errant congregation itself (members within congregations are expected to be introspective, to be sensitive to the cues of the larger Seminole Baptist community). Offerings are made on behalf of the congregation, and when acceptance is given, the corrective process is completed. The process appears to be unidirectional. The equivalent of a revitalization movement would be required for an individual or congregation to challenge the community.

Congregational face work is not independent of individual face work. Members may be performing work that is designed to influence one's own as well as the congregation's face. Often a member not directly involved in an incident will nevertheless make an offering on behalf of the well-being of the social group that has been publicly associated with the incident. Goffman (1967:27–28) is useful here: "When a face has been threatened, face-work must be done, but whether this is initiated and primarily carried through by the person whose face is threatened, or by the offender, or by a mere witness, is often of secondary importance. Lack of effort on the part of one person induces compensatory effort from others; a contribution by one person relieves the others of the task. . . . Resolution of the situation to everyone's apparent satisfaction is the first requirement; correct apportionment of blame is typically a secondary consideration." When incidents are left uncorrected, they will bring about a state of *disequilibrium* to the social group (Goffman 1967:19). Disequilibrium is uncomfortable and destabilizing. Long-term disequilibrium is costly to a social group as well as a community. Notwithstanding, interchanges may drag on interminably, resulting in an established disequilibrium.

Participants in the Seminole Baptist churches are often in states of disequilibrium—tensions run hot, and incidents may go on for weeks, months, or years before being resolved. What ensures the continuation of the Seminole Baptist community is the obligatory nature of church gatherings. Members continue to gather in spite of interpersonal tensions because they "must fulfill the work." This imperative secures church community maintenance by obligating members to face-to-face encounters in which consideration of face forces at least a functional level of cooperation.

The cultural symbols (conceptual frameworks) that organize Seminole Baptist social occasions structure a common, binding universe of meaning for the participants. However, the cultural symbols that govern social situations are persistently exposed to reinterpretation and redefinition to meet contingencies. Members regularly negotiate strategies of organization from available options. Some of these strategies (innovations?) are judged efficacious and are adopted by a portion of a community (among Seminole Baptists, this would be one or more congregations). Others are rejected outright or are sampled briefly, only to be rejected later. Of the successful strategies, some are recognized as especially propitious and are ultimately adopted by a substantial portion of the whole community (the adoption of Christianity was historically such an innovation). Negotiated reinterpretations and redefinitions of cultural symbols within the churches might be interpreted as a strategic manipulation of impressions by a constituency to enhance one's congregational face within the larger church system. Or, to use an organic analogy, they might be interpreted as "variations" that are "selected" to promote "fitness" that will ensure the survival of the Seminole Baptist community—as adaptive responses to a changing socioeconomic environment.

In this chapter I will detail the social life of one congregation within the Seminole Baptist church system: Eufaula. The primary social actors in this study are those people who are active members of the Eufaula congregation. "Active members" are those whose names are registered on the church membership books and who were usually in attendance at the social occasions I observed during my field experience (1990–94). (Some of the members are shown in figures 11, 12, and 13.) The members' attendance at the social occasions was remarkably consistent. With a minimum of seven social occasions that a parishioner is obligated to attend each month, members attended every one of those meetings unless there was a pressing reason for absence: recovery from surgery, car trouble, visiting out-of-state relatives, or special circumstances (impres-

Fig. 11.   Church leaders (a pastor and three deacons). Photo by author.

Fig. 12.   A deacon under the arbor before services, with the pulpit visible in the lower-right corner. Photo by author.

Fig. 13. The youngest members at Eufaula Church. Photo by author.

sion management), as described below. One deacon said, "There are no good excuses from church." Unlike many Anglo parishes, Eufaula has a very clear line dividing the active from the nominal members.

When I began fieldwork, the pastor of Eufaula was Rvro ("Fish").[1] Rvro is in his early seventies. He is *Ahalvhvlke* ("sweet potato") clan. Rvro grew up in the Seminole Baptist tradition at a church near Sasakwa, Oklahoma. He says that he "married into" Eufaula because his wife, Fuco ("Duck"), was a member at Eufaula. After he became a member at Eufaula, the church appointed him to be a deacon, then ordained him as a minister in 1971 and as pastor in 1973. He says that he never sought the position of minister or of pastor but that the church "found him." While he was serving in the role of minister, his secular employment was that of a commercial truck driver. His retirement from truck driving coincided with Eufaula's need for a pastor, and the congregation appointed him to serve in that role in 1973. Soon after I met Rvro, his wife of forty-seven years, Fuco, died. Rvro lives alone in Fuco's camp house on the church grounds. His present income is an army pension and social security.

The minister at Eufaula is Cesse ("Mouse"). He is about sixty years old and is *Katcvlke* ("tiger" or "cougar") clan. He grew up in Eufaula Church, but as a married adult, he left Eufaula for several years with his wife, Eco ("Deer"), and he was ordained as a minister in a Seminole Presbyterian church near his wife's home. While serving in the Presbyterian church, he was stricken with a brain tumor. He tells how during the surgery, he had a vision in which God gave him three directives: "return to your first love"; "find your work"; and "get your house in order." The first of these he interpreted as a sanction to return to Eufaula; the second was "fulfilled" when he was ordained as a layman and then later as a minister of Eufaula; the third would be fulfilled during the social drama described below. When my field experience began, Eco was undergoing training to become a women's leader. Cesse receives a modest pension, the result of a job-related disability. Eco sews upholstery for a small business affiliated with the Seminole tribe. Their daughter, who is in junior college, does not attend Eufaula. Cesse is a first cousin to Cufe ("Rabbit").

Cufe is the head deacon. In his midseventies, he is *Ecvlke* ("deer") clan. Cufe's father was a deacon, a minister, and then later the pastor at Eufaula. Cufe's mother was a women's leader. Cufe grew up in Seminole County and was raised with church as an important part of his life. He describes how in his youth, his parents would load him and his siblings into horse-drawn wagons for cold winter rides to attend the various church meetings. The further churches took two days of travel to reach, requiring camping en route. He recalls Big Meeting weekends at Eufaula, where members and visitors slept in the church building and in tents around the church grounds because the camp houses had not yet been erected. He laughed as he told how irritated his mother would get with his father for butchering a hog for each of the Big Meetings.

Cufe was in World War II, Forty-fifth Infantry, and after returning, he participated in the Voluntary Relocation Program,[2] moving to St. Louis with his wife, Pose ("Cat"), for a little over a year. He soon missed home and returned to Seminole County. He worked as a custodian before retiring. Cufe has kin at Eufaula. He is first cousin to the minister, Cesse, the deacon Sokhvhvtke ("White Pig," i.e., "Possum"), and the head women's leader, Fuswv ("Bird").

Cufe's wife, Pose, is Cherokee. She is not a member of Eufaula; however, she attends regularly and sets up camp at Cufe's camp house during Fourth Sunday Meetings and Big Meetings. She and Cufe met while they were both students at Chilocco Indian School near Ponca City. They have nine children, none of whom are active at the church. Cufe and Pose are raising one of their grandsons, whose mother (their daughter) was killed in an auto accident several years ago. Their grandson attends church with them regularly.

The other deacon is Sokhvhvtke. He is about forty-five years old and is *Katcvlke* ("tiger" or "cougar") clan. He drives a school bus for one of the community schools. His wife and their two teen-aged children are members at a neighboring Seminole Baptist church. They attend Eufaula infrequently as visitors.

Kono ("Skunk"), about sixty-five years old, is a deacon trainee. He is *Hotvlke* ("wind") clan. His family is from Seminole County, and he grew up in Eufaula Church. His wife, Penwv ("Turkey"), is a Creek from Okmulgee County. When I began my field experience, she was being trained as a women's leader. Kono and Penwv have six children, none of whom are active at Eufaula; however, they do have three grandchildren who attend. Kono's sister Tolose ("Chicken") was being trained as a women's leader when I began my field experience. She lives next door to Kono and attends with him and Penwv. Tolose has an adopted daughter, who was recently baptized at Eufaula. Kono's family sets up camp during Fourth Sunday Meetings and Big Meetings. They usually host refreshments following the Prayer Meetings each week.

The youngest worker is Nokose ("Bear"). He is in his midthirties and is employed as a delivery truck driver in a neighboring city. Nokose's father was a deacon at Eufaula, and Nokose is a deacon trainee. Nokose's mother, Wasko ("Chigger"), is in her late sixties and was going through training to become a women's leader at Eufaula when I began my field experience. Wasko and Nokose are *Vktv hvkcike* or *Kapikcaki* ("water people," although sometimes referred to as "alligator," "snake," "otter," or "beaver") clan. Nokose's wife, Esko ("Ground Squirrel"), is *Ecvlke* ("deer") clan. She is employed in a part-time service job. They have two daughters, twelve and seven years old, who attend church with their parents.

Fuswv, in her midseventies, is head women's leader. She is *Katcvlke* ("tiger" or "cougar") clan. Two of her granddaughters usually accompany her to the grounds and occasionally participate in the services. Fuswv's family sets up camp during Fourth Sunday Meetings and Big Meetings.

Lvmhe ("Eagle"), in his late sixties, lives permanently in one of the camp houses at the grounds. He is *Hvlpvtvlke* ("alligator") clan. Although his name appears on the membership list, he is considered apostate. He attends only occasionally, sitting in the "listeners' section," yet is frequently around for refreshments and often interacts with the members. He regularly provides services to the church, such as cutting the grass and making minor repairs. Lvmhe is Wasko's uncle.

Two other members died early in my field experience. The first, Cvpose ("My Grandmother"), in her midseventies, was the widow of the pastor before Rvro. The second, Opv ("Owl"), in her late sixties, was Fuswv's sister.

These are the active members of Eufaula and the primary actors in the social life I will chronicle. Other significant people will be introduced as necessary.

The social life of Eufaula may be depicted as a series of overlapping *interchanges* involving all of the members of the congregation. I will recount various episodes of *challenge*, *offering*, *acceptance*, and *gratitude*. Some of the *incidents* drew the attention of the larger church community to the point that the congregational face of Eufaula was being damaged and required remedial face work with the community. The social life of Eufaula also contains an element of competition among three men and the single position of pastor.

My first exposure to public conflict was during a June Prayer Meeting under the arbor. I had been attending Eufaula gatherings for about eight months. All of the members were in attendance—even Lvmhe was present. He sat quietly in the listeners' section throughout the service. Four visitors were also present, all from Sand Creek. When it came time for the announcements, Lvmhe stood up and expressed his concern over Kono's recent purchase of a riding lawn mower. Lvmhe reminded the congregation that he, not Kono, had been given the authority by the church to purchase a mower. Lvmhe's immediate concern was with the lack of a bill of sale for the records. Kono stood in defense and said that he would be happy to write one. Lvmhe refused that suggestion and reminded Kono that the bill of sale had to be from the person who sold the mower. Cufe and Eco, each standing in turn and addressing the pastor, stated that church decisions should be followed and that Kono was in the wrong for going against it. Kono countered, and there was discussion back and forth between several members. Cufe finally suggested that the discussion continue at the next business meeting. The pastor agreed, the discussion was ended, and the service continued. It is interesting to note that during this rather animated discussion, the four nonmembers present arose almost simultaneously and stepped away from the arbor, out of earshot. They rejoined the gathering only after the contentions had ceased, during the song following the announcements. Apparently, conflict is frequent enough that there have been proprieties established to manage it. The visitors knew precisely when to exit and when to return, creating a discrete private territory for intracongregational negotiation of face without impinging on the public face of the congregation as a whole.

The discord surrounding the purchase of the mower was not quickly resolved, however. The incident was readdressed during the monthly business meeting.[3] Kono was held responsible for "going against the church." In his opinion, what he did was for the church (he saw a good deal and took advantage of it). Several members grumbled that this is the way that Kono often acts: he goes against what the church directs and acts according to his own desires. Nothing was resolved during the business meeting; rather, the incident was shelved, with hard feelings remaining among several members. This unresolved incident impeded the work of the congregation.

When the grievance over the lawn mower was voiced during the Prayer Meeting, the issue became an incident. It was given "accredited status," warranting official attention. Lvmhe's complaint was a *challenge*, the first move in an *interchange*. Kono's response was an *offering*. He provided a rationale for his actions and offered to rectify the situation by writing a bill of sale. His offering was viewed by the others as inadequate. There was no *acceptance* and no *gratitude*. The incident was raised at the next business meeting, and the challenge was reissued. This time Kono refused to provide the necessary offering. Participants found themselves in a state of ritual disequilibrium.

During the ensuing weeks, gatherings were held as usual; however, members continued to express their feelings of discontent. Other incidents also remained in abeyance. The lawn mower incident in some way triggered the public airing, or accredited status, of other interpersonal disagreements. Some, no doubt, were initiated well before my arrival, and thereby remain unknown to me, yet some other unresolved incidents were brought to my attention. When Cufe had been hospitalized earlier that summer, Kono took charge of the offering money during a Fourth Sunday Meeting, without church authority. The money turned up missing. Kono claimed that he had left it in the church and argued that someone must have taken it. He later replaced the money ($55) from his own pocket. In addition, Penwv, Tolose, and Eco, trainees for women's leaders, had earlier criticized the head women's leader and the pastor for not providing them with proper training for their roles. The pastor was also being blamed for Eufaula's dwindling membership.

The tensions crested during a Prayer Meeting the week before the September Big Meeting. During the announcement segment, someone suggested that the Big Meeting should be postponed because the church was not "in complete unity." The head deacon, Cufe, lamented, "Members just aren't getting along, not working together." One member objected to the postponement; another voiced his support of it. There was little discussion, but it was agreed that the pastor would need to make the final decision by the next day so that the word could be spread to the neighboring churches. The Prayer Meeting continued. Members had ceased to feel obligated to support one another's faces, thereby halting the work of the congregation.

After refreshments later that evening, members independently explained their view of the situation to me. Cufe saw the root of the problem as Kono. "He's just making trouble." The lawn mower purchase surfaced again. Kono meanwhile complained: "We're not of one accord. It's coming about like my grandfather said." He went on to describe another time of turmoil in the life of Eufaula Church. In 1926, when Kono's grandfather was a minister at Eufaula, members were not getting along—"lots of complaining, backbiting." The minister addressed the congregation and warned them that they needed to work together because he had seen in a vision the demise of the church: "One day the arbor will shade cattle, and the church would hold hay." It appeared to Kono that the vision was about to be fulfilled. The next day the decision to postpone the Big Meeting was ratified by the pastor. The word was passed among members that the following weekend meeting would be a regular Fourth Sunday Meeting.

The incidents surrounding the cancellation of the Big Meeting became so eruptive that members recognized that their congregational face was being threatened. Steps were taken to correct for the effects. Postponement of a Big Meeting is quite serious: there must be a broadly felt dissatisfaction and concern within the local parish.[4] Postponing a Big Meeting has wide consequences, since it must be announced to the larger church community (that is, the other churches in the rotation). Postponing a Big Meeting is a public admission that the local conflict is indeed serious. The postponement also signals to the congregation that the situation must be resolved during the next three months (before the next Big Meeting), for it would be a major loss of congregational face to cancel consecutive Big Meetings.

In this instance, or incident, the challenge was issued from within. Members of Eufaula recognized the threat to their congregation's face. Attention had been called to misconduct—not only to the initial, individual misconduct (such as Kono's "going against the church") but also to the reaction of the others ("We're not getting along"; "We don't seem to care for one another anymore"). Corrective steps needed to be taken. The suggested offering was the postponement of the Big Meeting, an action that signaled to the members the need for face work. Unfortunately for the members, acceptance and resolution would entail several more challenges and offerings.

Eufaula's Big Meeting was postponed, and instead a regular Fourth Sunday Meeting was held. From the beginning of the morning service, Sokhvhvtke, the deacon, had been sitting in the listeners' section; his cane, the sign of his office, was absent, and he did not fulfill any of his ordinary tasks as deacon. Following the message, he responded to the invitation and went forward. In his statement he said: "I have not been as faithful as I should. I want to rededicate and strive to better fulfill my work." There were no questions of his motivation, nor were any challenges issued. The deacon was restored to fulfill his work, and his cane was returned to him by the pastor.

This was the first time that I had witnessed a deacon come forward. At this Fourth Sunday Meeting, which was supposed to be a Big Meeting, many visitors (i.e., members of the larger

Seminole Baptist community) were present. As was discussed previously, Fourth Sunday Meetings are not usually the occasion for rededications—Prayer Meetings serve that role more frequently, particularly for leaders. The deacon's coming forward marked something unusual. The deacon had, no doubt, felt that he personally had not been as faithful as he should. So he came forward. However, he may also have been responding to the disequilibrium that the congregation was feeling. Perhaps he was making an additional offering to the visitors who were present, attempting to assure them that corrective measures were being taken.

Perhaps more so than others, members in leadership positions support individual faces that are closely identified with the face of the congregation. Consequently, the leaders respond in personal ways when the congregation's face has been threatened. It is interesting to note that during the period of ongoing disequilibrium at Eufaula, the deacons and deacon trainees responded to invitations no less than six times, and the head women's leader responded once. During this same period, only one layperson came forward. As representatives of the congregation, leaders have more at stake than do the laity. Leaders are necessarily sensitized to the face that the congregation projects, and leaders are most often the ones directly involved in the congregation's external face work. Lack of effort on the part of an offender will often be compensated by the efforts of others, particularly leaders. Sokhvhvtke was making an offering in the corrective process of the congregation's face work.

In the days following that meeting, discontent was being expressed regularly and openly by the members. The corrective process was not completed—disequilibrium was still felt among the congregation. A sufficient offering was still lacking. Not too surprisingly, critical comments were being directed toward the congregational leader, the pastor. There was, however, enough resolution during the next three months to host the December Big Meeting in good conscience.

The next round of incidents, not disconnected from the first, centered around the pastor. Eufaula is one of the growing number of Seminole Baptist churches that appoint pastors for one-year terms. The more usual practice, though, has been for congregations to select pastors and install them for life. The decision regarding the pastor at Eufaula is made each January.

The congregation's choice of pastor is critical. The pastor's personal face tends to be closely identified with the face of the congregation and vice versa. He is the prime bearer of the congregational face. As a result, the pastor's behavior is closely monitored by the congregation. The pastor is expected to "toe the line," "to walk the chalk line." Rvro had been serving as pastor for about twenty years. The selection the past January had been a routine endorsement of him in his role. This year, however, the situation was different. In addition to the tensions that resulted in the cancellation of the September Big Meeting, longer-term problems with the congregation's low attendance and aging membership complicated the temporary resolution that allowed the December Big Meeting to take place. The pastor was being held accountable for these additional problems as well. Eufaula's face was still in need of repair, and it was imperative that the pastor be up to the challenge. There was talk about getting someone else in that position—namely Cesse, the only other man qualified. With members regularly voicing dissatisfaction with the way things were in the church, disequilibrium was still being felt.

Early in January 1992, while I was visiting Cufe, the head deacon, at his home, Cesse and Eco stopped by for a pastoral visit. As we sat around the table, Eco said that Sokhvhvtke, the other deacon, had reminded her to be in prayer for the upcoming decision regarding the installation of the pastor. Eco and Cesse were concerned about how Rvro was performing his role. They accused him of playing favorites. Eco said, "One member [Kono] was taking his role of trustee too far; he's becoming too interested in controlling the money. This is not according to the Bible." She faulted the pastor for not admonishing Kono. At the same time she was tacitly lobbying for her husband, the other eligible candidate for the position, to replace Rvro as pastor. Cufe invited us all to stay for supper. After the meal, we attended the weekly Prayer Meeting.

At this Prayer Meeting, the first of the new year, Cesse, the minister, warned during his message: "You need to *publicly* confess your sins. If you don't, they'll still be in you and you may not receive forgiveness." This statement was significant. He was saying that private disagreements must be publicly resolved for the work of the church to go forward. The warning was received by the congregation with a chorus of "*Eman.*" Unlike many non-Seminole Americans who consider religious expression a private matter, Seminoles feel that religious expression is very corporate and communal. Following the message, Kono answered the invitation. Considering how often Kono was being mentioned as a source of conflict within the church, I thought his coming forward would be significant. Perhaps he was making an offering—accepting some responsibility and seeking to put things right—that would bring about some resolution. Perhaps he was also asking others to come forward because his offering alone was not sufficient to resolve a communal problem.

When asked to make a statement, Kono responded that his reason was "renewal of his vows." The pastor said to the deacon Cufe, "You've heard his statement, what do you think?" Cufe stood up and, in Mvskoke, said: "We've heard his statement. It's good to rededicate, we'll accept him back, no reason we shouldn't." The pastor then asked the congregation to "give witness to the rededication by raising your right hand." Kono's coming forward lacked the usual show of emotion and remorse, however. Perhaps he felt that coming forward to renew himself would provide some solace, but by couching it the way he did, he did not accept responsibility for specific deeds. Afterward he spoke to me about it. He said he had heard a New Year's Eve message urging rededication at this time of year. He said he didn't like to go forward at other churches, so he had waited until Eufaula's Prayer Meeting. Kono risked little face with his offering, yet an offering was made.

In general, offerings are very carefully made. It is as if face is a limited commodity that is accumulated, hoarded, budgeted, and risked only when return is guaranteed. Kono was hesitant to make an offering (almost four months after multiple challenges against him), and when he did, he did it carefully, safely. He made an offering during the semiprivate Prayer Meeting and explained that it was an annual venture, not the direct result of misbehavior or damaged face. His offering was nevertheless accepted, at least officially. No one challenged his motive or his statement when given the opportunity, and all of the participants approached him and shook his hand.

The next week, the Prayer Meeting was the stage of an intense social drama. Nokose, a deacon trainee, came forward at the invitation. He had been sitting in the listeners' section up to that point, signaling his contrition. Through heavy sobbing and tears, Nokose said he had fallen away, "misrepresented my Lord Jesus Christ," and wanted to rededicate his life. Again, a leader made an offering. He was welcomed back and given his regular seat with the believers. Then during the announcements Fuswv, the head women's leader, stood up to voice a concern. Without mincing words, she spoke very critically of the pastor. She accused him of failing to fulfill his work as pastor; she called him lazy and blamed him for the current problems of the congregation. She reminded him that he was responsible to all of the members and not just a few. She accused him of "playing favorites" by failing to admonish "some members." Fuswv issued a challenge. The pastor, seated next to her, only stared at the floor during her harangue. When she finished, he offered no defense. He made no offering.[5] After a few moments of uncomfortable silence, the Prayer Meeting continued.

The following Wednesday was the business meeting at which the pastor was to be installed for the coming year.

During the meeting Fuswv "chewed Rvro up" again, telling him that he was not performing his duties and did not even deserve the title of pastor. She had said similar things the week before at the Prayer Meeting, but in this more private gathering she castigated the pastor with great vehemence. Kono commented, "She said a lot of things that shouldn't have been said." The meeting got quite heated, with criticisms exchanged between many members. At least two other challenges were issued: Eco criticized the pastor for failing to lead the congregation, and Kono censured Fuswv for her disparagement of Rvro. Rvro still made no offering. The meeting was adjourned without a pastor being installed for the coming year. It was decided that Cesse would serve as chair for the future gatherings until the incidents involving the pastor were resolved. That Friday's Prayer Meeting was fulfilled uneventfully.

The following Wednesday another business meeting was held, again to vote on the reinstatement of the pastor for the coming year. This meeting was less animated, and apologies were extended. However, Fuswv was not in attendance at the meeting. Because she was a major player in the incidents, the tension was far from resolved, and again no person was put up for the position of pastor. I met with Kono in his home that Friday evening. He spoke for almost an hour on the "strife" the congregation was having. "We're just not caring for each other anymore. It used to be that church members took care of each other and looked after each other. It's not that way anymore. We're getting slack." Kono described the events of the previous two business meetings. He said they were very upsetting, to him as well as to other members. Kono felt that Fuswv was particularly out of line and that she needed to make a public apology to begin to set things right. He said that he and his wife and his sister would not be attending Eufaula's Prayer Meeting that evening: "Things just aren't right there, and some apologies need to be made." Kono felt that the situation at the church was indeed an incident. His challenge was issued in the form of a boycott. As I was leaving his house to go to the Prayer

Meeting, he intimated that other members were going to boycott the meeting as well.

Contrary to Kono's expectations, the Prayer Meeting was well attended—twenty people were present. It was a Fourth Sunday Meeting weekend, and there were many visitors. Indeed, all of the active members were present except Kono, his wife, and his sister. Cesse acted as chair. Rvro had no "work" that night, and he sat as far south as he could, against the wall. During refreshments, several members commented about Kono's absence. Cufe asserted, "We need to work together, to work this out." Kono's family's actions were challenged by Cufe.

The contentions continued. Several people echoed the accusation that the pastor was not doing his job. Cesse and Eco accused Rvro of adultery, "and he hasn't owned up to it." Cufe lamented, "We just don't care for one another anymore." The next Prayer Meeting was chaired by Sokhvhvtke. Cesse and Eco did not attend. The pastor came in late and sat in the minister's bench as far south as possible. His participation was minimal.

Fuswv attended this Prayer Meeting, and during invitation she came forward. Since Rvro was the only minister present, he had to preside over the rededication ritual. He approached Fuswv at the mercy seat and asked her for a statement. In a trembling voice, she offered an apology for hurting anyone's feelings and for offending anyone with the things she had said. No one challenged her motivations or her statement. The ritual continued with handshaking and reinstatement. A prayer song was sung, and Rvro stood to deliver the second message. His message was uncharacteristically introspective and brief. He was candid about the turmoil that the congregation was experiencing and about how feelings were running hot. He concluded his message by stating that outside forces were acting against them all. "Someone wants us to stumble, they want to see us fall." He stated that someone was "witching" Eufaula.[6]

Rvro's appeal to witchcraft may be viewed as an attempt to move the onus away from himself and the congregation. The situation at Eufaula was indeed serious. By fixing the blame away from the participants themselves, there would be perhaps less personal risk to face and therefore more willingness to work for resolution. Laying the blame elsewhere, however, does not preclude the need for the corrective process; rather, it only delays the process. Interpersonal disagreements would continue to accumulate and would be made public again.

Eufaula's disequilibrium was quite entrenched. Goffman's (1967:19) observation is helpful: "The image of equilibrium is apt here because the length and intensity of the corrective effort is nicely adapted to the persistence and intensity of the threat." Eufaula's enduring ennui would require intense corrective effort; a substantial offering was needed. Fuswv's offering was necessary, yet in itself it was not enough to bring about the next move in the corrective process: acceptance and resolution. After the meeting, I spoke with Rvro and Kono about the service. I asked if they thought that Fuswv's apology would begin to make things right. They responded, "She always apologizes, but still goes on and does it again." Neither expressed much hope that anything was changing.

When it was beginning to appear that the situation would go unchanged indefinitely, a new actor, Wotko ("Raccoon"), entered the drama. Wotko appeared at a Prayer Meeting that next month. In his midfifties, Wotko is Rvro's stepson, the son of Rvro's deceased wife, Fuco. Wotko's wife, Hvlpvtv ("Alligator"), is "wind" clan. She and Wotko have several children, but it is their two grandchildren who accompany them to church.

Wotko grew up in Eufaula Church and was ordained there as a deacon and then later as a minister. His inclination to travel about leading revivals got him into trouble with his family as well as his church. His mother, Fuco, felt that he was spending too much time traveling, and she publicly urged him to serve at Eufaula. He ignored her pleas. Soon after, Wotko's mother became ill, and Rvro had to take her to a hospital in Texas. Since Rvro's absence would leave Eufaula without a chair for the upcoming Big Meeting, Rvro asked Wotko to "fulfill the pulpit" while he took Fuco to the hospital. Wotko refused because of his commitment to lead a revival in Oklahoma City that weekend. A pastor from a sister church explained, "Wotko went against the church and went up there, and that's what they tied him up on, cause he was disobedient to the church." Eufaula circulated letters to the area churches, stating that Wotko was "disobedient to the church" and that Eufaula no longer endorsed him as a minister. Wotko had a falling out with his mother and left town without warning. He went on to pastor two different non-Seminole churches. He had been away from the Seminole Baptist community for about seven years before his return.

At the invitation during that first Prayer Meeting he attended, Wotko responded and came forward. In his carefully worded statement, he said that he came forward to repent "if he was in need of it." He said he was aware that some people thought that he needed to repent, although he did not feel the need. In his view he had been absent from the Seminole Baptist community "carrying on the Lord's work as a missionary among the Indian people of Oklahoma." Having fulfilled that work, he was "returning to carry on the work at Eufaula." After his statement, the head deacon did not challenge him or question his motives. To the contrary, he said he was pleased that Wotko was back and welcomed Wotko. Several other members voiced their assent. Others, particularly Rvro, sat silent, perhaps remembering the unresolved face work leading to Wotko's departure.

Wotko became an immediate player in the social life of the congregation. Only a few members held his past sins against him. Within two months, Wotko was placed in the rotation, along with Rvro and Cesse, for chairing meetings. Wotko is a relatively young man, and he has a lot of energy. He is a dynamic, charismatic preacher who greatly inspires listeners. After Wotko's return, stated concerns about the congregation were less public, and the positive outlook appeared to have much to do with Wotko's charisma and leadership. He provided a distraction from the conflicts the church was in the midst of, and many members expressed renewed optimism. However, there were still unresolved incidents, and still no pastor had been appointed for the current year.

There were now three potential candidates for the position of pastor: Rvro, Cesse, and Wotko. Rvro was the most likely person for the position, given that he had been pastor for about twenty years. Surely he had weathered similar social storms during that time. However, the current situation was disruptive enough that a pivotal move (offering) needed to be made, and Rvro had been the target of many of the recent challenges. Perhaps another man was needed to provide the necessary leadership to restore equilibrium and, hence, repair the damaged congregational face. For this reason, Cesse was a viable candidate for the position. He had been faithfully fulfilling his work as minister at Eufaula for the previous three years. He was very deliberate in his work, though he lacked the sophistication and charisma of Wotko. Thus Wotko was also a strong candidate. His dynamism, optimism, and freshness were contagious. Only a few members were not yet willing to trust him completely, but more time was necessary for him to prove himself.

Tacit campaigns were under way. Members openly voiced their opinions about who should be Eufaula's pastor. The candidates' preaching was becoming more expressive. Rvro was preaching longer than usual and spoke with greater emphasis. Cesse began preparing sermons in advance, consulting Bible commentaries and often awkwardly quoting from them in his sermons. Neither man, though, could match Wotko in preaching ability. Wotko's reputation was widening. Visitors commented regularly about the "good messages" he preached. Wotko was especially persuasive when he was visiting neighboring churches for their Fourth Sunday Meetings.

During refreshments after a March Prayer Meeting of a Big Meeting weekend, the conversation turned toward witchcraft. Rvro, knowing that I was learning Mvskoke, offered me a list of Mvskoke words. I went through the list with Cufe and Rvro. Cesse and Sokhvhvtke were also in on the conversation. Most notable was our discussion about the two Mvskoke words for "owl." *Opv* is the barred owl, and *'stekene* is the great-horned owl. Rvro said the great-horned owl is the one that says " *'stekene e e*," and he imitated the sound. Cufe responded, "So that's you making that noise out here." Rvro went on to tell me that *'stekene* is the same word that is used for "witch," that is, one who can manipulate supernatural forces to his or her advantage. Cufe said, "They say that a witch can turn himself into an owl, that's why I asked Rvro if it was him making that noise." Additional witchcraft stories were then told. One person said that the way the witch was able to fly as a *'stekene* was to first disembowel himself, leaving the entrails behind when he flies off. This prompted the story of the *'stekene* who could not remember the proper medicine song and so could not get his entrails back inside his body.

When a medicine song is sung, it is imperative that it be sung without error. Should an error be made, the singer stops the song at the point of the error and sings the song backward until the beginning, where the song is begun again. The *'stekene* of the story had sung the song almost entirely through when he lost his place. As a result, he was only partially successful in putting his entrails back into place, and feathers could still be seen on the back of his neck. He walked home, holding his entrails in place with his hands. He arrived home, and his family saw him clutching his partially removed entrails and rushed him to the clinic. While waiting in the emergency room for the doctor to see him, the *'stekene* remembered his place in the song and sang it backward to the beginning, where he began anew. This time the song was sung correctly. His entrails were restored, and the feathers on his neck were replaced with hair. The *'stekene* then walked out of the clinic as a man.

During a lull in our conversation, I heard Nokose, at the other end of the table, talking about a white-footed dog (also a form that a witch can take) that he had seen recently walking on Eufaula grounds. Wotko joked that when it left, he saw Cufe's footprints. Rvro said that some witch doctors get there power from Satan. He went on: "They want to hurt people. They are jealous. If they see something you have, they'll try to tear you down, make you lose it, little by little." He described how people will hang a specially prepared owl feather above the main door of their homes to warn of approaching supernatural dangers. "If they've been doctored by someone who knows how, they will let you know if someone is trying to put you to sleep.[7] They'll flap on the wall, it will sound just like a bird in flight. It will keep making the noise until you wake up. If they put you to sleep, they'll scratch you, I don't know with what, and they'll leave four, not three, not five, but four lines on your leg or arm. The scratches will show up in four days."

During another lull, we heard Wotko narrating, with great animation, an event he had recently experienced: "So I said to him, 'I am a Christian, this is a Christian home, I don't want any of your ungodliness around and if you don't leave, I'm going to call down God on you and you know what he'll do, he'll burn your tail, now you just leave and never come back.'" At first I thought Wotko was talking about some drunk who had come to bother him. As the conversation continued, it became clear that he had been speaking of (to) a 'stekene.

In another account, Penwv told of a friend who lived by a Stomp grounds. This friend had been sitting on her porch when she saw a dog walking by. The dog walked over to the neighboring house (the house of a young pastor who partici-pated in Stomp grounds activities). The dog climbed up on the porch, and the woman said that "in the time it took her to blink," that dog had become the pastor (the dog was the pastor in the form of a dog). The conversation continued with state-ments to the effect that pastors can be witches and that there will be pastors in hell. Wotko offered: "There is strong power from the devil. It is easier to fly around than walk a straight path." In these conversations, it was interesting to note who, through joking behavior, was implicitly accused of the possi-bility for witchcraft. Certainly, witchcraft was on the members' minds. It would soon again be used as an explanation for the disequilibrium being experienced.

Two days later was the Eufaula Big Meeting. During the afternoon break Penwv, the church secretary, prepared letters to be distributed to representatives of the neighboring Seminole churches. These letters were the official announcements that Wotko was in full fellowship again and had full authority to preach. Members of other area churches remembered the events resulting in Wotko's hasty departure years earlier, and they needed to know that Eufaula had at last resolved the incident amicably.

The next month and a half were unremarkable. Rvro, Cesse, and Wotko rotated chairing the meetings. The campaigning for the position of pastor had become less aggressive. Rvro and Cesse were back in their more familiar preaching forms, whereas Wotko continued to impress visitors with his preaching. Rvro announced that the women's leader trainees had fulfilled their training and would be installed the following month.

Now, five months into the year, the members were finally prepared to appoint a pastor, at the monthly business meeting. Members expected that Rvro, Cesse, and Wotko would be placed in the running and that a majority vote would put one of them in the position. As it turned out, Wotko was not even in the contest. Repeating his previous transgressions, Wotko failed to attend this important business meeting, choosing instead to preach at a revival that night. Cufe reported that Wotko was not even considered because he put the other church commitment in front of his commitment to his own congregation. Cufe thought it likely that Wotko would have won the voting had he been present at the meeting. To further compound the matter, Cesse suggested that the church simply appoint either Rvro or himself rather than hold an election. Rvro balked at this suggestion and called for a "race" between Cesse and himself.

The actual selection process was embroiled in controversy. According to Rvro, he requested that a vote be taken so that the winner would receive a clear mandate to serve. Cesse and Eco interpreted Rvro's request for a race as a show of his confidence, knowing that he would defeat Cesse "in the fleshly way." A vote was taken and resulted in a tie. The normal procedure for breaking a tie is for the pastor to cast a vote. (This is the only time the pastor votes in business meetings.) However, because the issue being considered was the selection of pastor, Penwv—who, as secretary, does not normally vote—offered to break the tie. At this point Cesse abruptly withdrew his name from the race. Rvro, if by no other means but attrition, was installed to serve as pastor for the remainder of the year. Cesse and Eco left the meeting angry.

At the lightly attended Prayer Meeting (Kono, Penwv, Tolose, and Sokhvhvtke were conspicuously absent) two days after this business meeting, members were still unsettled about the decision. At least three of the members present at the business meeting told me that Cesse had in fact received more votes than Rvro and had then immediately and inexplicably "resigned" from the position. Cesse and Eco, though, told a different version of what had occurred. Cesse said that he knew how Penwv was going to vote and so, to save face, he withdrew his name before the final vote was cast.

While refreshments were being prepared for this Prayer Meeting, a remarkable event occurred. Several men were engaged in informal conversation when their attention was directed to some movement on the dirt road coming into the church grounds. Under the bright streetlight, right next to an empty camp house, a solitary animal was behaving curiously. One of the men suggested that the animal was a possum, since there were plenty of them around. Another thought it was a skunk. But it was neither. The strange animal walked upright, pacing like a small man with arms folded behind his back, moving in small circles. It would stand motionless for a few moments and then circle again. Distracted conversation continued as the animal's curious behavior demanded attention. Suddenly the animal leapt from the ground, took wing, circled the streetlight, and flew away from sight. Cesse declared, " *'Stekene!*" The animal walking around in the light had been a great-horned owl, or in Mvskoke, *'stekene* ("witch"). The group of men immediately dispersed. Cesse hurried to warn the others at the camp house where refreshments were being prepared. The news of this *'stekene* and its peculiar behavior was then spread among all those present. The children were warned to get into Fuswv's camp house, where refreshments were being prepared, and stay there.

Greatly concerned, most of the members gathered in Fuswv's camp house. The gathering was unusually quiet. Eco and Fuswv refused to go back outdoors, sending some men out to the car to get things that they normally would have gotten themselves. While the participants were gathered for the meal, someone observed that Rvro was conspicuously absent. Although it was not voiced explicitly, the simple inquiry into Rvro's whereabouts in the current context was a tacit accusation that he may have been the witch that had appeared as the *'stekene.* Cesse ate refreshments quickly and then went back out, announcing that he would keep watch for the *'stekene.* It did not return that evening. Refreshments ended early, and people departed quickly.

In the next weeks, members puzzled over these events. Wotko missed several Prayer Meetings. At least one member thought that his absence was a direct response to his disappointment over not being selected as pastor and that he was expressing his disappointment to the congregation. However, he was present during the installation of the women's leaders. The installation service attracted many visitors. Wotko's attendance was likely motivated by his concern for Eufaula's congregational face. Cesse and Eco, still upset about the selection of pastor, participated in the Prayer Meetings yet departed without sharing in the refreshments. Eco said: "Some people only come for the refreshments. That's not church anyway."

A pastor was in place, even if he was not the one that members had thought would be serving in the position. Witchcraft was again being blamed for the "strife" the congregation was experiencing. The presence of the 'stekene only reinforced suspicions. A heles hayv ("medicine maker") was engaged to search the church grounds to find the "medicine" that was causing the strife. On several occasions I asked about the results of this search and was informed, "I will tell you when things cool down a bit." Eventually the heles hayv found what he claimed was the source of the strife. His explanation was apparently adequate: his pronouncement may be interpreted as an acceptable offering in the corrective process. The "strife" abated, and Eufaula's social life proceeded, for a time, without public incident. Equilibrium was reestablished; interpersonal conflict was no longer at a level requiring public corrective interchange.

For the time being, the competition for the position of pastor subsided. Rvro fulfilled the position without innovation or surprise. Wotko's decision to attend the revival rather than the business meeting proved to be a risky venture. It is difficult to speculate about his motivation for missing the meeting at which the pastor would be appointed. Perhaps Wotko thought that the congregation would be impressed (i.e., that his face would be enhanced) by his service to the larger church community. Or perhaps he discounted the congregation's impressions because of his effect within the larger Seminole Baptist church system. Perhaps Wotko was trying to enhance his face vis-à-vis the larger church community. Wotko may view himself as an "evangelist," that is, one known for his dynamic preaching abilities, a circuit preacher, rather than as a congregational pastor. At this time the community does not sustain such a position. Eufaula members saw his action as a blatant disregard of the congregation's authority, the same sin that he had previously succumbed to. Certainly Wotko must have realized that if he desired to achieve congregational and community endorsement—that is, to support his social face—he would have to do so through the established avenues. His credibility had to be the result of his effectiveness as a Eufaula minister or, better still, pastor.

Cesse revealed to me later that he viewed his withdrawal as the only avenue he had to save his face in that situation. He felt that the members had already decided against him, and he desired to avoid the humiliation of a public defeat. He still wanted to serve as pastor but felt that the congregation was not being sensitive to the "urging of the Spirit" and that their choice was based on *vpeswv* ("flesh") rather than *poyvfekcv* ("spirit"). He and Eco faulted the members for the way the selection process occurred.

During the Prayer Meeting the week after the installation of the women's leaders, Sokhvhvtke, who had been sitting in the listeners' section, came forward during the invitation. He stated that he was being tempted to "return to the world." His confession referred to his temptation to participate in such worldly behavior as drinking alcoholic beverages, playing softball, stickball, or bingo, or participating in Stomp grounds activities. Sokhvhvtke's offering may have been the result of a challenge to his behavior (though there was no public challenge at this or the previous Prayer Meeting), or it may have been "preventative" face work, warning the congregation that he was tempted to participate or had participated in the forbidden behavior. The head deacon accepted his statement and offered no challenge. He was reintegrated with the handshaking ritual, and Rvro returned his deacon's cane to him at that time.

The next few months were relatively uneventful in the social life of Eufaula. A Big Meeting was hosted, and Fourth Sunday Meetings were routine. The more exciting incidents were occurring at neighboring Seminole churches. On the way home from a Fourth Sunday Meeting at a neighboring church, Cufe mentioned various Seminole churches and the problems they were having. He noted that many churches were having trouble with their pastors. He said that it was not right for a pastor—or anyone else, for that matter—to leave his church as the result of some interpersonal conflict. The situation needed to be "made right, settled," before a person moved on. Too many pastors and members, he said, were not following that ideal. Cufe explained that up until 1989, Eufaula had a rule on the books[8] that said its members could never leave that church and transfer to another. Now it was possible for a person to transfer; however, it had yet to be done at Eufaula.

Neighboring churches, however, were a different story. At one sister church, two teenage boys got into a fistfight on the church grounds. The father of one of the boys then allegedly beat up the other boy. This event split that church into two factions (along family lines). One of the factions stopped attending the church. At another church, two members, one of them a deacon, came to blows during a business meeting. The deacon left that church and took a few of its members with him and started a new church, Hvcce Rvkko ("Big Creek"). Clearly, disruptive incidents are not unique to Eufaula. It should be noted also that in both of the above situations, even though individual members withdrew from a particular congregation, they nevertheless still participated within the larger Seminole Baptist system. The obligatory nature of the gatherings constrains Seminoles to continue interaction even if it is within a different congregation.

Meanwhile at Eufaula, affairs progressed uneventfully. Under Rvro's leadership the situation was stable, if uninspired. The membership was still aging, and the number of members was still low. The congregation's face, though not in need of correction, was in need of enhancement.

Wotko again began taking a more active role, occasionally chairing Prayer Meetings and some Fourth Sunday Meetings. Wotko was becoming more comfortable with life at Eufaula and was beginning to assert himself in the social life of the congregation. He was gaining favor with some members, and his reputation in the larger Seminole Baptist community was spreading. In an August Prayer Meeting, Wotko made an interesting announcement. He said that he was going to be preaching things that people might not have heard before, and he added that they might not like to hear what he had to say. He said: "The elders didn't have it all right. I respect the elders, and I know that this church would not have been here if it wasn't for the elders, but they didn't have the depth of understanding. You see, God was merciful to them because they couldn't read. They didn't have all the resources available to them that explains the Bible. You may not like to hear what I'm preaching, you may not have come to hear this kind of message, but this is the message that I'm going to preach." Wotko was engaging in preventative face work, preparing the people to consider innovations in the conceptual frameworks that organize their social situations. Wotko, viewing himself as a reformer, was inviting the congregation to join him in a crusade to revitalize Eufaula's stagnant face.

Two months passed without any significant events. In December 1993, members prepared to appoint the pastor for the coming year. The appointment would occur in January, and the members were determined to avoid the repeated postponements of the previous year. The sentiment seemed to favor the appointment of Wotko for chair. At the second Prayer Meeting of December, after Cesse's preaching, Cufe went forward. He said he felt he needed to be "recharged and reenergized." He added that he had not been working as he should have been. Perhaps Cufe's coming forward was preventative face work, an attempt to thwart any tensions regarding the upcoming selection of the pastor. The typical routine followed for giving him the handshake of fellowship.

That next month the congregation made a bold move. During the January business meeting the members decided to appoint a new pastor. Wotko had garnered enough support to be elected as Eufaula's pastor. The decision was unanimous— inevitable, according to some. Given Wotko's penchant for leading revivals, the congregation appointed Rvro to serve as the assistant pastor with the directive to "fulfill the pulpit" when Wotko was absent.

Rvro did not appear too distressed over his lost position. When I spoke to him about it, he said that he was actually relieved. "There's just so much backbiting. Now I can step back and let someone else take it for a while." He concluded by saying that this was the church's decision and that he would go along with it.

Eufaula's appointment of a new pastor may be interpreted as a strategy of *congregational face enhancement*. Some members were eager to revitalize the congregation: membership numbers were down; few young people were ever present at the gatherings. Wotko, himself a relatively young and cosmopolitan man, might appeal to the missing generation. It was generally agreed that his sermons were quite stirring and inspiring. Increasing attendance was a sure avenue of congregational face enhancement. The new pastor held the potential.

The first two months of the new year were ones of optimism and renewal. Attendance at the Fourth Sunday Meetings was higher than in the previous year. Even Lvmhe began coming to Prayer Meetings. He rededicated one evening and was given his seat back among the believers. Wotko's reputation for preaching a stirring sermon was gaining. Eufaula members spoke with confidence about the potential for the congregation's growth. Wotko chaired the meetings with great energy and charisma.

Interpersonal conflict was not consuming the energies of Eufaula at this time. Wotko took advantage of this calm period and of his leadership position. He began to assert his authority to institute a program of change. If he could revitalize Eufaula by attracting more Fourth Sunday visitors and new members, both the congregation's and his own face would be enhanced. Wotko's experience in non-Seminole churches gave him a catalogue of options, or innovations, to promote within Eufaula.

In late February, Wotko instituted a "Second Sunday Meeting." The meeting format was to be identical to that of a Fourth Sunday Meeting except that it occurred on the second rather than the fourth Sunday of the rotation. This meeting was not intended to replace the Fourth Sunday Meeting; rather, it would provide an additional opportunity for gathering. Wotko explained his rationale for the institution of the new meetings:

"There is no convenient place for Eufaula members to attend on the second Sundays. Members are scattered everywhere. Here we can gather in one place." During a Prayer Meeting, Wotko also suggested that the congregation should begin a "puppet ministry" to attract the children into church life. He suggested several other ideas to revitalize the congregation.

At a summer Prayer Meeting, during the deacon's meeting when the work was being distributed, Cufe asked Kono to fulfill a work (to take up the offering basket after the collection and to count the money). Kono refused and said, "The Lord has laid it on my heart to come forward to rededicate." After Cesse's message, Kono came forward for a rededication. Following the ritual, Wotko, from the pulpit, said that he wanted to clear something up. "I don't want to put anyone down, I don't want to offend anyone, but the Bible says when a person repents, his sins are forgotten." He went on to say that Kono should have fulfilled the work because whatever Kono had done was forgiven and forgotten. "Maybe Kono had heard otherwise. I just want to make sure that there is understanding here. I didn't learn this teaching from the *stehvtke* ["white people"] or the *stelvste* ["black people"] but from right here" [pointing to the Bible]." After he finished, Fuswv, the head women's leader, stood up and addressed the assembly. She said: "What Kono did was right. He probably heard it from the old people." She recounted how long ago, two deacons who were to be ordained failed to show up at their ordination. The church dropped them. "It only took one sin, and they were gone. This is where Kono heard it. I know that in the old days people were a lot more strict and that things have changed, but this is how we used to do it and this is what we believe." She was very emotional when she spoke, almost coming to tears. Wotko was attempting a reinterpretation of established practice, but Fuswv and the others refused to accept it.

In another attempt to innovate, Wotko read from the Bible in his devotional reading at an October Prayer Meeting: "Don't rob the storehouse of God or you will be cursed." He went on to say that the Indian churches were cursed because they had not been giving their tithes and offerings. "*Osketowa?* [What are we going to do?] The old people left us this church, and it was a thriving church. What are we going to leave our young ones?" He told stories of how at Bowlegs they offered a tithe to the pastor, but the pastor said he didn't want it, that his rewards were in heaven. Wotko said: "That sounds good, that sounds very religious. But it's against what God says to do." He said: "Indian churches have too many treasures. We need to line up with God's Word. We need to stop using the three offering baskets and go to one. Some people say that will mean less money, but that's not so. We need to take a percentage out of this offering to pay the gas and lights, and so fourth. We make New Year's resolutions, maybe this should be one. I'll give you three months to pray about this, and come January we'll see about this. I'm giving you plenty of warning." He concluded his devotion by saying, "You need to take care of your pastor." Members later interpreted this statement as an intimation that Wotko was asking them to pay him for his services as pastor, just as Anglo pastors were paid.

Several members began to voice dissatisfaction with Wotko's approach. Following a Prayer Meeting of a Fourth Sunday Meeting weekend, Rvro, Cufe, and Kono gathered while refreshments were being prepared. Jokes were told and news was shared. The conversation turned to the Fasting service to be held the next morning. Wotko would not be around to lead it, and he had asked Cufe to chair it. This rankled the three, especially Rvro. He was critical of his stepson, stating that although Wotko is considered a good preacher, he "doesn't practice what he preaches." He concluded his critique of Wotko by saying to me, "The church is getting slack, becoming more like yual's [the Anglo's] church." Cufe added: "You know what's going on here? He's [Wotko] trying to phase this service out." The Second Sunday Meetings were also addressed. These three men concluded that Wotko was working to move Eufaula toward the Anglo model of weekly meetings, Sunday school, and no

Fasting services and at the same time remove Eufaula from the Fourth Sunday rotation.

Wotko came into Eufaula with ideas of how to revitalize the congregation. Members characterized Wotko's innovations as an attempt to make Eufaula "more modern," that is, like Anglo churches. He was not the first to attempt this strategy. It had been tried by several other congregations within the rotation, to varying degrees of success. In fact, one can rank the various churches on a continuum of "modernization": Spring Church is on one end, whereas Eufaula is toward the other end. This "modernization" is not simply acculturation; rather, it is an aspect of a process to adjust cultural structures to a changing socioeconomic context.

The structures that govern social occasions are dynamic. Cultural symbols are continually being reinterpreted, phased out, or introduced to better meet changing circumstances. Members experiment with various symbols, redefining and reinterpreting them to ensure their continued efficacy and to bolster congregational face. What remains constant is that these cultural symbols and categories maintain the social community. Cultural symbols are the syntax of social organization. Social participants continuously negotiate the meaning of these symbols.

How well the symbols fit or anticipate the changing situation is certainly a factor in the congregation's face. "Modernization" is a strategy used in varying degrees in all of the churches. Certainly the adoption of Christianity was a modernization. A Stomp grounds participant recently spoke of the practice of Communion in churches as a "modernization" of taking medicine at the Stomp grounds. At issue is how far the congregation is willing to pursue that strategy and how far the larger Seminole Baptist community is willing to allow them. Spring Church has taken this route the furthest, at the expense of being marginalized by many of the other congregations. Many Seminole Baptists do not consider Spring Church as an option within the rotation because it is viewed as an Anglo church (during a Fourth Sunday Meeting one visitor suggested that I, an Anglo, would be more comfortable at Spring Church).

Wotko continued to attempt innovations, and the congregation continued to refuse them. Second Sunday Meetings were held for only four months before being abandoned. Rather than becoming like Fourth Sunday Meetings, Second Sunday Meetings looked and felt like Prayer Meetings, and the composition of the participants mirrored that of the weekly Prayer Meetings. They were attended almost exclusively by members, with no more than three visitors at one of these meetings. The rest of the church community did not consider the meetings to be an option in the rotation, and the innovation was dropped.

In October, the opportunity arose for Eufaula to enhance its face without "modernization." Instead, drawing from the past, they hosted a Memorial service for a Eufaula member, Opv, who had died the previous year. This Memorial service was the first that Eufaula had hosted in more than forty years. It took place during the afternoon services of Eufaula's Fourth Sunday Meeting. More than seventy-five people attended, including five visiting pastors. Cesse explained the purpose of a Memorial service: "Sometimes a person just carries a memory in his pocket that he can't let go of. The Memorial helps him to lay that person to rest." The service format resembled that of Fourth Sunday Meetings, with the addition of eulogies. The front pews were reserved for family members (and clan kin) of the deceased. The Communion table was situated in front of the pulpit and was draped in black cloth. On top, a photo of the deceased was displayed between flowers. Two visiting pastors eulogized her, and the second pastor gave an invitation.

At the beginning of the Memorial service Wotko, who chaired the meetings, apologized in advance for any errors that might be made, since this was his first Memorial service to chair and it had been many years since Eufaula had hosted one.[9] Given the high attendance at the service, it was apparent that the Memorial service was valued by the larger Seminole Baptist community. Eufaula's face was being enhanced, and Wotko's apology was a bit of preventative face work.

During this same month a request came in to Eufaula from a neighboring church, Nvrkvpv Hvcce ("Creek Middle"), to "loan them Cesse" for a six-month term as pastor. This church was experiencing its own conflicts. Years ago this church "came up on its own," meaning that its break from the mother congregation was not amicable. The pastor who had founded the church left his wife and married another woman (Seminole Baptist pastors are not allowed to continue to serve if they go through a divorce). That pastor later left Nvrkvpv Hvcce, and the church was without a pastor for almost three years. During that time deacons usually chaired meetings.

Eufaula members voted to allow Cesse to serve as interim pastor. After a month of serving as pastor, Cesse described the situation at that church: "You've seen how [dead] snakes lie in pieces on the ground, each joint is separate, laying here and there and the head maybe way over there. But if you put them all together and join the head, the snake will come together and crawl off. Now that the church has a head, it's coming together."[10] Cesse saw himself as that head.

During these weeks another incident arose at Eufaula. There had been rumors that one of the deacons, Sokhvhvtke, was playing bingo. This is considered inappropriate behavior for any member, but particularly for a worker. During a deacons' meeting Wotko confronted Sokhvhvtke about it. Sokhvhvtke "owned up to it" and admitted that he had been playing bingo. Wotko asked for his cane. Sokhvhvtke agreed to refrain from his deacon duties until this "got worked out." He was to continue as a member but not serve as a deacon. However, after that meeting, Sokhvhvtke did not return to a Eufaula gathering. Rather than concede an offering, Sokhvhvtke withdrew from the congregation. Members soon got word that Sokhvhvtke, after a few weeks of apostasy, was back Stomp dancing and was involved with a group that was trying to resurrect the defunct New Tulsa Stomp grounds. This was quite a radical move, yet not unprecedented. It represented a reinvestment in an alternate, competing form of the Seminole community. Sokhvhvtke was now relying on a different set of individuals to define his social face.

The next three months were rather calm at Eufaula. One notable event occurred during a Prayer Meeting when a young woman, Tolose's adopted daughter, "accepted Christ" and requested baptism. Rather than the ritual handshaking of a rededication, Tolose and Fuswv escorted her back to the sacristy and spoke with her for a few minutes to communicate to her the seriousness of her request. While the new convert and the women's leaders were in the sacristy, the congregation rose for a prayer of thanksgiving and help for the new convert. The three came back and reported that she was sincere and desired to be baptized as soon as possible. She had requested that Wotko fulfill the work of baptism.

In January the congregation voted to repeat the selection of pastor from the previous year: Wotko would serve as chair, and Rvro would be his *vpoktv* ("twin"). By early February, however, Rvro was no longer preaching. In fact, he was sitting as a floor member. On inquiry he explained: "Oh, I removed my name for a bit, they didn't remove it. I felt that I needed to until things got straightened around. I was humble for a long time. Then I couldn't take no more. I had all I could stand." Later Cufe explained that Rvro had stopped preaching because of "lust of the flesh" (adultery). Rvro was accused and later confronted about it by Wotko. Cufe went on: "Rvro owned up to it. So the church asked him to sit out until all the parties involved could make peace. That hasn't happened yet. The church didn't put any deadline or anything. It just has to be worked out." The completion of the corrective process was contingent on "peace being made." This meant, Cufe explained, that Rvro and his mistress would publicly confess their sin and that Wotko would pronounce absolution. Rvro was unwilling to do this and was content instead to participate as a floor member. Rvro's absence from the pulpit was causing a few hardships, however.

Wotko continued to be called on to lead revivals and was often away during Eufaula Prayer Meetings. When this happened, Eufaula called on the pastor of a sister church to chair these meetings.

Cesse's interim service at Nvrkvpv Hvcce was nearing its end. Nvrkvpv Hvcce wrote to Eufaula and requested to use Cesse for another six months. Yet though the Eufaula members had been quite willing to let him go for the first six months, things had now changed. The head women's leader lamented, "We had three chairmen, now we don't have one." Wotko was often off leading revivals, Rvro had stepped down from the pulpit, and Cesse was serving another parish. The members were reluctant to let Cesse go. Regarding Cesse's desire to serve as pastor, many members asked: "If he wanted to be pastor, why did he refuse it?" As noted earlier, when Cesse and Rvro had been placed up against each other for the position of pastor at Eufaula, Cesse withdrew after a tie vote was cast. Many members interpreted his action as turning down the position. The talk was that Eufaula would deny the Nvrkvpv Hvcce request.

After much discussion in the business meeting devoted to this issue, it was suggested that the best solution would be to have Cesse remove his name (transfer his membership) from Eufaula and take it to Nvrkvpv Hvcce. This way he could do what he thought was right, and Nvrkvpv Hvcce could then appoint him as pastor with full authority. Cesse did elect to remove his name from Eufaula.[11] He left Eufaula as a floor member and was to be reordained at Nvrkvpv Hvcce. Cesse and Eco felt quite strongly about fulfilling the work at Nvrkvpv Hvcce. Cesse said that he was fulfilling the third directive he had received in his hospital vision. He was "getting his house in order" by leaving Eufaula and by serving as pastor of Nvrkvpv Hvcce, his new *Mekusvpkv coko* ("prayer *house*").

The social life of Eufaula, as well as that of several other Seminole Baptist congregations, is fraught with interpersonal conflict, yet the church system has mechanisms in place to ensure Seminole

Baptist community maintenance. Eufaula's social life consisted of episodes of face work by participants within the social occasions. Appeal to face, both personal and congregational, during occasions provides the dynamic mechanisms to manage conflict and promote cooperation within the congregation and the community. As shown, the episodes can be analyzed in terms of Goffman's corrective interchange: challenge, offering, acceptance, and gratitude. Social occasions—namely, Prayer Meetings, Fourth Sunday Meetings, and Big Meetings—are the setting for the face work. The entire Seminole Baptist church system is built upon the obligatory nature of social occasions, which participants refer to as "fulfilling the work." This mechanism compels members to interact, to expose face to other members and subject it to scrutiny and affirmation or correction. The corrective interchange, a vital aspect of these occasions, has become institutionalized and conventionalized: sermons and announcements give occasion for *challenges*; the invitation allows for penitents to make an *offering*; the ritual handshake is a vehicle for *acceptance*; and participation within the congregational life allows those who have been restored to express *gratitude*. The social life of Eufaula demonstrates specific uses of these mechanisms to accomplish social work. This social life is interdependent with cultural structures.

Cultural symbols structure a common, binding universe of meaning. They provide an integrating set of definitions that organize gatherings. These symbols, as was shown in the above account, are not static structures but are subject to reinterpretation and innovation. Members regularly negotiate the meaning of symbols, ensuring a viable response to the changing contexts. Suggested innovations are often rejected. What is important, however, is that negotiations are ongoing and that innovations are adopted when the congregation and the community judge them beneficial.

The Seminole Baptists may be understood as a *traditional* community in spite of continuous cultural change. The real demarcation of community is the interactions of people—not patterns of traits. For Seminole Baptists, cultural structures supporting church occasions obligate people into face-to-face social interaction. Cultural and social elements are mutually interdependent in maintaining a *traditional community*, that is, a dynamic social group sharing a history and demonstrating adaptive vitality.

It has been more than a year since Cesse left Eufaula and since Rvro stepped down from preaching. Recently, Sokhvhvtke, the deacon, returned from his apostasy. He came forward for a rededication and is attending Eufaula as a floor member. Some members would like to see him restored to his position as deacon. Wotko, still serving as pastor, insists that Sokhvhvtke needs to prove himself for a time before being reinstated. Cesse was ordained at Nvrkvpv Hvcce and is currently serving as pastor. He and Eco visit Eufaula regularly. Rvro is attending Eufaula as a floor member and shows no sign of providing the necessary offering to complete the corrective process that would return him to a leadership position. Wotko's enthusiasm is predictably quenched. He continues to lead revivals, yet the promise of increased membership and vitality at Eufaula appears to be unfulfilled. The sister congregation that split as a result of a fistfight has come to a reconciliation, and both factions are gathering together again. The new church, Hvvce Rvkko, is still holding meetings. It remains to be seen if the church community will recognize its legitimacy.

CHAPTER 8

Discussion and Conclusion

Communities require maintenance. A dynamic process fraught with peril, social life is inherently precarious. Conflicting self-interests, varying personnel, and changing contexts require ongoing investment to sustain groups. The principal investment consists of culturally structured face-to-face encounters, gatherings, and social occasions involving group members. These encounters—formal and informal, focused and unfocused—must be of adequate frequency and duration to establish social identities and to integrate individuals. As group members interact, their behavior is subject to evaluation and is exposed to community sanctions. Individual and group behaviors are interpreted, expectations are manipulated, and social action is effected. Community maintenance is a dialectical process involving cultural and social factors: people come together and negotiate mutual expectations (situational proprieties), which in turn govern their interaction. The preceding chapters have demonstrated the interdependent cultural and social processes involved in the maintenance of the Seminole Baptist community. This chapter will contextualize the previous account, discussing other Native American adaptations of Christianity, the relationship of Seminole Baptists to the greater Baptist community, and the association of the Seminole churches with the contemporary Stomp grounds and the larger Seminole community.

Christianity among Other Native Americans

The Seminole Baptists, though of course Christian, are not assimilated into the dominant Anglo world. They maintain and participate in a community distinct from the non-Seminole world. The Seminole Baptist "Christian element" (Howard 1984:161) does not embody assimilation; rather, it is, in fact, a vehicle of *traditional* Seminole community (*traditional* implying a people with a history of social interaction adapting their cultural framework to changing external circumstances).

Given the Seminole Baptist example, it may be safe to assume that other Christian natives are not necessarily assimilated into the dominant system and that Christianity is not necessarily antithetical to tradition. Christian churches may function within other native communities to maintain social interactions structured in distinct ways and thus may be instrumental in maintaining their larger community. Unfortunately, there is little contemporary ethnographic treatment of Native American Christianity. There are, however, a few historical studies that allow some comparisons.

First, it should be conceded that, indeed, historically many natives did adopt Christianity as a vehicle for moving toward assimilation. Berkhofer (1965), among others, describes how natives embraced Christianity as a way of embracing "civilization." During the historical period, Christianity and civilization were not often separated, and no doubt, many individuals and bands successfully converted to civilization. Berkhofer (1965:11) describes how the dress and hairstyles of Native American converts reflected the assumption of "civilization." The spiritual dynamics of the inner man were understood such that when people had been touched by the gospel, their whole life was changed, including their culture, subsistence, values, language, and associations. Christianity implied a way of acting, dressing, speaking, and thinking. For many then, and perhaps for many now, adoption of Christianity is assumed to be an "either/or" proposition: either native pagan or civilized Christian, the outward appearance testifying to the inward change.[1] But as the present study has shown, there are other forms of native Christianity.

A very interesting historical account is William G. McLoughlin's work on the Cherokees (1994). While describing the adoption of Christianity by the Cherokees as being sporadic and at times discordant, he demonstrates how Christianity for the Cherokees, as for the Seminoles, became a vital element of Cherokee survival and revitalization. Among the Cherokees (as among the Seminoles), Methodist and Baptist missionaries had the most success of all the churches, probably for many of the same reasons as they did among the Seminoles (described in chapter 3). But neither church was completely successful, and a strong conservative faction of the tribe remained. McLoughlin (1994: 219ff) describes the unique Cherokee solution that melded this conservative faction with the full-blood Cherokee Christians into the Keetoowah Society, which functioned politically and socially. He convincingly demonstrates the connection between Cherokee Christianity and politics. Adoption of Christianity by the Cherokees did not bring about immediate social-structural change. Their incorporation of Christianity allowed traditional social and political structures to continue to function. McLoughlin's discussion provides some interesting comparisons; unfortunately, his account of the Cherokees ends in 1870. Hopefully, a contemporary account of the Cherokee situation will be forthcoming.

Another interesting account is Raymond J. DeMallie's (1984) discussion of perhaps the most famous Native American Christian, Black Elk, a Lakota Sioux. DeMallie (1984:92) makes some interesting observations: "Conversion to Christianity must not be understood as indicating loss of faith in traditional religion. . . . For Black Elk, as for most Lakotas, the acceptance of Christianity seems to have been a pragmatic decision, not an emotional conversion. . . . After the Christian religion came to be firmly established on the reservation, and Christian rituals and prayers became routine, it seems that for many Lakotas the sharp differences between traditional religion and Christianity began to blur." One of the pragmatic aspects was that in the early reservation days, Indians were required to belong to a church in order to receive ration books (Powers 1986:192). DeMallie recognized that for many Native Americans, adoption of Christianity did not necessarily imply loss or abandonment of tradition. Incorporated Christian beliefs may be interpreted as cultural innovations that are adaptive to changing social situations. DeMallie (1984:15) wrote:

> It is possible that one of the attractions that led Black Elk to Christianity was the access it provided to the social and material benefits of church life. From the beginning of the reservation period, the government had systematically suppressed all traditional social institutions. . . . Christian churches provided institutional structures that were not merely tolerated but encouraged by the government. . . . Such men's and women's sodalities as the Roman Catholic St. Joseph and St. Mary societies could function as replacements for traditional men's and women's societies that had been fundamental social building blocks in earlier times.

Moreover, for the Lakotas, "whole tiyospaye [bands] tended to join the same church, whatever denomination had established itself in the community" (Powers 1986:192). In these examples, the historical Lakota social institutions were converted into culturally meaningful ways through Catholic church-based societies and congregational membership. These church-based social groupings were acceptable from both the Lakota perspective and the dominant, federal government perspective. Similar to the way that the Seminole Baptist churches fulfill the social uses of the historical Seminole *etvlwvlke*, the Lakota social uses of church membership generally and the Catholic men's and women's societies particularly reflect the social uses of traditional Lakota social structures.

From these two additional examples it should be clear that Native American Christianity does not necessarily bring about acculturation and assimilation, even when that is the goal. More important, the examples expose the fact that other, non-Seminole groups of Native Americans have used Christianity to achieve traditional social goals. Certainly, more ethnographic treatments of contemporary Native American Christians are warranted.

One such contemporary Native American community whose investigation would no doubt prove fruitful is the Choctaws of south-central Oklahoma. Early in my field experience, I had a conversation with a Spring Church member whose wife is a Choctaw. This man frequently attended Choctaw Presbyterian churches with his wife. He described the church structure (based on a fourth Sunday rotation) as being very similar to that of the Seminole Baptists. The most notable exception that he noted was the obvious fact that the Indians were Choctaw, not Seminole, and therefore the services (including the hymns) were conducted in the Choctaw language. Recently I have spoken with a young Choctaw man who grew up in the Choctaw Presbyterian church system near Coalgate, Oklahoma (just south and east of Ada).[2] He identified the eleven-church presbytery as "Choctaw Cumberland Presbyterian." Church members in this system are almost exclusively Choctaw; its pastors are not seminary-trained but are locally identified and selected. Regarding these churches he said, "That's where all the Choctaw people were at." The young man tells how as a child, he was "surprised to find out that white people went to church." In his experience, "church" was this Choctaw church system. He observed that it is impossible for him to conceptualize his identity as Choctaw without consideration of his church life. For him, as for the Seminole Baptists, the Indian church system serves as a source of ethnic identity.

Additionally, the historical Choctaw society was centered around local family *iksa*. *Iksa* were "lineages based on common matrilineal descent" (Champagne 1992:26). Collections of *iksa* formed local villages, which maintained political autonomy. It would not be surprising to find a relationship between the social uses and affiliations of the historical *iksa* and the contemporary uses of and associations with specific churches of the Choctaw Cumberland Presbyterian system— in a way similar to the relationship between the Seminole Baptist churches and the historical *etvlwvlke*.

Seminole Baptists' Relationship to Non-Seminole Baptists

The highway that led me to Eufaula Church went past several non-Seminole Baptist churches, one of them just a few miles from Eufaula. When I first began my fieldwork in 1990, before I understood the social uses of the Seminole Baptist churches, I wondered why the Seminoles did not participate in these other Baptist churches. The location of these churches was more convenient for some members, the churches were well maintained, and they appeared vibrant.

Since the churches are identified as Baptist, I assumed that whether Seminole or not, these Christians would recognize some sense of shared identity, and indeed there are similarities. Yet these churches were not included in the Fourth Sunday rotation of the Seminole Baptists: cultural similarities do not necessarily result in shared social arrangements, just as shared cultural elements may not be interpreted in the same way by different groups. Culture and social interaction are interdependent in the maintenance of a community. Both must be shared by a group if there is to be some sense of community.

Although there are many similarities between the Seminole Baptists and their non-Seminole Baptist neighbors, there are also profound differences. The cultural differences between Seminole Baptist churches and non-Seminole Baptist churches are apparent from the onset. The arrangement of the physical compound of the Seminole Baptist churches is unique, understandably so, with the arrangement coming out of Seminole history. Non-Seminole Baptist churches do not have an attached arbor for outdoor services, nor are they necessarily oriented to the east. Inside the churches, the differences continue. Non-Seminole churches do not have pews along the walls and do not separate the sexes, the visitors and uninitiated, and the leaders. Few non-Seminole Baptist churches mark the beginning of their services with the ringing of a bell. The use of a cow-horn or seashell is unknown outside the Indian churches. In non-Seminole churches, Communion is usually distributed among the seated members; the altar at the front of the church serves as the table and is not moved to the physical center of the ceremony. Leadership positions in non-Seminole churches are also different, and again this is understandable considering that the Seminole positions were developed out of the historical leadership of the *etvlwv* system. In non-Seminole Baptist churches, the terms "pastor" and "minister" are synonymous. Most people (pastors may be women) who hold this position have been trained in a seminary or a Bible college. Although deacons are found in both traditions, there are no ordained women's leaders who oversee the spiritual and social life in the non-Seminole Baptist congregations. Anglo churches generally have instrumental accompaniment by organs and pianos. And of course, non-Seminole Baptists have Sunday services each week. The Fourth Sunday structure comes out of the Seminole tradition and is not found in the Anglo churches. Again, this difference results from the unique Seminole history from which the Seminole Baptist churches arose.

The Seminole Baptists and their non-Seminole Baptist neighbors do share much rhetoric and many customs. The most obvious is their mutual identification with the symbol "Baptist." This in turn implies a host of other similarities. Notable is the centrality of Jesus Christ as Savior, the prominence of Satan, an understanding that the Bible is the Word of God, public prayer, congregational autonomy, the preeminence of the pastor, preaching styles, many popular gospel hymns, temperance, postsermon invitations, and baptism as initiation into full participation in the community. However, many of the similarities are only apparent.

DISCUSSION AND CONCLUSION

It may be reasonable to assume that when an individual or community adopts foreign symbols, the underlying meanings of those symbols are also adopted, but such is not always the case. The primary symbols of the introduced Baptist faith—such as Jesus Christ, Satan, the Bible, prayer, the role of leaders, hymns, and baptism—may have been incorporated by the Seminoles, yet the meanings of the symbols and, perhaps more important, their use are profoundly different for the non-Seminole Baptists (as has been described in the previous chapters).

Even shared cultural elements do not provide a base substantive enough to build a community. Community requires both cultural and social dimensions. There is something more occurring at church gatherings than simply the rehearsing of beliefs. The social life that is constructed around the gatherings is of great significance, even if that function is not recognized by the participants themselves. If a church were only a gathering place to meet "spiritual needs" and did not effect any other function, then perhaps one might see participation by Seminoles in non-Seminole churches. However, as I have demonstrated, the social elements are at least as important as the "religious" elements. Gatherings at churches are the social situations that a community uses to form some sense of identity. The social consequences preclude random participation from geographical neighbors. Seminole Baptists may share cultural elements with Anglo Baptists, but they do not share a significant social life. This accounts for the rift separating the Anglo Baptists from their Seminole Baptist neighbors.

Many rural Anglo Baptist churches serve as a community for local participants. Members associate voluntarily. The social dynamics would no doubt be similar to those described at the Seminole Baptist churches: marked by conflict, cooperation, competition, and collaboration. But as a social unit, the church is bounded by rules of participation. The boundaries drawn exclude as well an include. Few Seminole members participate within those churches, since few would find a place within the community that is being represented. Discrimination, different expectations, and conflicting cultural attitudes would certainly make a shared social life difficult if not impossible.

From the Seminoles' perspective, there is little involvement with the larger Baptist system. One pastor explained to me why his church was independent: "We don't take no money from the Missions board because if we do they'll expect something back." Although some of the more "modern" pastors and floor members participate in conferences and revivals, most Seminole Baptists have no formal contact with other non-Seminole/Creek Baptists. Some of the more progressive pastors view participation in the larger assembly as being a positive thing, and some churches collect money that is donated to the assembly and is used in various missions. A few of the Seminole Baptist churches use printed materials in their gatherings, but these are generally limited to Sunday school curricula. For most members, the direction is toward the Seminole community.

It is interesting to note that the larger Baptist assembly does include Seminole churches in its own counting of members.[3] A roster is kept of the churches and their pastors (although much of the information is neither accurate nor current). These churches have been counted by the larger assembly throughout their history, apparently as a way of documenting the Baptist progress while allowing the native churches to continue in their local enclaves of development.

The mutual identification with the symbol "Baptist" does occasionally serve as a uniting element. Occasionally, neighboring Anglo Baptists will visit, en masse, a Seminole congregation. On these occasions the Seminoles accommodate. The Anglo ministers are given the opportunity to preach. The interactions are cordial, if uncomfortable. During these times, the Seminoles emphasize, whether intentionally or not, their similarities with the outsiders (services are conducted in English, and the songs are generally popular English gospel hymns). When participating in such events, I was struck by the contrast between the brash, extroverted Anglo preachers and the more restrained, unobtrusive Seminoles, although these style differences do not appear to be distasteful to either camp. The profound cultural and social differences, as well as the differences in beliefs, do not arise in these encounters. Surface similarities are more apparent than are the deeper differences. This is no doubt a function of the brief nature of the encounters, although I think both groups like to leave the encounters feeling their similarities rather than their differences. In pluralistic America in general, and for American Baptists in particular, a certain level of difference is allowed, if not expected, between different religious expressions. Even so, the shared symbols are the ones emphasized in these encounters.

Even though some symbols may be shared, this does not mean that a symbol's significance is shared. Should the two groups have any sustained interaction, these different significata would no doubt be recognized. However, in the brief, cursory interactions, the shared symbols—not the symbols' meanings—become the focus. The religious symbols' adaptive power, which allowed the Seminoles to reinterpret their own traditions into new Christian expressions, also allowed the non-Seminoles to extend Christianity to include the Seminole Baptist expression. Religious symbols, although traditionally credible, are inherently ambiguous, permitting diverse interpretation.

Ironically, for many the promotion of Christianity among the Seminoles was an attempt to assimilate the indigenous group into the dominant culture (some would say that Christianity was even an attempt to destroy the native cultures), yet it appears to have had the opposite effect. Apparently, Christian missionaries and other agents of the dominant state failed to see the interdependence of cultural and social factors. Non-Seminole, even civilized cultural features (a set of beliefs, values, symbols, and ideas) were offered to the Seminoles while the social uses that could be made of them were ignored. And now the Seminole Baptist churches are a primary source of Seminole ethnic identity.

Seminole Baptist Churches and Contemporary Stomp Grounds

My research with the Seminole Baptist churches precluded my direct participation in the Seminole Stomp grounds (the churches discourage participation in Stomp grounds activities).[4] Yet some comparisons should be made. Considering the shared history of the people composing the churches and the Stomp grounds, cultural and social similarities may be expected between them. At Stomp grounds gatherings, the Mvskoke language is spoken; foods that were described for the church refreshments are prepared at the Stomp grounds as well. Though utilized by churches, clanship is more important at the Stomp grounds, since it orders certain obligations in the ceremonies. Many of the beliefs described in chapter 4 are held by Stomp grounds members; in fact, at the Stomp grounds, one regularly hears prayers addressed to *Cesvs* ("Jesus"). For Stomp grounds participants, the consumption of medicine is a "communion," ensuring the well-being of the whole. Conversely, interpersonal conflict is viewed as a threat to the whole.

As described in chapter 2, the physical layout of the church grounds resembles that of the Stomp grounds. The ceremonial center of each is surrounded by a ring of camp houses. The functions of these houses are similar as well, providing temporary domestic residences for the participants. However, the social groupings of those using these camps differ. Among the churches, these camps are maintained by particular families but are often used by other members—refreshments are served after the gatherings, and visitors and members assemble at the camp houses. At Gar Creek Stomp grounds, the ten to fourteen camps serve as the basic social unit for participants. In addition to their function as temporary domestic residences and as the location of meals for visitors, the camps define participatory social groupings. There is little social interaction between people of other camps. Of course, people of different camps fulfill with each other the ritual obligations (e.g., the dances, consuming medicine) that are the focus of their gatherings, but there is little other social interaction between camps.

Many of the social dynamics that I described for Eufaula are similar to those at the Stomp grounds: Stomp grounds occasions bring together community members, exposing face to sanction. This is true for individual as well as corporate face (grounds participants represent their grounds to the larger community). However, two sources of conflict that occur in the churches are virtually nonexistent among the Stomp grounds. The first source of conflict among churches is the competition between churches. Since there is only one Seminole Stomp grounds, there is no competition between grounds. People do not shift membership as a result of interpersonal conflict in the grounds, as they often do in the churches. Instead, grounds participants view churches as their competitor.

A second source of conflict within churches arises from the filling of leadership positions, particularly the position of pastor. In the Stomp grounds, there is little conflict over the leadership positions, since they are not as fluid as in the churches. About the only time there is a shift in personnel is after a death creates a vacancy, and then the person who will fill the position is usually already known. This prescience is in large part due to the prescribed pool from which replacements are chosen in the Stomp grounds. Unlike the churches, where leaders may be drawn from the whole congregation, the grounds restrict leadership to certain lineages and clans (see Swanton 1928a:192ff). In fact, within the Stomp grounds the institution of clans serves more-defined functions than in the churches. For example, seating in the ceremonial arbors around the central fire at the grounds is assigned by clans.

Another significant difference between the churches and the grounds is that unlike the churches, Stomp grounds do not have the option of starting up new grounds. Churches may experience a fission with a faction of an established congregation and may start a new congregation. In the grounds, the only recourse for a dissatisfied faction is to revive a defunct grounds (such as the recent efforts to revive the New Tulsa Stomp grounds). But such grounds have histories, reasons they are presently defunct, and previously designated leaders and customs (even if dormant). Perhaps this lack of option forces members to work out interpersonal conflict within the Stomp grounds rather than abandon the relationships involved, the latter being an option that some churches have chosen.

The Seminole Baptist Church and the Greater Seminole Community

A very significant aspect of the church network, one that up to this point has only been alluded to, is the role of the church system in the maintenance of the larger Seminole community. Of the social occasions presently available to the Seminoles, the Baptist church system involves the greatest portion of Seminoles. Because it is the widest-reaching of all Seminole social occasions, the Baptist church system serves as the principal vehicle for the integration and maintenance of the larger Seminole community. Historically the Stomp grounds provided the vehicle for community reproduction and maintenance, but since there is currently only one active Seminole Stomp grounds, Christian churches are at present more important to the maintenance of a Seminole community. Thus Seminole Baptist churches sponsor the primary social occasions available to Seminoles to be Seminole.

The churches can provide this integrating function even for those not directly involved. Many Seminoles do not participate in the churches. Yet because of the church occasions, Seminole identity is maintained and provides a referent for nonparticipating Seminoles. By pointing to this distinct community, marked by its language, attention to clan obligations, worldview, gatherings, foods, and values, even nonparticipating Seminoles can identify with the Seminole community.

The Seminole Baptist churches integrate the Seminole community in ways not possible for the Seminole Methodist and Presbyterian churches. I have described how these latter churches generally follow an Anglo model of organization and structure. There are, however, individual Seminole members within those churches who regularly participate in the Seminole Baptist church system. The Methodists and Presbyterians who participate in the Baptist system are those who seek identification as Seminole, for Seminole Baptists do not attend those same Methodist and Presbyterian churches. The Seminole Baptists complain that the Methodists and Presbyterians are "too modern," meaning they follow a model that is too non-Seminole or Anglo. Seminole Baptist churches, however, are recognized by both Baptist and non-Baptist Seminoles as the locale of something distinctly Seminole.

Churches are not the only stage for maintaining Seminole identity. Stomp grounds provide a parallel alternative. The general social functions of both the grounds and the churches are very similar. Like churches, Stomp grounds gatherings structure interpersonal interaction and provide regular opportunities for individuals to expose face. The theme of "unity" drives both Stomp grounds gatherings and church gatherings. Both grounds and churches provide culturally structured occasions that guide Seminole behavior. The ideologies supporting the occasions may be conflicting, but the occasions of both function structurally in the same way.

Many Seminole Christians participate in Stomp grounds activities and occasions (consider the deacon Sokhvhvtke, discussed in the previous chapter), and many Stomp grounds participants attend (at least during some part of the year) church gatherings and occasions. Mutual participation is discouraged by leaders of both institutions, yet there is an adequate amount of interaction between the Seminole church members, Baptist and non-Baptist, and the Stomp grounds participants that a single, shared Seminole community is sustained. Together, the church system and the Stomp grounds integrate and maintain the larger Seminole community. The two institutions are parallel social structures that regulate the interactions of individuals, tacitly cooperating to organize and maintain Seminole identity.

Conclusion

In recent years, Seminole Baptist church participation appears to have been waning. Members frequently make comparisons between congregational life today and congregational life when they were children. The most notable difference is attendance. A deacon recently observed: "The church today is getting slack. The elders used to go all night long during Big Meetings. We quit after supper. And our church houses were full. They would sing so loud it could be heard a mile away. We would have to set up chairs all around the arbor, and even then there would be people without seats." Needless to say, many of the older members are quite distressed about the decline in participation. Members attribute this decline to young people not participating in congregational life. Congregational participants fear that the church will die out with its aging members.

If the church system is today the primary means for maintaining Seminole identity, then a decline in participation is indeed quite serious. With the decline in church and Stomp grounds participation and with no alternative set of social occasions, it appears that continued Seminole identity is at risk. Will there be another generation of Seminoles? Of Seminoles under the age of seventeen, fewer than 375 speak Mvskoke. Fewer than 150 of those speakers live in Seminole County. Most Seminoles no longer live in Seminole County.[5] Perhaps "Seminole" identity will give way to a more generic "Indian" identity. At Seminole Days, an annual event celebrating Seminole culture, one can find tepees, Indian tacos, fancy dancers, Plains-style lazy-stitch beadwork, and a Seminole princess who speaks no Mvskoke.

Declining church participation may also include an economic dimension. Verdery (1976:192) has suggested that there is a close relationship between ethnicity and economic inequities. Whether ethnicity is a cause or an effect of economic inequities is less important, however, than the fact that the Seminoles' move toward fuller participation in the Anglo economy certainly affects the Seminole social organization. Seminole subsistence farmers during the first half of this century had much more control over their time. Monthly meetings that extended from Wednesday night through Sunday evening were economically possible because of the nature of subsistence farming. Event though the church today does not require a participant to camp over a Fourth Sunday Meeting weekend, participation in the church community still requires a considerable investment of time. It is difficult for those Seminoles today who are employed full-time in service and production positions to take the time to "fulfill the work."

Will there be another generation of Seminoles? Consider this prediction, made in 1935: "It may be expected that culturally speaking the Oklahoma Seminole will be identical with the surrounding poor Whites in another generation. Any opportunity for the field ethnologist to work with them must be taken immediately" (Hadley [1935] 1987:158). But the community has survived and no doubt will continue to do so. The tribal government and community members are currently devising a language program designed to maintain fluency. Another group is currently working to reopen the closed New Tulsa Stomp grounds, sponsoring stickball games and fund-raisers to generate interest and income. And churches are not simply withering away. Although participation may be down, members are actively responding to and negotiating adaptations and innovations designed to reappropriate wide community participation. It is also likely that the replacement has simply not yet reached maturity. Members today speak of their "younger, wild days" before they were church members. Many members who grew up in the church left congregational life at early adulthood and did not return until midlife (when they were in their forties and fifties). They speak of how they then "settled down" and began attending church. Perhaps the replacement generation will yet grow into the church. Nevertheless, members today continue to "fulfill the work."

Thus today's members of the Seminole Baptist church system assist in the integration of the larger Seminole community. The social life that is organized, replicated, and sustained in the Seminole Baptist gatherings and occasions reaches beyond the local congregation and extends into the larger Seminole community, sustaining it and giving it vitality. Communities, as social entities, are held together by face-to-face social interaction among members. For a community to experience solidarity, maintain order, and reproduce its social units, this social interaction must be of an adequate frequency and intensity. For Eufaula members specifically, and for Seminole Baptists generally, the social occasions of the church system (Prayer Meetings, Fourth Sunday Meetings, and Big Meetings) provide frequent opportunities for participants to interact. The obligatory nature of the occasions ensures that members will attend and therefore will interact with other individuals, enhancing community maintenance.

Social life is not simply a collection of idiosyncratic actors who operate from veiled, disparate motivations and who just happen to share the same space. Rather, as the social life of Eufaula demonstrates, people act in accord with the regulations of their social units. Thus, an individual's behavior becomes understandable when placed in a social context. Behavior at Eufaula during gatherings, social occasions, and any other social encounter is regulated by the mechanism of face. The strategic consideration of face provides the dynamic internal mechanism by which the Seminole community is equipped to maintain and reproduce itself even in the midst of changing external circumstances. In the social life of Eufaula, actions were undertaken with a sensitivity to the social consequences of those actions. Individuals cannot simply behave as they please without risking their social identity. This is as true for leaders of the congregation as for floor members (consider the removal of the pastor, Rvro, who had served Eufaula for more than twenty years). The behavior both of individuals and of the social unit (i.e., the congregation) was monitored and regulated in Eufaula's social life by the strategic consideration of face.

For Seminole Baptists, face—both individual and congregational—is exposed during various gatherings and occasions. Weekly Prayer Meetings provide a relatively private arena for initiation into the congregation (by "accepting Christ" and being baptized) and for socialization (proper behavior is modeled by those older participants "situationally present" and is also the subject of most sermons). Fourth Sunday Meeting participation compels members of individual congregations to engage in an additional level of social interaction. Individuals are held to shared standards of conduct that define their Seminole Baptist community. Fourth Sunday occasions expose not only an individual's face but also the face of his or her immediate social unit (congregation) to the scrutiny of the larger community. Big Meetings, sponsored by congregations quarterly, involve the broadest base of Seminole Baptists. These occasions occur throughout the entire geographic region of the Seminoles, bringing together a mixed assortment of congregational members in such a way that the entire community does not need to gather at one time. The very structure of Big Meetings *requires* members of various congregations from around the Seminole community to "fulfill the work." The underlying theme of unity, cooperation, and concord consolidates individuals and congregations into a larger Seminole Baptist community.

It is in the ongoing, obligatory social occasions that the interdependence of cultural and social factors is displayed. Culture and society form a dialectic: groups negotiate structures and meaning, which in turn pattern interactions, which manage social activity. All social occasions are governed by shared, culturally specific expectations that define a social situation.

For the Seminole Baptists, the expectations of proper behavior organize church meetings. The church meetings supply a meaning base of cultural patterns that allow participants to interpret each other's behavior, serving as a matrix for social cohesion and action.

During the brief time span represented in this account of Eufaula's social life, its organizational arrangements built upon previous patterns to sustain Seminole identity. For such there is a long history of precedence: the adoption of Christianity itself may be viewed as a response to changing external circumstances, an option that was acceptable to a portion of the community and that later became established as an appropriate cultural expression. The historical adoption of Christianity is better understood as an adaptation of cultural patterns than as a structural shift in their basic social patterning.

It is the task of the community to be self-perpetuating. Throughout their history, Seminole Baptists have withstood countless assaults against their community. Yet their community was able to adapt because of its dynamic, internal mechanisms. And the community has continued to self-replicate, with the necessary adaptations. Each generation looks and behaves a little differently, yet the traditional community will no doubt continue as long as the Seminole Baptists continue to gather to "fulfill the work."

Mvskoke Orthography

The Mvskoke words used in this book are written in *italics* using the traditional orthography for the language. This traditional spelling system for the Mvskoke language was developed in the nineteenth century and is still in use by literate Seminoles and Creeks. In general, consonants are consistently represented with the orthography; vowels, on the other hand, are often problematic, with considerable variation between sources.

Some Mvskoke vowels occur in long and short forms. These are the vowel pairs *A a, V v, Ē ē, E e,* and *O o, U u.* Ideally, *A a* represents the long form (as in f*a*ther) and *V v* the short (as in b*u*t). The symbols *Ē ē* are inconsistently used in some historic texts to denote the long form (as in b*ee*t) and *E e* for the short form (as in b*i*t). And finally, the long form is represented by *O o* (broad as in r*o*de), the short form by *U u* (as in p*u*t). However, the short form *V v* is sometimes pronounced as f*a*ther; the short form *E e* may be pronounced as s*ea*t; and the short form *U u* is sometimes pronounced as r*o*de. In these instances, the long and short distinction designates the relative length of time, or duration, that the vowel sound is maintained. Many non-Mvskoke speakers do not distinguish these differences (although these differences are significant and may change word meaning), and many native speakers do not use the alternate symbols to designate the two forms. Therefore, the orthographic symbols designating long and short forms are often arbitrarily interchanged.

An additional source of confusion is the symbol *I i*. During the nineteenth century this symbol was apparently pronounced as in l*i*ke, but a sound change has occurred, for speakers today pronounce it as in s*ay*. In various sources either sound may be represented with the same symbol. To further confuse matters, some sources represent the two sounds inconsistently and interchangeably with the symbols *ay, vy,* or *ey*. In this text *I i* is pronounced as s*ay*; the sound in l*i*ke is designated with the diphthong *ay*.

While teaching the Mvskoke language at the University of Oklahoma, my co-teachers (both native speakers) and I attempted several innovations to the orthography to simplify and clarify some aspects of the spelling and pronunciation. Although many students found the innovations helpful, we later abandoned the changes, recognizing our presumptuousness. We found that virtually all native speakers insisted on maintaining the traditional uses and spellings even at the expense of clarity and ease of reading. In this text, I have elected—at the risk of a loss of clarity—to maintain the traditional and contemporary uses of the symbols as used by the Seminole community. The reader must thus allow a certain level of ambiguity in the representation of the words.

I have spelled Mvskoke words in this text to represent as faithfully as possible the language with the traditional orthography pronunciations used by contemporary Mvskoke-speakers. The spellings were reviewed by my language co-teacher, Linda Alexander. In most instances my spelling is identical to that of Loughridge and Hodge (1890a; 1890b). Should one desire to compare Mvskoke words from other sources with those in this text, one must be mindful of the vowel difficulties and should try substituting the various symbols to find equivalents.

Orthography Used in This Text

A a   as in f*a*ther
C c   as in *ch*eese or ca*ts*; between vowels as in *j*udge

E e	as in b*i*t or s*ea*t. Some historic texts inconsistently include the symbols *Ē ē* to denote a broad sound, as in beet. In this text, *E e* are used to represent long and short forms of the vowel.
F f	as in *f*our; between vowels as in *v*ery
H h	as in *h*ot; always pronounced
I i	as in s*ay*
K k	as in *k*ing; between vowels as in *g*um
L l	as in *l*ike
M m	as in *m*uch
N n	as in *n*ight
O o	as in h*o*pe; or broad as in r*o*de
P p	as in *p*in; between vowels as in *b*in
R r	no English equivalent, close to fou*rthly*
S s	as in *s*ome; between vowels as in *z*oo
T t	as in *t*ake; between vowels as in *d*ark
U u	as in p*u*t. In some sources this symbol represented the short form of *O o* and thus was pronounced as h*o*pe; at other times it represented the sound as in p*u*t. Contemporary Seminoles generally use this symbol for the sound in p*u*t; the short form of the vowel is designated with *O o*.
V v	as in b*u*t, but can be as in h*o*t
W w	as in *w*e
Y y	as in *y*ou

Diphthongs Used in This Text

ay	as in w*i*ne
ue	as in *we*

Note: When consonants are doubled, both are pronounced or the sound of the consonant is held slightly longer.

Big Meeting Weekend Format

Thursday Evening

Informal visiting
First bell
Informal visiting
Deacons' meeting
Participants seated
Second bell
Prayer songs
Devotional reading
Prayer song
Message
Invitation
Prayer song
(Second message)
(Second invitation)
Prayer song
Offering
Announcements
Prayer song
Blessing and dismissal
Handshaking
Refreshments

Friday Morning Fasting

Informal visiting
First bell
Informal visiting divided by gender
Second bell
Men's meeting
Women's meeting
Third bell
Women's prayer song
Pastor's prayer song
Devotional reading
Prayer song
Devotional readings
Prayer songs
Blessing and dismissal

Friday Evening

Informal visiting
First bell
Informal visiting

Deacons' meeting
Participants seated
Second bell
Prayer songs
Devotional reading
Testimonies
Prayer song
Message
Invitation
Prayer song
(Second message)
(Second invitation)
Prayer song
Offering
Announcements
Prayer song
Blessing and dismissal
Handshaking
Refreshments

Saturday Sunrise

First bell
Informal visiting
Second bell
Prayer songs
Devotional reading
Prayer songs
Dismissal

Saturday Midmorning

First bell
Informal visiting
Second bell
Prayer songs

Devotional reading
Prayer songs
Message
Invitation
Prayer songs
Blessing and dismissal

Saturday Evening

Informal visiting
First bell
Informal visiting
Deacons' meeting
Participants seated
Second bell
Prayer songs
Devotional Reading
Prayer song
Message
Invitation
Prayer Song
(Second message)
(Second invitation)
Song
Offering
Announcements
Prayer song
Blessing and dismissal
Handshaking
Refreshments

Sunday Morning Sunrise

First bell
Informal visiting
Second bell

Prayer songs
Devotional reading
Prayer songs
Message
Invitation
Prayer songs
Blessing and dismissal

Sunday Morning

Informal visiting
First bell
Informal visiting
Deacons' meeting
Participants seated
Second bell
Prayer songs
Devotional reading
Prayer song
Message
Invitation
Prayer song
(Second message)
(Second invitation)
Song
Offering
Announcements
Prayer song
Blessing and dismissal
Refreshment break

Sunday Afternoon

Informal visiting
Deacons' meeting

Participants seated
Bell
Prayer songs
Devotional reading
Prayer song
Message
Invitation
Prayer song
(Second message)
(Second invitation)
Song
Offering for pastor
Announcements
Prayer song
Blessing and dismissal
Light refreshments

Communion Service

Participants seated
Table prepared
Prayer songs
Devotional reading
Pastor's prayer
Consecration of bread
Consecration of wine
Prayer songs
Consume bread
Prayer songs
Consume wine
Prayer songs
Handshaking ritual
Prayer songs
Blessing and dismissal

Notes

Preface

1. All of the members I interviewed were competent in English. Most were bilingual (English and Mvskoke), having learned Mvskoke as their primary language. My competency in Mvskoke was developed over the four-year period of fieldwork while the community members encouraged, assisted, and prompted me in their language. Also, during that time I taught the Mvskoke language courses for foreign language credit at the University of Oklahoma; I was aided in these classes by two native speakers: Margaret Mauldin and Linda Alexander. My translations of longer texts in this book were reviewed by Mauldin and Alexander.

2. The Mvskoke nickname I received was 'Panhvtke ("White Boy"). The term used here for "boy" is a contracted form of *Cepan*. This term was historically used to describe a younger member of one's own clan (see Swanton 1928a:84; Spoehr 1942:60). Now it serves as an endearing term. Several Seminoles translated it into English as "Sonny Boy."

3. I did not choose which church to attend; I simply accompanied Eufaula members to churches of their choice.

Chapter 1. Introduction

1. See, for example, the series "Culture Element Distributions" in the journal *Anthropological Records.*

2. The "traditional religion" of the Seminoles is identified in the literature under varying titles: e.g., "Stomp grounds religion," "busk" (Swanton 1928a, 1928b), "Stomp Dancing" (Howard 1984), "conservatives," "stomp dancers," "Snakes" (Opler 1972). This ritual expression is extant among Seminoles and Creeks and is often viewed as being in direct competition with the Seminole and Creek churches. The Mvskoke word for the ceremonial grounds is *coko rvkko* ("big house"). In the present study I have chosen to identify the cere-

monial center of these rituals with the English gloss that the majority of the older Seminoles use: "Stomp grounds." The title generally reflects the importance of the ceremonial, or square, grounds and the activities and rituals surrounding it. Participants of the Stomp grounds are called *sayatkv* (pl. *sayatkvlke*, "all nighter"). I will identify them as "Stomp grounds participants."

3. One pastor told me that when he was a younger man, he used to fully participate in the Stomp Dances. As a mature man, he seldom participated but did frequent the Stomp grounds with his wife (a women's leader at church), who did participate. The pastor's wife died about four years ago. He has not visited a Stomp grounds since that time. He said, however: "It's not that I don't dance. I could never say that. It's just that I haven't danced for a while. If I say that I don't dance, then the devil will make sure to draw me back."

4. I have heard at least three ministers say that even before the white man came with the Bible, the Seminole people knew Jesus; however, they called him *Hesaketv emese*.

Chapter 2. A Brief History of the Seminoles

1. This history is a synthesis of a variety of sources, including Champagne (1992), Chaney (1928), Debo (1940, 1941), Fairbanks ([1978] 1987), Foreman (1932), Kersey (1987), Lancaster (1994), McRenolds (1957), Opala (1980), Sattler (1987), Spoehr (1941, 1942), Sturtevant (1971), Swanton (1922), Welsh (1983), and Wright (1986).

2. The term *etvlwv*, or "band," has narrowed in its meaning. It is generally used by Seminoles today as a political label defining hereditary voting units within the Seminole tribe, although I once heard it used to identify the gathering of people at a congregational Friday-night Prayer Meeting.

3. Stickball is a game similar to modern lacrosse (which is itself based on an Iroquois variant of stickball). In the Southeast, stickball players use pairs of ball sticks to hurl a small ball through a goal. See Howard (1984:181–205) for a detailed description of the game, complete with figures and plates.

4. Most often incest involved marriages within one's own clan and not marriages with one's biological kin.

5. After I had spent countless hours within the community, one pastor assigned a clan, his clan, to me: "If you're around Indians all the time, you claim one of them clans. Well, first thing you know—it's like a grass fire—you go around and all these Indians will know you by your clan." This was during refreshments after a church meeting, and the topic was clans. After I was assigned *Ahalvhvlke* ("potato") clan, the people who were gathered around the table announced their clans to me and the accompanying relationship (e.g., "sister," "brother," "daddy"), if there was one. One of those present punned that my clan was really *Ahalvhvtke* ("white potato")!

6. The statistics in this paragraph come from U.S. Bureau of the Census, *1990 Census of Population and Housing* (Washington, D.C., 1990): "Summary Social, Economic, and Housing Characteristics, Oklahoma," Tables 17 and 18; "Summary Population and Housing Characteristics, Oklahoma," Tables 3, 17, and 18; "Characteristics of American Indians by Tribe and Language," Tables 3, 5, 6, and 17.

Chapter 3. Christianity among the Seminoles

1. Sources for this history include Foreman (1951), Honey (1937), Kiker (1932), Lancaster (1994), Marks (1911), Methvin (1937), Ramsey (1857), Routh (1932), Smith (n.d.), Walker (1937), and Welsh (1983).

2. From the missionary Joseph Samuel Murrow's papers, 1884–90, quoted in Marks (1911:100): "Rev. Monday Durant, a Negro Baptist preacher among the Creeks, began visiting and preaching to the negroes among the Seminoles. He was not a slave; but was an earnest and good preacher. A church was organized in 1854, at first composed wholly of negroes."

3. Seminole National Records, Roll 3, Oklahoma Historical Society, Oklahoma City.

4. Rarely today does church meeting attendance reach over two hundred. Church meetings were once one of the few social gatherings available for Seminoles. As the Seminoles have moved toward participation in the Anglo economy, other social options have become available (those of the Anglo world). With that move comes decreased participation in Seminole gatherings, as the declining church participation of the present generation attests.

5. Several members made it clear to me that just because a person may be "credentialed" from some Baptist organization, such as Oklahoma Baptist University, he will not be recognized as being qualified or eligible for the position of pastor in one of the Seminole Baptist churches. It is the duty of the local congregation to select men for the position. See chapter 5 for additional discussions on the role and ordination of pastors.

6. The name "Eufaula" is fictitious. In the hope of preserving the privacy of the individuals of the focal congregation, I have elected to use pseudonyms throughout this study. I chose to use "Eufaula" because it is such a common name among Seminoles and Creeks: it names a city and tribal grounds, and several churches include Eufaula as part of their name.

7. The earliest documentation I have seen is Lewis (1937:227), which mentions the church by its Indian name.

Chapter 4. Beliefs

1. By "rationality," Weber meant more differentiated, comprehensive, and systematic. See Weber 1993; also Berger 1967:53ff for use of the term.

2. Acts 26:28, after Paul's testimony.

3. Professor Morris Foster, personal communications, August 1996. The concept of prayer itself appears to be an introduced practice, both for Seminole Christians and for Seminole Stomp dancers. The Mvskoke word for Christians is *Mekusvpvlke* ("the people who *pray*"). I attended the Ribbon Dance of Tallahassee's Green Corn Festival. One of the older women participants explained to me that the red ribbons adorning their dresses represent the "flowing blood of Jesus."

4. This idea of *Hesaketv emese* as the single creator has also been incorporated by the Stomp grounds.

5. During the two messages given in Mvskoke at one Prayer Meeting, I compared the number of times *Cesvs* was said with the number of times other names were used for the deity. *Cesvs* was used four times; *Hesaketv emese*, *Hesaketv*, or *Pocase* ("Our Lord" or "Our Owner") was used more than seventy times.

6. He was speaking in English and so used these glosses. When I asked him to clarify, he used the Mvskoke terms *Hesaketv emese, Pocase* ("Our Lord"), and *Cvrke* ("My Father").

7. *Nakcokv Esyvhiketv* (Muskogee Hymns), p. 70. See chapter 6, note 6, for a description of this songbook.

8. Specific botanicals used for various ailments are described in detail in Swanton (1928b: 655–70) and Howard (1984:20–70).

9. Capron (1953:174) records an identical belief among the Florida Seminoles: "Sleep, to the Seminole, is a kind of little death. In it the ghost comes out of the anus and, unhampered by physical laws of time and space, goes about having experiences. These experiences, remembered when the ghost reenters the body and the person wakes, are dreams."

10. Many feel that "on the last day" the *poyvfekcv* will be reunited with the resurrected body. Others feel that only the *poyvfekcv* (not the body) will have an afterlife.

11. Some disagree, however. One pastor commented: "A lot believe that spirits can leave paradise and come back to earth. But I think the place of paradise is a place of rest."

12. One pastor reported that long ago, people would drill holes in the casket of the deceased to facilitate the movement of the spirit to and from the body.

13. This refers to the custom of many Seminoles to orient their beds so that their heads are to the east. It is when they are dead that their heads are placed to the west.

14. See Swanton 1928b:490–95 for a description of the various snakes, both natural and supernatural, and their place in historic Seminole and Creek tradition. For Seminole Baptists, snakes are generally associated with Satan,

or at least bad luck. See chapter 6 for an episode of snake activity and its interpretation.

15. The Seminoles and Creeks tell turtle stories that speak of the turtle's perseverance, patience, and endurance. One story explains the patterns on the back of a common box turtle. Long ago the turtle was crushed by a woman's *kecvpe* ("corn-pounding pestle"). The wounded turtle crawled off and sang a medicine song that miraculously knit its shell back together.

16. In the Seminole tradition, the possum does not "play dead" when provoked; rather, it "pouts" (*elesketv*, "to pout").

17. *Opv* is the barred owl. This is not *'stekene*, or the great-horned owl, which is identified with witches.

Chapter 5. The Church Setting

1. Camp houses are "consecrated to the church," meaning they are the property of the church; however, specific families are responsible for their maintenance. During a message, the pastor noted that a camp house had been removed from another church ground that day to be used as a private residence. He condemned this act and warned that "they will suffer the consequences." He added, "The camp house belongs to the church and it should not be removed from these holy grounds."

2. The prayer grounds are used less frequently these days than in the past. The deacons' meeting is now usually held in the church sacristy or in a quiet place outside the church building. Prayer grounds are spoken of with great reverence. Members tell how on many nights throughout the year, one can hear emanating from the prayer grounds the voices and songs of the "elderlies who have passed on."

3. The eastern orientation is quite important among Seminole Christians. During prayers when circling to kneel, many Seminoles pause while facing east.

4. The placement of pews at Spring Church, near Sasakwa, does not fit this pattern. Its pews are all arranged to face the pulpit, as in Anglo churches. Men and women tend to sit together here as well. Spring Church is considered to be "modern," that is, like Anglo churches. During the meetings that I attended at Spring Church, almost 40 percent of the participants were non-Indian.

5. In Seminole churches there is a difference between ministers and pastors—the terms are not interchangeable. All pastors have been ordained as ministers, yet not all ministers are pastors. There is one pastor in each congregation. He is the "shepherd," the *obliktv liku*, or "chairman." The ministers are to assist the pastor, primarily as preachers. A similar relationship exists between a Stomp grounds *mekko* and his *speaker*.

6. See chapter 6, note 3, for a discussion of the use of the cow-horn.

7. The Mvskoke term translated as "ordained" is *yekcetv* ("to be strong or bold"). The sense is that the ordained person has the authority or right to fulfill the office. People who are ordained have been selected for the position by the congregation, trained, and then ordained or consecrated to fulfill the role during a public gathering held for that purpose.

8. Sometimes this title is contracted into *obliktv obliku, obliktolikv,* or simply shortened into *obliketv.*

9. There does not appear to be a Mvskoke term for this position.

10. The deacon's cane, *setekketv* ("to brace one's self with"), is a sign of the office. He is supposed to carry it at all times, particularly at church gatherings. After having been selected for the office, the deacons are to fast and pray in the woods while searching for a proper stick to make the *setekketv.* A deacon explained: "When we spot one, that's when you start thinking and praying again. You're praying and thanking the Lord for the tree that you have to, not exactly destroy, but cut to use to do your work for the church . . . it's got to look right. I never have seen one really that crosses here [at the handle], I guess that represents a cross. It's hard to find one." The wood used to make canes are pecan, hickory, or ash.

Chapter 6. "Fulfilling the Work" at Church Gatherings

1. The attendance figures are typical of those of the churches in the system, though there are differences, of course. Spring Church, near Sasakwa, has the largest membership and attendance. The report of the "1992 Minutes of the Muskogee, Seminole, Wichita Baptist Association" (Gaskin Baptist Archives, Baptist Building, Oklahoma City) lists membership at over 500. Sunday attendance is around 200.

2. The appropriate number of bell rings to begin a service is about a dozen. One deacon laughed as he told of a deacon trainee who was given the task of ringing the bell for the first time. The trainee rang the bell so many times that after the service, members asked him who had died (after a funeral, the bell is often rung until all of the cars in the funeral procession are out of sight of the church grounds). The next time, afraid that he would ring too many times, the trainee rang the bell only a few times. After this service, members said to him, "I thought we were going to have refreshments before the service" (the bell is rung two or three times to announce that the camps have been prepared and refreshments are about to be served).

3. Early in my field experience, I noticed the cow-horn hanging with the deacons' canes in the corner of the church. I asked the deacon about it. He replied: "I used to carry one around with me. I would practice blowing it so that I would be ready if anyone should ask me to blow it." He went on to

describe its use: "The deacon appointed for this work stands outside the church house, faces east, and blows the horn four times. This is just like ringing the first bell. He does it again just before the service begins." He said that at least one Seminole church uses a seashell horn. The deacon said he would not like to be called on to use the horn but that it is "not right to refuse if the church asks you to do something." Only once did I actually see the horn blown to begin a service. The deacon, facing east (which is, by the way, the same orientation that the deacon assumes when ringing the bell), blew the horn four times. He sustained the note as long as his breath allowed, the volume increasing toward the end. The result was really quite dramatic.

4. The deacon said: "In our church we tend to give the visitors the best seats. Members have their own seats." A new convert is instructed in proper church behavior by the men or women leaders (according to the convert's gender) immediately after baptism. At this time the convert is assigned a specific seat in the sanctuary, where he or she is expected to be seated for each church meeting.

5. The first time that I visited Eufaula, the three people who had invited me (one of whom was the pastor and another the head deacon) to attend the gathering were all absent. None of the people present in the church had seen me before. I came into the service late, and the deacon seated ne in a neutral area (second row, on the east end). The visiting pastor interrupted the service to have me introduce myself. The first question he asked me was if I was a minister.

6. All of the hymns in this work are printed in a pocket-sized songbook used by many members of the Seminole Baptist churches. *Nakcokv Esyvhiketv* (Muskogee Hymns) was first published by Westminister Press and was reprinted by the Department of Cooperative Missions, BGCO, and the Muskogee-Seminole-Wichita Indian Baptist Association. I have generally maintained the text as written in the songbook, correcting obvious misspellings and typographical errors where necessary. For some of the songs, I have also included additional verses not recorded in the songbook. "Vnokeckvt Omecaycen" is found on page 47 of *Nakcokv Esyvhiketv* (Muskogee Hymns).

7. *Nakcokv Esyvhiketv* (Muskogee Hymns), p. 70.

8. *Nakcokv Esyvhiketv* (Muskogee Hymns), p. 92.

9. The New Testament and the Old Testament books of Genesis and Psalms were translated in the mid–nineteenth century by Rev. R. M. Loughridge and others serving as Presbyterian missionaries among the Creeks. *Testament Mucvsat* (New Testaments), published by the American Bible Society of New York, are still in print and are frequently used in churches today. The books of Genesis and Psalms are no longer in print, however, and are relatively scarce.

10. *Nakcokv Esyvhiketv* (Muskogee Hymns), p. 73.

11. Depending on his audience at the gathering, a preacher will primarily use either Mvskoke or English, whichever is more appropriate. This sermon was spoken in both English and Mvskoke. The pastor switched from one language to the other, saying essentially the same thing in each. This is a verbatim transcript of the English sections.

12. Two different Mvskoke terms are used to identify this concept. The first, *ehasatecetv*, means to "cleanse one's self"; the second, *emahericetv*, implies fixing or repairing something (namely, one's self).

13. An elderly pastor provided the rationale for the mercy seat:

> I know when I need to rededicate. . . . We don't put on a shirt and wear it forever. We take a bath. We need to put on clean clothes. It's the same way with faith. Faith gets old. I believe it's II John or III John that says it—whosoever says I don't sin, making God a liar. So we were born with the seed of sin. We got to learn to control it with Christ's help. And he says that's why you can be forgiven, not seven times, but seventy-seven times seven. That's a lot, see? So that Mercy seat, it's something too. They fast and build these Mercy seats in these Indian churches. And the Old Testament says when Moses talked with God direct, when they built that—it's not a temple, but he called it something else—a place of worship, he told Moses, said next time you come to this synagogue or whatever, build a Mercy seat. And have two cherubim angels standing there at the end of them facing each other. Said you come sit there, then I'll talk to you. A person needs to pray on that and think on it. It really gets down to—Moses was his chosen vessel. He was dealing with him face to face, so to speak. He talked to him direct. But still yet, he wanted Moses to come and sit on this Mercy seat. How about us? He don't talk direct to us, Jesus talks to us through his spirit. You know they want us to come renew our vows.

14. *Tosina* is pork side meat. This is the meat usually used for bacon, but as side meat it is not smoked.

15. *Vpvske* is a traditional beverage made of parched, pounded corn; *vpvske nerkv* ("seeds") refers to the food dish made with the larger kernels of *vpvske* corn boiled with pork hocks, pigs' feet, or chicken.

16. *Taklik kvmokse* means "sour corn bread." The cornmeal batter, mixed with a little milk, is left to sour for a day or so before it is cooked.

17. This is a type of large, flat biscuit made in a pan. It is also called "cowboy bread" or "buffalo bread."

18. The English gloss is "blue bread." This is a dumpling made with corn-meal and ashes. When mixed with a particular type of ashes (such as those that result from burning the husks of green beans), the cornmeal turns a deep blue, hence the English name.

19. *Tvfvmpuce* are wild onions fried with grease and eggs. Prepared when the wild onions are in season (early spring and sometimes late fall), this dish is served with fry bread.

20. These are called "grape dumplings" in English. Flour and wild grape juice are mixed to form dumplings, which are then boiled in wild grape juice.

21. *Sofke*, or *Osofke*. is a beverage made of hard corn boiled in water and ash drippings. It is served either cold or warm and is eaten with a spoon, out of a cup or bowl. Many people prefer it sweetened with sugar. Occasionally it is served as "sour *sofke*," meaning it has begun to ferment.

22. With such a motivation to attend the gathering, it is understandable that attendance is a high priority. I was at one gathering when an elderly woman stood and told the congregation of her present illness and upcoming surgery. She told the congregation that even though the doctor had advised her to stay home and rest, she was in church all week for the revival. The congregation responded with a hearty *"Eman"* ("Amen").

23. Baptisms are usually performed the day after a person makes his or her "decision." Most of the Seminole churches do not have a baptistery, so the baptism is performed in a local pond. Baptisms are performed in spite of inclement weather. Deacons speak, somewhat fondly, of chipping holes in a frozen pond to perform a baptism. The entire local congregation is expected to attend the baptisms that its pastor performs.

Baptism ceremonies begin with the singing of prayer songs and prayers. The deacon enters the water and walks around the section that will be used. He is to circle the area four times. He is in an attitude of prayer, and while he wades in the pond he is looking for any debris that may interfere with the ceremony. After making sure that the area is clear, the deacon returns to the bank, and he and the pastor assist the convert into the water, where the actual ritual is performed. After the baptism, additional songs and prayers are sung and spoken. The members all return to the church for refreshments. At the church grounds, the neophyte is briefly instructed in proper behavior.

24. After the baptism, the participants reconvene at the church, where the convert is reminded of the church's expectations. An elderly pastor described the situation:

We set him behind the pulpit, tell him the church orders, you know, if they want they're welcome to build their own camp. They're welcome at the boards or business meetings. Then they can partake the Lord's Supper; they're eligible now, which they wasn't. You tell him all these little things like that, you know—when is church meeting, when is fasting day. You tell him all the church rules, of this church here, independent church. And you tell him all this and that. And then when they get through—oh, when I first walk up to him to tell him all of this, I will ask the church—I will ask this person to stand up and make a statement what church he want to put his membership in. If he says High Springs Church, then I turn and tell the church that he wants to put his membership in this church. I leave it up to the church, and the church will make a motion that will accept him in full unity, with this church. And then they'll all raise their hand and accept him in. And then I'll exhort to him—what all of us got to tell him. Then we give him a fellowship handshake. Then we'll give him a chair; they'll appoint him a chair. Those that are just baptized at the beginning—it used to they'd put him in the last chair. They go up. The older they get they come up, one at a time. He's leading songs, leading prayers, getting that way, they're liable to scoot him up. Another one gets baptized, well, they will scoot him. Another one gets baptized, they'll scoot him, till he's usually up front. And that seat they'll appoint him. It's always his, as long as he lives. When he dies they usually put a black cloth where he sits. That's during when his body's here, but after he's buried, then that seat is free. Them deacons got to remember and that pastor got to know where he used to sit, where he was appointed to, who they appointed that chair to. They'll tell you this during the Lord's Supper—you have to get in your own stall. Jesus compared Christians to sheep. Sheep know their own stall when they go to feed. They go into their own stall; they won't go into another. Goats is the one that fights trying to get in. So we are compared to sheep—they go to their stall when they're going to be fed. When we go to drink that wine and eat that bread, well, they want each one to get in their chair, where there was appointed to him. Be like each one getting into their stall.

25. "Worldly behavior" includes missing church, drinking, playing ball, attending powwows, and Stomp dancing. One participates in such behavior at the risk of personal and congregational face.

26. Early in my field experience, I spent several days with a *heles hayv*. On my first visit he offered me a small bundle of objects; he assured me that if I carried them, everything would go well for me. The bundle contained four types of medicine, all properly prepared with the appropriate medicine songs to infuse the items with specific power: *vcena* ("cedar"), "to keep you always looking good"; *cvto cvsakwe* ("pebbles"), "to keep you heavy . . . your enemy will get light and float away"; *heles hvtke* ("ginseng"), "to bring you luck, and a friend in the time of need"; *pasa* ("black root," one of the ingredients in the "black drink" of the Stomp grounds), "to give you protection from harm." Throughout my field experience, I realized that many members used these same medicines to effect the same objectives.

27. This figure is from *1990 Census of Population and Housing*: "Characteristics of American Indians by Tribe and Language," Table 3.

28. This is the only money that the pastor receives for his services.

29. Members disagree about which churches are primarily Seminole or primarily Creek. The consensus states that those churches in Seminole County south of a line drawn from Wewoka to Seminole are Seminole. Other members, however, include churches outside of Seminole County, particularly those around the Holdenville area of the adjacent Hughes County.

30. Stomp grounds participants use this same term to describe their participation at neighboring grounds.

31. This list should not be assumed to be exhaustive. In east-central Oklahoma there are an additional thirty Creek Baptist churches that Seminoles could theoretically attend. This list represents only those churches that were attended by Eufaula members or whose members attended Eufaula during my field experience.

32. Only one congregation is known to do this presently. Second Christmas (known in other Christian churches as Epiphany) is twelve days after Christmas and commemorates the visitation of the Wise Men to the infant Christ.

33. Easter services include an Easter egg hunt, in which all members may participate. The finder of a golden egg is rewarded with a special prize, usually a new, leather-bound Bible.

34. This holiday is commemorated with a service resembling a Prayer Meeting. Refreshments are highlighted by serving turkey and dressing in addition to the usual food.

35. At Eufaula, following the Prayer Meeting closest to Halloween, a costume party is held. Judges are chosen to select the ugliest costumes, and food prizes are awarded. The party includes much tomfoolery, giggles, and laughter. At one such party a deacon trainee explained: "Jesus said that children would inherit the kingdom and that we should be like children. This time is set aside for the children so that they would have a good feeling about the church, because they are the church of the future. They need to know that church is a safe place and that God has great love for them."

36. This is different from the *Soletawv Mekusvpkv* ("Service for the Armed Forces") described previously. The Veteran's Day service is held near the national holiday and is a Prayer Meeting that includes recognition of veterans. Following the devotional reading, a candle is lit in memory of those veterans who have died or who gave their lives in battle. The sanctuary is decorated with flags and with red, white, and blue ribbons.

37. The "wine" is actually bottled grape juice. In the context of Big Meetings, however, it is always referred to as wine.

38. This term was explained by one pastor: "*Ohhoyvnkv ohhompetv*, it's a Passover meal. Passover, like in the Old Testament. Jesus came and killed it, the Passover, before he ate with his disciples. That's a burnt offering. He killed that and put us under grace. He defeated Satan. He had to do that. It's

symbolic of his body and blood, when we take that wine and bread. He did away with the sacrifice. No more bull blood or goat blood. He's the passover."

39. The phrase "words of encouragement" is used frequently among the church members. It most often refers to a person standing singly in a gathering and expressing appreciation for the opportunity to gather with the others present and giving a testimony of his or her perception of God's goodness. The term may also refer to personal words spoken in a less public social gathering. People will speak of their interpersonal problems, and others will respond with some positive, spiritual "words of encouragement"—such as "continue striving." A "word of encouragement" may also be a simple "God bless you" during a rededication.

40. "Exhortation" implies some reading or sharing of biblical injunctions and commands that believers are under an obligation to fulfill.

41. The first time that I participated in a Fasting service, I committed a situational impropriety. There was an uncomfortable pause when it came time for me to lead a song and prayer. I was unaware that I was required to do so. The pastor came to my aid and saved my face by attributing my inaction to ignorance. After the service, the pastor and a deacon explained that each man is expected to lead a song and prayer and thus "fulfill" the work. I apologized, and during the next Fasting service I fulfilled the work. To make sure that I did not commit the impropriety again, the pastor explicitly invited me to lead the song and prayer when it was my turn.

42. The Green Corn Festival is called in Mvskoke the Posketv, which means literally "to fast."

43. A minister described fasting:

You're not suppose to tell nobody you're fasting. Your wife would know, but like I wouldn't tell you that I'm fasting today. Or I wouldn't tell you that I'm going to fast tomorrow. That's got to be a secret. And when you fast and go before the public—like I'm fasting this morning (I'm just saying an example, now) if I'm fasting this morning, do you know me real well that I smoke and if I had long hair you know how I part it and keep it combed. I could wash and comb my hair, but I can't exercise my fasting before you. You know, such a way as to show it, to let you know I'm fasting—I can't do that. I got to go my regular way. But you'd probably notice our minister or any member that you see smoking that won't smoke. They won't even take a aspirin or anything. There aren't many ways you can tell they're fasting. They won't tell you. They won't volunteer and tell you, but can tell.

44. The *heles hayv* later explained that this spit "breaks up" the bad medicine left by the snake.

45. During other services, members sit in their appointed seats scattered throughout the sanctuary. During this service, all of the male members sit next to each other in one pew and all of the female members sit in one pew opposite the males. The deacons attempt to seat visitors from the same congregation together.

46. This is referring to the "medicine" taken at the Stomp grounds.

47. At Eufaula, the case for the chalice and paten happens to be a bowling ball bag.

48. *Nakcokv Esyvhiketv* (Muskogee Hymns), p. 54.

49. *Nakcokv Esyvhiketv* (Muskogee Hymns), p. 101.

50. *Nakcokv Esyvhiketv* (Muskogee Hymns), p. 16.

51. In a manner analogous to the variation accompanying the transfer of genes from one generation to the next, social groups include variation in their repertoire of cultural expressions. Members of a social group can negotiate (or select) strategies from the variety, allowing an adapted social system that can reproduce itself into the next generation.

52. This theme of unity is maintained as well in the contemporary Stomp grounds.

Chapter 7. Social Life at Eufaula

1. All of the names used in this account are fictitious, in an attempt to protect the privacy of the individuals. Following a Seminole practice of nick-naming, all of the fictitious names are Mvskoke terms for various animals and birds.

2. See chapter 1 for a description of this program.

3. During business meetings, held monthly, administrative business is discussed and decisions are made. Business meetings are open only to church members; therefore, all of my accounts of events that transpired during the meetings are based on secondhand information.

4. During my field experience, there was only one other Big Meeting postponed, by another Seminole Baptist church. This postponement was also the result of unresolved interpersonal conflict—two members of the church had come to blows during a business meeting.

5. I later learned that this is the posture that many Seminoles take during such an encounter. The Seminole word for the pastor's reaction is *eyasketv* ("to be humble, meek, or mild-mannered"). Once, during announcements in one Fourth Sunday Meeting, a visitor from Sand Creek apologized for being late to the service. He said many things had prevented them from getting there on time. He said they came with "great humility, we were being humble all the way here." During refreshments he explained to me that when he had first come into church life, he and his wife would always fight while they were getting ready to come to church. He said that since then, he had

learned that he needed "to be humble during that time"—he and his wife would simply not speak to each other. Rvro overheard our conversation and interjected that he always has to confront conflict with "humility." "I just don't say nothing," he said. *Eyasketv* is a valued posture. A line from a popular hymn states, "*Eyasketvt omecicen hvlwe tvlofvn apeyakvres*" ("On account of humility [*eyasketvt*] we are going to heaven").

6. See chapter 4 for a discussion of witchcraft and witching. Accusations of witchcraft are quite common in Seminole and Creek circles. The most common way for "witching" to occur is for the practitioner to perform a ritual on some object, thus infusing the object with the power. This object is then hidden on the property of the person to be witched. Some people control the antidote to witching, and their services can be purchased.

7. Some people are believed to have the power to "put someone asleep," that is, to magically induce a trancelike sleep. The victim may then be taken advantage of (robbed or raped, for example).

8. This "book" is only figurative. The term refers to rules and practices that have been passed down from the elders.

9. After the service, Cufe and Cesse reminisced about Memorial services they had attended at Eufaula as children. They described how members would gather at the camp house of the deceased and how a family head man was appointed to exhort, then lead, the family and the other members to the church, singing a hymn. The members would process through the eastern end of the arbor and then into the church, where chairs had been set up for the family in the middle. The service would then continue.

10. Cesse said that he had once seen snake bones do just that. As a boy, he was out doing some farmwork with his uncle. They saw a dead snake lying in several pieces. Cesse's uncle warned him not to touch the snake bones, explaining that the snake is strong medicine and that it would "pull itself together." They walked away from it, but soon Cesse's curiosity was piqued and he went back to take a look. The snake was gone.

11. Eufaula members told me that he was the first member to do this. Only recently (within the last four to five years), at the suggestion of the women's leaders, followed by a majority vote, has Eufaula allowed people to withdraw their names. Before that, when one joined Eufaula, the only way to officially leave was through marriage or death.

Chapter 8. Discussion and Conclusion

1. Many converts, however, soon found that conversion did not bring about incorporation into the Anglo sphere, as they had hoped. Adopting Christianity did not mean incorporation into the dominant political and economic system. Discrimination was just as profound for Christian natives

as for non-Christian. Others, finding "white culture to be one of the least attractive weeds in the garden of history" (Opler 1972:59), became apostate.

2. This young man is Raymond John, office assistant in the Sociology Department of Oklahoma State University.

3. See, for example, the lists of Indian churches, particularly Seminole churches, in the *Proceedings of the Baptist General Convention of Oklahoma.* Copies of these *Proceedings* are located at the Oklahoma Baptist Historical Society, Oklahoma City.

4. Several anthropologists are currently working with the Seminole and Creek Stomp grounds of Oklahoma. Most notable is Professor Morris Foster, from the University of Oklahoma, who has been working with Gar Creek, the only remaining Seminole Stomp grounds, for almost nine years. The following comparisons were gleaned from my conversations with him regarding the social life of the grounds.

5. Figures in this paragraph are drawn from *1990 Census of Population and Housing:* "Characteristics of American Indians by Tribe and Language."

References

Manuscripts

Chaney, Margaret A. 1928. "A Tribal History of the Seminole Indians." Master's thesis, University of Oklahoma, Norman.

Honey, Willie. 1937. Interview 5337 in Indian-Pioneer History, Grant Foreman Papers, vol. 5:159–62, Oklahoma Historical Society, Oklahoma City.

Kiker, Ernest. 1932. "Education among the Seminole Indians." Master's thesis, Oklahoma State University, Stillwater.

Lewis, D. B. 1937. Interview 7581 in Indian-Pioneer History, Grant Foreman Papers, vol. 61:223–30, Oklahoma Historical Society, Oklahoma City.

Marks, Luther Whitfield. 1911. "The Story of the Oklahoma Baptists." Manuscript, Gaskin Baptist Archives, Baptist Building, Oklahoma City.

Methvin, J. J. 1937. Interview 8186 in Indian-Pioneer History, Grant Foreman Papers, vol. 107:30–31, Oklahoma Historical Society, Oklahoma City.

Ramsey, J. R. 1857. "Missionary Correspondence." Oak Ridge Mission, Letter 101, Presbyterian Historical Society, Philadephia.

Sattler, Richard. 1987. "Seminoli Italwa: Socio-Political Change among the Oklahoma Seminoles between Removal and Allotment, 1836–1905." Ph.D. dissertation, University of Oklahoma, Norman.

Smith, Micah Pearce. N.d. "The Seminole Presbyterian Mission." Manuscript, M. P. Smith Collection, Western History Collections, University of Oklahoma, Norman.

Walker, Isaac. 1937. Interview 7016 in Indian-Pioneer History, Grant Foreman Papers, vol. 68:450–52, Oklahoma Historical Society, Oklahoma City.

Books and Articles

Adair, James. 1930. *Adair's History of the American Indians.* Edited by Samuel Cole Williams. Johnson City, Tenn.: Wataunga Press.

Barth, Frederick, ed. 1969. *Ethnic Groups and Boundaries: The Social Organization of Cultural Difference*. London: Allen and Unwin.

Bartram, William. 1928. *The Travels of William Bartram*. 1791. Reprint. Edited by Mark Van Doren. New York: Macy-Masius.

Berger, Peter. 1967. *The Sacred Canopy: Elements of a Sociological Theory of Religion*. Garden City, N.Y.: Doubleday.

Berkhofer, Robert F., Jr. 1965. *Salvation and the Savage: An Analysis of Protestant Missions and American Indian Response, 1787–1862*. Lexington: University of Kentucky Press.

Blu, Karen I. 1980. *The Lumbee Problem: The Making of an American Indian People*. Cambridge: Cambridge University Press.

Boyd, Mark F., Hale G. Smith, and John W. Griffin. 1950. *Here They Once Stood: The Tragic End of the Apalachee Missions*. Gainesville: University of Florida Press.

Capron, Louis. 1953. *The Medicine Bundles of the Florida Seminole and the Green Corn Dance*. Smithsonian Institution, Bureau of American Ethnology Bulletin 151, 155–210. Washington, D.C.

Champagne, Duane. 1992. *Social Order and Political Change: Constitutional Governments among the Cherokee, the Choctaw, the Chickasaw, and the Creek*. Stanford: Stanford University Press.

Debo, Angie. 1940. *And Still the Waters Run: The Betrayal of the Five Civilized Tribes*. Princeton: Princeton University Press.

————. 1941. *The Road to Disappearance: A History of the Creek Indians*. Norman: University of Oklahoma Press.

DeMallie, Raymond J. 1984. *The Sixth Grandfather: Black Elk's Teachings Given to John G. Neihardt*. Lincoln: University of Nebraska Press.

Fairbanks, Charles H. [1978] 1987. "The Ethno-archeology of the Florida Seminoles." In *A Seminole Sourcebook*, ed. William C. Sturtevant, 163–93. New York: Garland Publishing.

Foreman, Carolyn Thomas. 1951. "John Jumper." *Chronicles of Oklahoma* 29(2):137–52.

Foreman, Grant. 1932. *Indian Removal: The Emigration of the Five Civilized Tribes of Indians*. Norman: University of Oklahoma Press.

Foster, Morris W. 1991. *Being Comanche: A Social History of an American Indian Community*. Tucson: University of Arizona Press.

Fowler, Loretta. 1987. *Shared Symbols, Contested Meanings: Gros Ventre Culture and History, 1778–1984*. Ithaca: Cornell University Press.

Goffman, Erving. 1959. *The Presentation of Self in Everyday Life*. Garden City, N.Y.: Doubleday.

————. 1961. *Encounters: Two Studies in the Sociology of Interaction*. Indianapolis: Bobbs-Merrill.

———. 1963. *Behavior in Public Places: Notes on the Social Organization of Gatherings*. New York: Free Press.

———. 1967. *Interaction Ritual: Essays on Face-to-Face Behavior*. Garden City, N.Y.: Anchor Books.

———. 1969. *Strategic Interaction*. Philadelphia: University of Pennsylvania Press.

Grimes, Morris W. 1870. *Annual Report of the Board of Indian Commissioners, of Indian Affairs to the Secretary of the Department of the Interior, 1869*. Washington, D.C.

Gumperz, John. 1982. *Language and Social Identity*. London: Cambridge University Press.

Hadley, J. N. [1935] 1987. "Notes on the Socio-economic Status of the Oklahoma Seminoles." In *A Seminole Sourcebook*, ed. William C. Sturtevant, 133–59. New York: Garland Publishing.

Hawkins, Benjamin. 1980. *Letters, Journals, and Writings of Benjamin Hawkins*, vol. 1:1796–1801. Edited by C. L. Grant. Savannah, Ga.: Beehive Press

Howard, James H. 1984. *Oklahoma Seminoles: Medicines, Magic, and Religion*. Norman: University of Oklahoma Press.

Hudson, Charles. 1976. *The Southeastern Indians*. Knoxville: University of Tennessee Press.

Kersey, Harry A., Jr. 1987. *The Seminole and Miccosukee Tribes: A Critical Bibliography*. Bloomington: Indiana University Press.

Lancaster, Jane F. 1994. *Removal Aftershock: The Seminoles' Struggles to Survive in the West, 1836–1866*. Knoxville: University of Tennessee Press.

Linton, Ralph. 1940. *Acculturation in Seven American Indian Tribes*. New York: Appleton-Century.

Loughridge, R. M., and David M. Hodge. 1890a. *English and Muskokee Dictionary*. Creek Mission, Indian Territory: n.p.

———. 1890b. *Dictionary of the Muskokee or Creek Language in Creek and English*. Red Fork, Indian Territory: n.p. [Reprinted with Loughridge and Hodge 1890a as *Dictionary: Muskokee and English* (1964), Okmulgee, Okla.: B. Frank Belvin, Baptist Home Mission Board.]

McLoughlin, William G. 1994. *The Cherokees and Christianity, 1794–1870: Essays on Acculturation and Cultural Persistence*. Edited by Walter H. Cosner Jr. Athens: University of Georgia Press.

McReynolds, Edwin C. 1957. *The Seminoles*. Norman: University of Oklahoma Press.

Opala, Joseph A. 1980. *A Brief History of the Seminole Freedmen*. African and Afro-American Studies and Research Center Papers, series 2, no. 3. Austin: University of Texas.

Opler, Morris E. 1972. "The Creek Indian Towns of Oklahoma in 1937." *Papers in Anthropology* 13(1). Department of Anthropology, University of Oklahoma, Norman.

Phelps, G. Lee. 1937. *Tepee Trails*. Atlanta: Home Mission Board, Southern Baptist Convention.

Powers, Marla N. 1986. *Oglala Women: Myth, Ritual, and Reality*. Chicago: University of Chicago Press.

Powers, William K. 1977. *Oglala Religion*. Lincoln: University of Nebraska Press.

Routh, E. C. 1932. *The Story of Oklahoma Baptists*. Oklahoma City: Baptist General Convention.

Sapir, Edward. 1949. *Selected Writings of Edward Sapir in Language, Culture, and Personality*. Edited by David G. Mandelbaum. Berkeley: University of California Press.

Spicer, Edward H. 1961. *Perspectives in American Indian Culture Change*. Chicago: University of Chicago Press.

Spoehr, Alexander. 1941. "Oklahoma Seminole Towns." *Chronicles of Oklahoma* 19(4): 376–80.

———. 1942. "Kinship System of the Seminole." *Anthropological Series, Field Museum of Natural History* 33(2): 31–113.

Sturtevant, William C. 1971. "Creek into Seminole." In *North American Indians in Historical Perspective*, ed. Eleanor Burke Leacock, 92–128. New York: Random House.

Swan, Caleb. 1856. "Position and State of Manners and Arts in the Creek, or Muskogee Nation in 1791." In Henry Rowe Schoolcraft, ed., *Information Respecting the History, Condition, and Prospects of the Indian Tribes of the United States*, vol. 5:251–83. Philadelphia: J. B. Lippincott and Co.

Swanton, John R. 1922. *Early History of the Creek Indians and Their Neighbors*. Smithsonian Institution, Bureau of American Ethnology Bulletin 73. Washington, D.C.

———. 1928a. "Social Organization and Social Usages of the Indians of the Creek Confederacy." *Forty-second Annual Report of the Bureau of American Ethnology*, 23–472. Washington, D.C.: Smithsonian Institution, Bureau of American Ethnology.

———. 1928b. "Religious Beliefs and Medical Practices of the Creek Indians." *Forty-second Annual Report of the Bureau of American Ethnology*, 473–672. Washington, D.C. : Smithsonian Institution, Bureau of American Ethnology.

Trigger, Bruce. 1986. "Ethnohistory: The Unfinished Edifice." *Ethnohistory* 33:253–67.

Verdery, Katherine. 1976. "Ethnicity and Local Systems: The Religious Organization of Welshness." In *Regional Analysis Volume III: Social Systems*, ed. Carol Smith. New York: Academic Press.

Weber, Max. 1993. *The Sociology of Religion*. Boston: Beacon Press.

Welsh, Michael. 1983. "The Missionary Spirit: Protestantism among the Oklahoma Seminoles, 1842–1885." *Chronicles of Oklahoma* 61(1): 28–47.

Wright, J. Leitch, Jr. 1986. *Creeks and Seminoles: The Destruction and Regeneration of the Muscogulge People*. Lincoln: University of Nebraska Press.

Wright, Muriel H. 1951. *A Guide to the Indian Tribes of Oklahoma*. Norman: University of Oklahoma Press.

Index

Layman, 95–96, 101, 103
Leadership positions, roles, 15, 28, 49, 56, 90, 91, 92, 99, 102, 104, 125, 157, 160–61, 211, 216. *See also* Deacons; Ministers; Pastors; Women's leaders
Lena, Willie, 6, 22
Lighthorsemen, 39
Lilley, Rev. John and Mary Anne, 46, 47
Linton, Ralph, 5, 6
Loughridge, R. M., and David M. Hodge (translators), 226, 239n.9

McLoughlin, William G., 207
McReynolds, Edwin, 22
Macro-sociology, 16
Maud, Oklahoma, 52
Medicine. *See* Black drink
Medicine maker. *See Heles hayv*
Mekko (band chiefs), 28, 33, 38, 40, 48, 94, 95, 97, 237n.5
Mekusukey Academy, 51–52
Memorial service, 199, 246n.9
Mercy seat, 121–23, 129, 134, 182, 240n.13
Methodists, 50–52, 56, 102, 160, 207, 218
Micro-sociology, 15
Ministers, 84, 92, 95, 97, 100–101, 103, 114, 121, 122, 131, 135, 153, 155, 237n.5
Missionaries, 30, 46, 49, 57, 59, 159, 214. *See also* W. P. Blake; David and Antoinette Constant; Rev. Monday Durant; Rev. John and Mary Anne Lilley; Rev. Joseph Samuel Murrow; Rev. J. R. Ramsey
Missions: Catholic, 50, 208; Methodist, 50, 207; Methodist Episcopal, 51; Oak Ridge Presbyterian, 46; Presbyterian Foreign Mission Board, 46, 48,

239n.9; Seminole Mission, 51; Southern Baptist, 47, 207
Murrow, Rev. Joseph Samuel, 47, 48, 50, 235n.2
Muskogean languages, 23, 24
Muskogee-Seminole-Wichita Association of the Southern Baptist Convention, 55, 238n.1
Mvskoke language, 3, 29, 34, 43, 44, 55, 60, 61, 63, 109, 114, 121, 140, 146, 185, 215, 219, 220, 225–27, 233n.1, 236nn.3,5,6, 240nn.11,12, 245n.1

New Deal Indian Program for Oklahoma Indians, 41

Oklahoma, 39, 40–43, 51, 136, 184
Oklahoma Indian Welfare Act of 1936, 41
Opala, Joseph A., 52
Opler, Morris E., 29, 246–47n.1
Ordination, ordained, 91, 95, 100–101, 196, 204, 235n.5, 238n.7
Osceola, 35
Owls, 70, 77, 186–87, 189–91, 237n.17

Pastors, 55–56, 57, 84, 90, 92–95, 97, 99–100, 101, 108, 113, 122, 123, 124, 131, 141, 178, 187, 188, 192, 197, 237n.5, 242n.28
Phelps, G. Lee, 53
Porrv ("witch"), 68, 70–71, 186–87. *See also* 'Stekene; Witchcraft
Posketv (busk or Green Corn Festival), 24–25, 56, 69, 75, 160, 161, 233n.2, 236n.3, 244n.42
Power, 63–64, 67–68, 146, 187, 246nn.6,7
Powers, William K., 5, 208
Poyvfekcv ("spirit" or "soul"), 66–72, 120, 192, 236nn.10,12

Prayer, prayers, 62–63, 76, 77, 83, 98, 109–12, 116–19, 127, 144, 238n.10
Prayer grounds, 83, 237n.2
Prayer Meetings, 12, 105, 106–32, 135, 143, 148, 156–61, 171, 173, 175, 177, 179, 180–84, 189, 190, 243nn.34,35,36
Presbyterians, 47, 48–52, 56, 102, 103, 160, 170, 209–10, 218

Ramsey, Rev. J. R., 47
Rededication, 121–22, 129, 130–31, 157, 164, 179, 180, 182, 196, 240n.13, 244n.39
Red Stick War of 1813–14, 33, 34, 35
Refreshments, 123–24, 134, 139, 144, 154, 189–90, 238n.2
Residences, 26, 45
Revivals, 140–41, 188, 191, 202, 204, 213
Revolutionary War, 32

St. Augustine, Spanish Florida, 30
Sapir, Edward, 9
Sasakwa, Okla., 50
Sasakwa Female Academy, 51
Satan, 64–65, 76, 119, 120, 121, 147, 211, 236n.14, 243n.38
Second Seminole War, 36
Second Sunday Meetings, 195–96, 197, 199
Seminole Baptist churches, 7, 16, 17, 39, 53–54, 79, 83, 137–40, 184, 198, 217, 245n.45; Arbeka, 53, 138; Ash Creek, 47; Big Creek, 193; Bird Creek, 139, 142; Cedar Creek, 137; Cedar River, 138; Cold Springs, 138–40; Green Leaf, 53; High Spring, 118, 138–39, 242n.24; Hill Top, 138; Hitchiti, 50; *Hvcce Rvkko* (Big Creek), 193, 204; Many Springs, 138–39; Mekusukey, 53; *Nvrkvpv Hvcce* (Middle Creek), 138, 200, 202, 204; Salt Creek,

138; Sand Creek, 116, 118, 137, 139, 173, 245n.5; Seminole Baptist, 138; Snake Creek, 138, 142; Spring Church, 49–50, 55, 57, 139, 198, 209, 237n.4, 238n.1; Trenton, 138
Seminole Baptists, 3–9, 11, 12, 14, 18, 44, 48, 56, 58–78, 91, 130, 141, 159, 164, 205, 221, 222–23, 243n.29
Seminole community, 6, 9, 13, 16, 18, 53, 136, 217–19, 221, 226, 246n.6
Seminole County, Okla., 20, 25, 38, 40, 41, 43, 44, 45, 50, 57, 79, 170, 171, 219, 243nn.29,31
Seminole Nation, 38, 43
Seminoles, 3, 5, 6, 19, 20, 21, 22, 27, 30, 225; in Georgia and Alabama, 23; history of, 30–45; history of Christianity among, 46–57; origins of, 30–32
Sermons, messages, 117–21, 127–28, 130, 146, 157
Singing, 47, 50, 68, 90, 108, 126–27, 144, 241n.23, 246n.9
Sioux, Lakota Indians, 207–208
Situational proprieties, 12, 16, 18, 79, 125, 156, 158, 205, 244n.41
Slaves, slavery, 20, 26, 30–31, 34, 36, 38, 47–48, 235n.2
Snakes, 76, 146–47, 200, 236n.14, 244n.44, 246n.10
Social occasions, 9, 11–13, 15, 16, 17, 18, 105, 125, 131, 158, 203, 205, 217, 218, 221
Social processes, 12, 17, 79
Social situations, 11, 12, 79, 105, 162, 212–13
Songs, 69, 90, 108–109, 110–11, 113, 114, 115–16, 127, 135, 144, 151, 152, 153, 186, 237n.15, 239n.6
Southeastern culture, 22, 29
Spanish, Spain, 30, 31, 32, 34

Speaker. *See Emponvkv*
Spicer, Edward H., 6, 8
Spirit. *See Poyvfekcv*
Spoehr, Alexander, 21, 53–54
'Stekene ("Great-horned owl" or "witch"), 71, 186–87, 189–91, 237n.17. *See also Porrv*; Witchcraft
Stickball, 25, 192, 220, 234n.3
Stomp dance, 5, 6, 160, 200, 233n.2, 234n.3, 242n.25
Stomp grounds, 5, 6, 9, 13, 16, 20, 27, 28, 39, 53, 56–57, 60, 61, 68, 70, 79, 88, 89, 97, 132, 154, 160, 192, 198, 200, 205, 215–20, 236n.4, 245nn.46,52, 247n.4; Gar Creek, 25, 215, 247n.4; New Tulsa, 217, 200, 220, 233n.2; Tallahassee, 236n.3
Sturtevant, William C., 32, 34, 36
Subsistence farming, 44, 220
Sunrise service, 148–49
Swan, Caleb, 60, 64, 65, 72, 94
Swanton, John, 5, 20, 21, 24, 27, 60, 61, 63–66, 68, 70, 72, 74, 75, 77, 88, 91, 95, 97, 98, 125, 145, 146, 161, 216
Symbols, 18, 96, 149, 212, 214; Baptist, 211–13; Christian, 9; cultural, 8, 9, 167, 198, 203; religious, 7, 58, 75, 78, 214; Seminole, 7, 60, 74, 88

Tecumseh, 33
Testimonies, 148
Third Seminole War, 22, 37
Thomas Town Church (freedmen church), 52
Town. *See Etvlwv*
Trade, 26, 30, 33; deerhide, 26, 32; fur trade, 30, 32

Traditional, 3–6, 12, 16, 18, 22, 58, 59, 60, 74, 75, 78, 158, 203–204, 206, 214
Treaties, 29; of Fort Gibson, 35, 36; of Moultrie Creek, 1823, 34; of Payne's Landing, 1832, 35
Trigger, Bruce, 6
Tvstvnvke ("warrior"), 28, 97

Union Army, 37–38
Unity, theme of, 25, 88, 105, 152, 154–56, 158, 161, 175, 218, 221, 242n.24, 245n.52

Verdery, Katherine, 220
Veterans, 41, 132, 140, 243n.36
Visitors, 70, 107, 108, 112, 114, 117, 123, 124, 125, 128, 131, 133–39, 141–42, 144, 154, 155, 158, 182, 195, 199, 215, 239n.4, 245n.45
Voluntary Relocation Program, 42, 171

War of 1812, 33, 34
Weber, Max, 59, 235n.1
Wewoka, Okla., 38, 48, 51, 243n.29
Witchcraft, 71, 182, 185–88, 190–91, 246n.6. *See also Porrv*
Women's leader, 84, 90, 97–98, 103, 124, 144, 171, 175, 177, 180, 188, 192, 196, 211, 246n.11
World view, 4, 5, 9, 12, 59, 121, 217, 246n.6
World War II, 40, 41, 44, 171
Wright, Muriel H., 160

Yamasee Indians, 30–31
Yamasee War of 1715, 31
Yuchi Indians, 31, 35